The Best of Lakewood Publications'
Strategies & Techniques for Managers & Trainers

Evaluating Training's Impact

Third Edition

Compiled By DAVE ZIELINSKI
from articles that have been published in

TRAINING
The Magazine Covering the Human Side of Business

Lakewood Publications

The Complete New Training Library:

Book 1	*Basic Training: The Language of Corporate Education*
Book 2	*Adult Learning in Your Classroom*
Book 3	*The Best of Creative Training Techniques*
Book 4	*Designing Training for Results*
Book 5	*The Training Mix: Choosing and Using Media and Methods*
Book 6	*Managing Training in the Organization, Book I*
Book 7	*Managing Training in the Organization, Book II*
Book 8	*Delivering Training: Mastery in the Classroom*
Book 9	*Evaluating Training's Impact*
Book 10	*Using Technology-Delivered Learning*
Book 11	*The Effective Performance Consultant*
Book 12	*Making Training Pay Off On the Job*

Bulk reprints of individual articles may be quoted and purchased through:

Reprint Services
315 Fifth Avenue N.W.
St. Paul, MN 55112
(800) 707-7798 or (612) 633-0578

LAKEWOOD BOOKS
50 South Ninth Street
Minneapolis, MN 55402
(800) 707-7769 or (612) 333-0471
Fax: (612) 333-6526
Web Page Address: http://www.lakewoodpub.com

Editorial Director: Linda Klemstein
Editor: Dave Zielinski
Production Editor: Julie Tilka
Production Manager: Pat Grawert
Cover Design: Julie Tilka
Proof Reader: Becky Wilkinson

Contents of this book copyrighted ©1996 by Lakewood Publications, Minneapolis, MN 55402. All rights reserved. No part of this publication may be reproduced, stored in a retrieval system, or transmitted in any form or by any means, electronic, mechanical, photocopying, recording, or otherwise, without the prior written permission of the publisher. Printed in the United States of America.

Lakewood Publications Inc. is a subsidiary of VNU/USA. Lakewood Publications Inc. publishes *TRAINING Magazine, Presentations* magazine, *Training Directors' Forum Newsletter, Creative Training Techniques Newsletter, The Lakewood Report On Technology for Learning Newsletter, Potentials In Marketing* magazine, and other business periodicals, books, research, and conducts conferences.

ISBN 0-943210-57-7

10 9 8 7 6 5 4 3 2 1

PREFACE

THE NEW TRAINING LIBRARY

Contemporary training and performance improvement ideas, strategies and techniques for managers and HRD professionals

Welcome to *The New Training Library*. Before you read on, there are a few things you should know about this series of books and how it came into existence.

Each book in *The New Training Library* contains articles originally published in *TRAINING Magazine, The Training Directors' Forum Newsletter, Creative Training Techniques Newsletter*, or *The Lakewood Report on Technology for Learning Newsletter*, all Lakewood publications that explore contemporary human resources development issues, trends and ideas from different angles and perspectives. While there is some overlap among the books in the series, each of them stands on its own.

Our editors selected articles to illuminate a particular theme or subject area — from the dynamics of adult occupational learning, to managing and running a corporate training function, to designing cost-effective training programs, to powerful performance consulting. And more.

The pervasive style of the selected articles is that of magazine and newsletter journalism, opinion and commentary. In this accessible, nonacademic style, the authors address the real and immediate challenges you face as practicing HRD professionals or as managers and motivators of people.

The edited articles are contained between the covers of the books in *The New Training Library*. Not, to repeat, as the definitive texts or final words on any one subject area, but as books that serve a different and (depending who you are) maybe even more useful purpose.

As the training profession evolves, it demands a solid understanding of the original ideas, theories and systems that shaped its development. Today's training professionals also must be prepared to absorb, assimilate and put into perspective an astonishing amount of new information. Like doctors, lawyers, bankers or other professionals, HRD professionals can never stop learning. Not if they want to be effective. Certainly not if they want to get ahead.

The publications that form the core of *The New Training Library* have become among the most widely read and influential in the field because their editors have never forgotten that fundamental need. In addition to featuring the best writers, theorists and practitioners in HRD, each publication also meets the HRD professional's need to understand the newest techniques, strategies and approaches to tough workplace challenges within the context of the established body of HRD knowledge.

Thus, each publication I've discussed here is carefully balanced to appeal to relative novices in HRD as well as to seasoned professionals. And so are the books in *The New Training Library*, which represents a comprehensive and systematic collection of current ideas and practical responses to meeting workplace challenges (in many cases, articulated by those who first formulated them) within the context of HRD's most enduring, time-tested fundamentals. In other words, these books manage to be both timeless and relevant to the challenges you now face in the rapidly evolving American workplace.

Plus, the books in *The New Training Library* are designed so you can find useful information fast. And with that information, you probably can meet a challenge, solve a problem or defuse a crisis right away. It's a fact that HRD changes constantly, especially today. But I think you'll find, due to the care with which the contents of these books were selected and to the editorial strengths of the publications in which this material first appeared, that *The New Training Library* series will be as useful many years from now as it is today.

Philip Jones
Editorial Director
Lakewood Publications

TABLE OF CONTENTS

CHAPTER 1

Evaluating Training at Levels 1-4:
Issues, Ideas and Models

Prove It! Does Your Training Make a Difference? 3
    By Beverly Geber
- Levels of Evaluation
- How Arthur Andersen Did a Level 4 Study
- Rx for Good Performance

Yes...You Can Weigh Training's Value 9
    By Jac Fitz-Enz
- The Fallacy of the Burden of Proof

Simplifying ROI 13
    By James Hassett

How to Escape Corporate America's Basement
    By John V. Noonan 17

Training for Impact 21
    By Dana Gaines Robinson

Measuring the 'Goodness' of Training 25
    By Jack Gordon

How to Calculate the Costs and Benefits of an HRD Program 31
    By Lyle M. Spencer Jr.
- Red Flag / Jack Gordon

The Dollars and Sense of Corporate Training 37
    By Michael Godkewitsch

ROI: What Should Training Take Credit For?
    By James R. Cook and Carol M. Panza 39

Decipher the Real Feedback on 'Smile Sheets'
    By Ron Zemke 43
- Fear and Loathing on the Evaluation Trail

Sins of Omission
    By Barbara Bowman 45

CHAPTER 2

BUILDING BETTER PRE- AND POST-TRAINING TESTS

One More Time: Test Trainees Before You Train Them 49
    By Paul Rahn
    • Wait to Correct Trainees' Tests

Six More Benefits of Pretesting Trainees 51
    By Bob Mezoff

Using Certification to Evaluate Training's Effectiveness 53
    By Scott Heimes

Add 'Then' Testing to Prove Training's Effectiveness 55
    By Robert G. Preziosi and Leslie M. Legg

Constructing Tests that Work
    By Marc J. Rosenberg and William Smitley 57
    • Using 'Dailies' to Keep Training on Target

CHAPTER 3

IMPROVING TRANSFER OF TRAINING TO THE JOB

28 Techniques for Transforming Training into Performance 63
    By Ron Zemke and John Gunkler
    • Transfer of Learning: The Laboratory Perspective

9 Ways to Make Training Pay Off Back on the Job 73
    By Ruth Colvin Clark
    • Measure Your Training Transfer Quotient

But Will They Use Training Back on the Job? 77
    By Dean R. Spitzer
    • Why IBM Trainees Practice What Trainers Preach

Measuring Back-on-the-Job Performance 79
    By J.B. Cornwell

CHAPTER 4

MEASURING THE PAYOFF OF SOFT-SKILLS TRAINING

Why Soft-Skills Training Doesn't Take 85
    By James C. Georges

ROI of Soft-Skills Training 89
    By Judith Pine and Judith C. Tingley

How to Make Level 3 Evaluation of Soft-Skills Training Pay Dividends 93
    By Dave Zielinski

CHAPTER 5

EVALUATING MANAGEMENT DEVELOPMENT AND SALES TRAINING

Measuring the Impact of Management Development 97
   By Ron Zemke

How to Get the Most Out of 360° Feedback 99
   By Gary Yukl and Richard Lepsinger

Teaching Johnny to Manage 103
   By Alex Mironoff
   • SIDEBAR HERE

How Do You Know It Works? 107
   By Matt Hennecke
   • Tying Training to the Bottom Line

Is It Really Leadership Training? 111
   By James C. Georges

Are Sales Training Results Measurable? 113
   By Ron Zemke
   • What to Measure to Prove the Effectiveness of Sales Training

Build Plenty of Evaluation Into Your Sales Training — Early and Often 117
   By Brian O'Hara
   • Yes, You Can Evaluate Bottom-Line Results / *Ron Zemke*

CHAPTER 6

USING TECHNOLOGY TO ENHANCE EVALUATION

If Used Correctly, Technology Can Reduce Cost of Evaluation 121
   By Elliott Masie
   • How Keypad Response Systems Can Improve Your Training Evaluations / *Scott Heimes*

Technology Makes Level 3 Evaluation Feasible and Friendly 123
   By Dave Zielinski
   • Delivering Evaluation Forms Via Computer Network / *Scott Heimes*

CHAPTER 1
EVALUATING TRAINING AT LEVELS 1 - 4

Issues, Ideas and Models

Does Your Training Make a Difference? Prove It!

Blame TQM, downsizing or impatient managers. Fact is, trainers are being pressured to evaluate training courses at much deeper levels

BY BEVERLY GEBER

Trude Fawson first noticed the renewed fascination trainers have with course evaluation as she tried to worm her way into a packed seminar room during a training conference. The unlikely title of the SRO session was "Cost-Benefit Strategies for Conducting Level 4 Follow-Up Evaluations." Fawson, manager of needs assessment and evaluation services within the AT&T School of Business, was the presenter.

Like any diligent classroom instructor, she had arrived early, before the previous session ended. What she found was a statuary of people crowding the door, protecting their positions so unbudgingly that the exiting participants from the other session could barely edge out.

By the time Fawson's presentation started, 150 people were crammed inside a room set up for far fewer. Curious, she asked why the throng hungered to hear about a topic that had generated only tepid interest at previous conferences. After all, doing Level 3 and Level 4 evaluation is the trainerly equivalent of flossing your teeth. You know you're supposed to do it, you know it's good for you, you know there might be dire consequences eventually if you don't, but let's be honest: How many people floss each day unless their dentists have warned them that their gums are flabby and their teeth are starting to wobble?

What Fawson discovered there at the annual convention of the National Society for Performance and Instruction is that a lot of dentists appear to be populating the line-management ranks at companies these days, and they're squinting suspiciously at the training department's gumline. The message these managers are delivering is that the training department had better be able to show concrete evidence that training is achieving its goals of changing behavior on the job (Level 3) and contributing to the bottom line (Level 4 — see box on p. 4). And they want to see results, not just

---

Trainers hearing the evaluation sermon would nod dutifully, go back to their companies and become overwhelmed.

---

for the easy-to-measure technical training courses, but for soft skills as well.

That was the explanation Fawson's participants reported most often for jamming into her session, but it wasn't the only trigger. Other attendees pointed to the influence of the quality movement and its emphasis on measurement. Some mentioned the pressure exerted by cost-cutting measures, which forces training departments to use money more wisely. Still others told of the rise of technology, which has eased much of the burden of data-gathering for evaluating programs.

It all adds up to a keen interest in evaluation in general, and in Level 3 and Level 4 evaluation in particular. Some large organizations have gone so far as to establish new evaluation units within their training departments. Fawson's unit at AT&T, for instance, was created two years ago. Motorola Inc. also formed its evaluation unit about two years ago, and recently responded to rising interest in the topic by adding a module on evaluation to the course it gives at Motorola University for trainers from customer companies who want to learn Motorola's secrets.

TRAINING's 1994 Industry Report also indicates great interest in evaluation. Of the respondents from organizations with 100 or more employees, 83 percent said they do a Level 1 evaluation of at least some courses (measuring trainee reactions); 66 percent said they do Level 2 (testing); 62 percent said they have done at least some Level 3 evaluation; and 47 percent reported doing Level 4 evaluation. What's more, of those who do at least some checking at Level 3 or Level 4, respondents said they do Level 3 evaluations on 45 percent of their courses and Level 4 probes of 44 percent of their courses. Those latter numbers, in particular, seem mendaciously high to many observers, and could reflect respondents' flossing guilt rather than their actual practices. But the numbers definitely imply interest in the topic.

A Paper Nightmare

For years, leading lights in the field have preached that if job-related training is to be done correctly, the training department ought to do Level 3 and Level 4 evaluation of at least some courses. Trainers hearing the sermon would nod dutifully, go back to their companies, become overwhelmed with the workload, and rationalize that Level 1 or Level 2 evaluations were sufficient.

There were good reasons to neglect doing deeper evaluations. For one thing, very few higher-ups wanted it done, perhaps out of ignorance that it could be done. For another thing, rigorous Level 3 and Level 4 evaluations are time-consuming and expensive. Measuring changes in on-the-job behavior can't properly be done in a slap-dash manner. It takes time and a chunk of the training department's budget to do it properly.

Fawson recalls that some years ago, her division of AT&T attempted to do Level 3 and Level 4 evaluation of an important course, but gave up after trying to assess just the first two groups of trainees. "It was a paper nightmare," she says.

But lately there has been a turn-about in attitudes toward evaluation. Marc Rosenberg, district manager for education and training in AT&T's corporate human resources department in Somerset, NJ, thinks that part of the change can be attributed to a growing maturity in the training field as trainers realize that their charge is to effect results, not just to put people in chairs. "Learning is nice, but it's inadequate," he says. "Learning that doesn't change the business isn't useful."

Some of this evolution reflects more professionalism in the field, says James Hite, a training manager with Northern Telecom's Learning Institute in Nashville, TN. Although people still enter the training department with no experience in human resources development, Hite says, there are more and more college graduates with advanced degrees in HRD who are signing on. Most of them are well-schooled in fundamental concepts such as the Kirkpatrick model.

Of course, this is not the whole reason for the evaluation renaissance, or even the greater part of it. Even the most conscientious, "professional" trainers have found it all too easy to sacrifice the long-term benefits of evaluation to their current workload.

What really fueled the surge of Level 3 and 4 evaluation at Northern Telecom, Hite says, was the company-wide push for continuous improvement. All over the organization, departments started to measure themselves in new ways. So it was natural for the training department to begin calculating results that were more meaningful than the number of happy trainees or the total training hours delivered.

Being able to demonstrate to line managers that training was making a difference on the job was in line with the training department's effort to be more customer-focused. But Hite readily admits that if the department hadn't made the effort, the metric-savvy line managers would soon have forced the issue. "The more they would get into continuous improvement, the more they would ask these questions of us," he says.

At AT&T, too, it became clear that new measurements were needed to gauge the results of training. Executives who were getting more sophisticated measurements from the rest of the company expected more from the training department as well. "When you tell a vice president of a business unit that on a scale of 1 to 5, trainees rated the effectiveness of the instructor as 4.1, they look at you and kind of say, 'That's nice,'" Fawson says. "We were very proud to have those averages go up each year, but it wasn't meaningful information to the decision-makers."

Paradox or Not?

It might seem odd that training departments would fall under greater scrutiny while much of the business world chants the mantra that Training Is Good. At many companies, executives now accept that training is not a cost, but an investment — at least, that's what they claim. And yet, if the response to Fawson's seminar is any indication, trainers have suddenly become obsessed with proving training's effectiveness.

Jim Robinson, chairman of the Pittsburgh consulting firm Partners in Change, sees no paradox. Robinson, whose firm specializes in evaluation, says it is generally true that management recognizes that employees are assets whose performance must be monitored and improved. That leads directly to training. "But we're also in a period in which resources are limited in organizations," he says. The confluence of those two forces produces an emphasis on course evaluation. "Management says we really need to make sure we're getting satisfactory return on our dollars."

This pressures trainers to wade into the deeper water of Level 3 and Level 4 evaluation. But besides the obvious benefit — finding out whether training programs are, indeed, contributing to important goals — there are other advantages.

For one thing, evaluation can be a "value-added" service to internal customers, a benefit training departments can use to sell their services to line management. Rosenberg says it's persuasive to tell managers that a

---

THE 4 LEVELS OF EVALUATION

The most widely used model for evaluating training programs is one proposed in 1959 by Donald L. Kirkpatrick, who is now professor emeritus of the University of Wisconsin and a consultant in Elm Grove, WI. He recently wrote his first book on the topic, *Evaluating Training Programs: The Four Levels* (Berrett-Koehler, 1994). The model is so closely linked to him that it's usually just called the Kirkpatrick model.

It is elegantly simple. Kirkpatrick maintains that there are four ways to measure the quality or effectiveness of a training course.

LEVEL 1. At the most primitive level of evaluation, we find the battered and bloodied "smile sheets." Kirkpatrick, however, does not deride them as do many trainers who sniff that smile sheets are not an indicator of whether the training worked. It's true; they are not. But Level 1 evaluation, which seeks trainee reactions to a course, is not useless. Trainees who are put off by some aspect of the course design are unlikely to ingest the learning points you've so carefully put in their trough.

LEVEL 2. Once you've determined whether they liked the course, it's useful to test what trainees learned. Sometimes this will take the form of a pencil-and-paper test; sometimes they'll be asked to demonstrate they can operate a piece of machinery. But the goal is to find out if they learned what you were trying to teach.

LEVEL 3. Here's where measurement gets tough to do. It's one thing to document that learners mastered the course content, but if they don't apply any of it when they return to the job, the course has wasted everyone's time. Level 3 evaluations try to measure behavior change on the job.

LEVEL 4. Most trainers profess that they want to tie training to the company's bottom line, and that's exactly what Level 4 evaluation attempts to measure. If a course achieved its objective by changing trainees' behavior on the job, did that change improve the company's business results?

team of independent evaluators will check to make sure that the training did its job. That's one reason AT&T formed a separate evaluation unit.

In addition, Level 3 and Level 4 evaluations can be instruments for overhauling an entire curriculum. If an evaluation shows that a course isn't improving the performance of workers or producing more bottom-line benefit than it costs, the logical move is to kill it or change it.

Intel Corp. is on a campaign to do Level 3 and Level 4 evaluations for its entire curriculum at Intel University, says Eric Freitag, training, evaluation and improvement manager for the corporate university in Chandler, AZ. So far, he says, about 5 percent of all courses have been eliminated, roughly 20 percent have undergone major modifications, and a substantial number have been changed slightly.

Another benefit of deeper evaluation is that it can uncover the barriers that prevent the training from being applied on the job, says Vickie Shoutz, a human resources planning representative with Hutchinson Technology in Hutchinson, MN, which makes computer components. When Shoutz and training specialist Julie Page did their first Level 3 evaluation nearly three years ago, their trainees were 150 workers in the company's tooling department. Employees were starting to work in teams and to interact more directly with customers; the department's manager thought their communication skills needed polishing.

Before the course began, Shoutz and Page assessed the employees' skill levels by surveying customers, supervisors and coworkers on how frequently the employees displayed certain behaviors, such as handling conflict smoothly. An identical survey done several months after the training showed that the workers used the appropriate skills about 75 percent of the time, compared with 50 percent of the time before the training.

That gave Shoutz and Page quantitative information, but they also wanted a "qualitative" component. So they conducted separate focus-group meetings with trainees and their customers, both before and after the training. That was when the two trainers heard about the kinds of barriers some workers faced on the job that might have prevented them from applying their new skills. For instance, one group of workers who had to work in a shadowy, cramped space told of how depressing it was to come to work and how much they envied their counterparts who worked in a bright, airy spot. Might that affect their ability to be model communicators on the job? No question. "We would never have learned that from a survey," Shoutz says.

Why Not Quick and Dirty?

Conducting a Level 3 or Level 4 evaluation seems daunting to most trainers. And it is, if it's done ex post facto. In other words, it's much easier to design evaluation into the scheme

---

Executives who were getting more sophisticated measurements from the rest of the company expected more from the training department as well.

---

as you're designing the course itself. It's much more difficult to go looking for the right measurements that will tell accurately if an existing course is working.

"Evaluation and front-end analysis are two sides of the same coin," says AT&T's Rosenberg. "If you don't do the right front-end analysis, then it's impossible to do Level 3 and Level 4 evaluation."

It's crucial to get the client involved in evaluation before the course is designed. The manager who requests training ought to be able to define the performance problem she's trying to solve (or the opportunity she's trying to grasp) and what kind of behavior she's looking for. If she can do that, she also ought to be able to suggest existing metrics that could help measure a change in behavior. Says Northern Telecom's Hite, "The key is to raise these issues early in the process so that the client will start thinking about how to measure the ultimate results. If that isn't raised immediately, then it may not come up until later, at which point you don't have any benchmark data."

With all the effort that's involved, it would be impractical for most companies to do Level 3 and Level 4 evaluations on every single course. How do you make the cut?

Rosenberg recommends that trainers concentrate on the most expensive programs or the courses that are dear to top management. Fawson uses a decision tree analysis in deciding which ones will get a full-court press at AT&T. She gives heavy weight to factors such as the number of students involved (the more students, the higher the total cost) and the strategic value of the course.

A lot depends on the kinds of courses that are being evaluated. Technical and "hard skills" training has always been easier to track, simply because persuasive data is more readily available. If you ran a safety course, did accidents and workers' compensation claims decrease? If you trained secretaries to use new software for word processing, did they produce more letters faster? In contrast, getting good numbers on a soft-skills course is harder. It can be difficult — some say impossible — to get hard data on the effects of a diversity-awareness program, for instance.

Robinson recommends that a Level 1 evaluation be done for all courses. He recommends a Level 2 evaluation for any courses in which trainees need to retain a particular body of knowledge or apply a specific skill. An example might be a safety course, in which an employer may need to show that workers not only were taught safety procedures, but understood them.

A Level 3 evaluation is called for in cases in which the objective is to change behavior on the job and the client is particularly interested in the results, Robinson says. For instance, in the deregulated telecommunications industry, telephone repair technicians do more than string wire and install phones. As front-line customer service technicians, they also must deal effectively with customers, and maybe even woo them into buying upgraded products. Those behavior changes would directly affect the company's fortunes, so it might be prudent to make sure that skills learned in customer service courses are in fact being used on the job.

A Level 4 evaluation should be done in those cases in which the results represent a top priority to the company and can be linked realistically to hard financial numbers. Empowerment may be important to the company, Robinson says, but it's almost impossible to measure the

HOW ARTHUR ANDERSEN DID A LEVEL 4 STUDY

You can do evaluation easy or you can do it hard. Actually, "easy" may be a misnomer if you're talking about measuring results at Level 3 or Level 4. But the path of least resistance is to plot evaluation while the training course is still a fresh idea. That was the approach taken by the Center for Professional Education in St. Charles, IL, the central training facility for the Arthur Andersen worldwide organization, in developing a Level 4 evaluation for a training course delivered to the accounting and consulting firm's tax professionals.

Darryl Jinkerson, director of evaluation services for the center, says that planning for the evaluation started as soon as the center learned that a course would be launched to support a new area of business for the company. Until then, the company's tax professionals were trained only to help clients prepare their federal taxes. But many clients also wanted help in preparing their state and local taxes, which the tax accountants agreed to do in the interest of serving the client.

Eventually, however, the company decided that so much state and local tax preparation was going on that it was necessary to make sure the tax accountants understood thoroughly the laws of the jurisdictions in which they worked.

The training center developed a five-week course, which included two weeks of self-study and three of classroom work. Before the first group of 60 students could be immersed, they took a pre-test to determine their knowledge of state and local tax affairs, and their confidence they could prepare the tax returns accurately.

Evaluators also tracked the tax accountants' billable hours before the course began, determining how many of them were spent in calculating clients' state and local taxes, as well as how much revenue was generated by the activity.

After the 60 tax accountants completed the course, evaluators again tracked billable hours and found that the accountants were spending more of their billable hours doing state and local tax work.

Jinkerson and other evaluators also compared the billable hours of those 60 trainees against the hours of tax accountants who were doing state and local tax work but who hadn't yet had training. The trained group produced more revenue than the untrained accountants, undoubtedly because they were much further along the learning curve and confident of their skills.

That was borne out by one more measurement. The evaluators surveyed the 60 trainees and found a significant improvement in their confidence that they could prepare state and local taxes. And they were much more willing to promote that expertise to clients.

Jinkerson won't give specific figures for the evaluation's findings, but says that after 15 months, the amount of increased revenue gained by the company more than offset the cost of the training. On average, the increase in revenue for the trained tax accountants was more than 10 percent.

— *Beverly Geber*

---

business results of any particular training course designed to support an empowerment strategy. "It's such a long-term payoff, and there are too many variables," Robinson says.

Level 4 evaluations need solid metrics, says Judith Hale, president of Hale Associates, a consulting firm in Western Springs, IL. Sometimes, she adds, those metrics are not that hard to locate. Suppose your accounting department averages receivables of $7 million a day. You could deliver a course teaching accountants better ways to track down money owed the company. Your Level 4 evaluation may require nothing more than checking to see if the daily receivables fell.

Workers Aren't Laboratory Rats

The Center for Professional Education, the central training location for the worldwide Arthur Andersen & Co. organization, is the acknowledged leader in training evaluation. Nearly 15 years ago, the center in St. Charles, IL, set up a formal evaluation group within its training function. Darryl Jinkerson, director of evaluation services, a 32-person unit, says evaluators look at the size and impact of a course before deciding how to evaluate it. Level 3 and Level 4 evaluations are reserved for large, high-profile initiatives or ones in which the stakeholders demand evidence of results.

At the center, all courses receive a Level 1 evaluation and about half get a Level 2 evaluation. Less than a third of courses receive a Level 3 evaluation and just 10 percent are evaluated at Level 4.

Taking the first steps toward a Level 3 evaluation can be frightening, and with good cause. Some experts believe that an evaluation at Level 3 is more difficult to accomplish than one at Level 4. The problem, says Donald Kirkpatrick, an Elm Grove, IL, consultant and author of the widely used four-level evaluation model, is that at Level 3, you're trying to measure human behavior; at Level 4, you're tracking some bottom-line figures that should already exist, such as productivity, quality, turnover, or the number of accidents. "But behavior is different," he says. "There are no existing figures on behavior."

And there are few how-to guides. The Kirkpatrick model, for instance, is descriptive, not prescriptive. This means that at Level 3, somebody has to invent methods of measurement for behavior.

It's a task that is hard, but not impossible, says Karen Neuhengen, senior training evaluation specialist at Motorola University in Schaumburg, IL. The key is to figure out the specific behaviors that represent a soft skill, such as leadership, and then track the changes in behavior that trainees exhibit. If you can reach consensus among the stakeholders on the set of behaviors — an arduous process for some courses — you're halfway there, Neuhengen says.

In the two years the evaluation unit has been operating at Motorola, about 20 Level 3 evaluations have been done or started, Neuhengen says. In one, involving a leadership training course for mid-level managers, the evaluators are using a 360-degree evaluation, a measurement method of choice for a Level 3 evaluation of soft skills. Motorola evaluators send a survey to the trainees, their bosses and their subordinates, which asks all three groups to rate the trainees on the frequency with which they display certain behaviors related to leadership. The survey is being done four times a year for two years.

Initially, says Neuhengen, evaluators will be looking for a decrease in variance between the three groups' perceptions as the hoped-for changes in behaviors become obvious to everyone. The surveys are supposed to serve as springboards to quarterly discussions between trainees and their bosses, in an effort to reinforce the principles of the leadership course. Consequently, evaluators hope to see the scores rise over the two-year measurement period.

There are some in the training field who would sniff at such a "measurement," saying that even if the scores rise, it won't prove that training worked. There are far too many variables that affect performance to credit only training for some improvement.

Course evaluators agree completely; but they respond that what they're trying to present is evidence, not proof. It is quixotic to think one could control all variables in the real world to prove conclusively that a training course was the sole reason that performance improved. But if a course sought behavior change or bottom-line improvement and subsequent measurements showed that the goal was reached, that's evidence that training made a difference.

Anne Marie Laures, corporate manager of training and development for Walgreen Co. in Deerfield, IL, has undertaken several Level 3 and Level 4 evaluations in the past three years. Initially, she wrestled with the "proof" question and worried that other factors could muddy results. She finally decided that "there isn't a pure laboratory setting when you're dealing with the real world, and I don't know that you will find any organization where the executives are looking for pure data."

She recognizes there is a debate in the field about how valid some Level 3 and Level 4 measurements are, but adds, "maybe sometimes we're just too hard on ourselves."

No Level 4 at Motorola

Some trainers believe that success in a Level 3 evaluation simply implies success at Level 4. Motorola, for instance, does Level 3 evaluation in order to make sure that its individual courses are working. But, says Neuhengen, Motorola doesn't do any Level 4 evaluation. Executives are willing to assume that if employees are exhibiting the desired behaviors, that will have a positive effect on the bottom line.

Arthur Andersen's Jinkerson says there's a difference between showing cause-and-effect and showing a relationship. Sometimes it's possible to show a fairly direct link between training and results. But in most cases, he says, it's necessary only to show a relationship.

Jinkerson and other Andersen evaluators are trying to link training to customer satisfaction, on the theory that if customers are completely satisfied with the work of Andersen consultants, they will stick with the company.

So Jinkerson gauges satisfaction by asking clients questions, such as: How satisfied are you with our particular skills? Our business acumen? Our knowledge of your industry? Jinkerson then examines the background of the Andersen employees who deal with the clients. He has found that the ones who had extensive training tend to have more satisfied clients. It may not be absolute proof, Jinkerson says, but "we don't think it's chance."

Andersen evaluators constantly troll for new ways to establish the relationship between training and results. In one recent case, the department used video cameras to do a

---

Rx FOR GOOD PERFORMANCE

The most thorough way to gauge whether a trainee is applying new skills on the job after training is to have an independent, skilled observer take copious notes while watching the employee work. Nice, but usually impractical.

So Anne Marie Laures, corporate manager of training and development for Walgreen Co., in Deerfield, IL, chose the next best option in evaluating a course for technicians working in the company's drugstore pharmacy departments. She asked the pharmacists to do the observing and note-taking.

Pharmacy technicians are the people who do the support tasks in a pharmacy. They wait on customers. They take refill information over the phone from doctors. At Walgreen's stores, they're also expected to offer customers generic drugs in place of brand-name drugs when the two are identical and when state laws allow it.

Until recently, techs received only on-the-job training from the pharmacists who hired them. But three years ago, Laures' department established a course for new techs that involved 20 hours of classroom training and 20 hours of close supervision on the job. Since the company has about 2,000 stores, the initiative was bound to be expensive. Laures wanted to ensure that it was worth the money. She set out to evaluate the course at Level 3 and Level 4.

After some individuals went through the program, she identified a group of techs who were in their third month of service; some were trained on the job in the usual manner, and others had gone through the training course. She sent surveys to the pharmacists who supervised the techs, asking questions about the new employees' performance. For instance, how speedily did the tech enter information into a computer? How often did the tech interrupt the pharmacist's work to ask a question? How often did the techs offer a generic drug substitute to a customer?

In almost all cases, Laures found that the formally trained technicians were more efficient and wasted less of the pharmacist's time than those who received only on-the-job training.

She then ran the results through a regression analysis and discovered that sales in pharmacies with formally trained techs exceeded sales in pharmacies with on-the-job-trained techs by an average of $9,500 annually. Considering that the cost of training was $273 per trainee, Laures concluded the program was a bargain.

— *Beverly Geber*

Level 3 evaluation of a two-day course for executives on the essentials of giving good business presentations. First the executives were videotaped giving presentations before the course began. They were taped again at the conclusion of the course. Then six months later, they were videotaped as they gave presentations to clients.

In the meantime, evaluators had defined the elements of giving good presentations as quantitatively as possible. They checked to see how many times the executives used nonwords, such as "uh." They counted the number of times the executives made eye contact with people in the audience. The evaluators even defined the size and frequency of hand gestures that represented good performance. Given that list of factors, each of which was matched with a number to represent good performance, it was easy to measure improvement.

Bomb Threats at Barbados

Devising quantitative measures is crucial to a good Level 3 or Level 4 evaluation, but AT&T's Fawson says qualitative information can enhance the picture. AT&T trainers are encouraged to report any post-course phone calls they get from trainees who have used the principles on the job and are delighted with the results.

For instance, a course the company delivered on how to prevent violence and terrorism had a dramatic impact on a telephone company office in Barbados, where the local telephone company is viewed as a symbol of the disliked government. The island's lone office was getting frequent bomb threats, which disrupted communications to the entire island and made the employees call in sick nearly as often as they worked.

The course taught employees how to discern whether a telephone bomb threat might be fake, and how to

---

The cost of evaluation can be trimmed by using measurements that have already been collected.

---

quickly and efficiently search the building. Soon after the course was delivered, the manager called to report that his employees were coming to work regularly again and the number of bomb threats had dropped dramatically. Apparently, bomb threats lost their thrill when employees didn't always evacuate.

Fawson writes up one-page synopses of these case studies and includes a couple with each Level 3 or Level 4 report to executives. "There are some people who like to see the statistics, but others want to see dramatic examples. I really think we need both," she says. "The case histories just communicate better than statistics."

No one who does Level 3 or Level 4 evaluation pretends that it's free. But it helps reduce the cost if trainers can use measurements that are already collected. Northern Telecom's Hite recalls a Level 4 evaluation he did with the company's finance department, whose members were being taught to use a new computerized system to reduce the time it took to derive financial analyses. The measurements were already there; the evaluation added just 5 percent to the cost of the training, which the finance department bore.

But Hite says that the more experience trainers get with finding and choosing the right measurements among ones that are already available, the less expensive it will be.

Says consultant Hale, "There is a perception that evaluation costs money. I disagree. It only costs money if you don't design it well. You can design it so that your line managers do it for you."

What she means is that the responsibility for improving performance on the job belongs to managers. By setting up a Level 3 or Level 4 evaluation, the training department is simply giving those managers the means to determine whether performance actually is improving. And it's not just the training department that's interested in that.

Notes:

Yes...You Can Weigh Training's Value

Even soft, interpersonal-skills training can be evaluated in dollars-and-cents terms. But you have to begin at the beginning

BY JAC FITZ-ENZ

The enduring belief that you can't quantify the benefits of a corporate training program has been punctured many times over the years. Yet the myth persists. We still hear incessantly that the effects of training interventions — especially "soft-skills" training — cannot be traced objectively and quantitatively to an organization's bottom line.

Once again, the myth has exploded. And this time, the evidence doesn't come merely in the form of a single evaluation project that documented the dollar value of a training program in a single organization.

In the fall of 1992, 26 companies joined forces to search for a universal method of training evaluation. After more than a year of model development, refinement and field testing, a standardized training valuation system (TVS) emerged. It is built around a relatively simple set of analytic tools and has been tested across a range of training interventions.

The system employs a four-step process, starting with an in-depth situation analysis (similar to a needs assessment) and concluding with the dollar value added to an operation by training or other causal factors. The methodology can be used to identify specific, current and potential values before training is conducted. It also measures value obtained after training. And if the training fails to produce the anticipated results, the method helps us determine why.

On the surface the process is deceptively simple. There is little in it that will sound new or surprising to anyone familiar with the literature of human-resources development or with the work of HRD Hall of Fame members Bob Mager, Thomas Gilbert or Joe Harless. But the most elegant solutions are the simplest. And the key to this approach is the relationship that develops between the trainer and the customer — usually a line manager — as a result of the situation analysis. The strengthening of that relationship is also a key benefit, one that may be as important as the evaluation itself.

> **Throughout the process the underlying question is: "What difference would that make?"**

The idea for what came to be called the Training Evaluation Project (TEP) arose from conversations in the summer of 1992 with training professionals at Miles USA, MCI, and Du Pont Merck Pharmaceuticals. For the umpteenth time we discussed the barriers to objective and quantitative evaluation of work-related training. We agreed that in its most basic terms the age-old evaluation demon in training has been the perceived inability to connect training outcomes to changes in organizational quality, productivity, sales or service. The question has always been: When people gain a new skill or enhance an existing one through a training program, how do we trace that change to one or more of the organization's key performance indicators?

That fall, 23 other companies joined the discussion. The method subsequently developed and tested in this project followed the classic outline: Analyze the performance problem — the gap between the results we're getting and the results we want; if training appears likely to solve the problem, develop and deliver the training; find out whether behavior has changed, back on the job, as a result of the training; and finally, determine the value of that behavior change to the organization. What made this initiative successful where others have foundered is the relationship that was forged with the customers (line managers and top executives) and the way the problem-analysis questions were structured. Both factors were critical; one without the other would not have been sufficient.

Objections

The ancient bugaboo preventing the sort of evaluation we wanted to do is the issue of proof: With so many variables affecting a company's overall performance, how do you prove that some particular gain resulted entirely from a training program and nothing else? We began by agreeing that this so-called obstacle is largely a straw man (see box on page 10).

The question is not, "How can we prove beyond the shadow of a doubt that a given training program produced a given result?" but rather, "What will we accept as persuasive evidence that the program produced the result?"

The answer is: We will accept the informed judgment of the line manager. Only the manager knows the vagaries of the work environment. If we assume that the manager is competent and honest, then that person's testimony must be acceptable.

The catch is that "informed judgment" requires the line manager to be intimately involved in the training initiative from the beginning. And the trainer needs to know how to help the manager dig out and specify the value that the training is intended to add to the manager's operation. Here we meet with three objections.

Objection A claims that most managers cannot be persuaded to take part in a needs assessment — what we call the "situation analysis" of the performance problem. This is really only an admission of the trainer's inability to strike a working partnership with the customer. None of the 26 companies in our project considered this a roadblock. Indeed, in many cases it was the customers who provided the evidence of success or failure of the trial programs these companies conducted and evaluated.

Objection B states that the manager naturally will want to justify his decision to invest in training. Therefore, the argument goes, he will be a willing co-conspirator in the trainer's attempt to prove that the course was worthwhile. Frankly, this is more often a specious excuse than a reasonable argument. But even if it were a fair criticism, it would be simple enough to bring in a third-party auditor to check the results.

Objection C asserts that even if the manager is willing and reliable, she will only be estimating the bottom-line value of the training program. The fact is that almost all line managers and professionals have a wealth of operating data sitting about unused. When asked in the right way, they are able to find data related to the process and outcomes in question. The operative phrase is, "in the right way."

These objections do not do the training profession justice. Managers and executives make value judgments every day, with far less analysis, about everything from paying for performance (How much is Judy's performance worth compared to Joe's?) to whether a quarterly sales increase is "caused" by the new marketing plan or merely a seasonal fluke. One can only conclude that the objections are obfuscations put forth by people who don't have the energy, imagination or courage to evaluate their training.

Having agreed that these barriers are self-imposed, the participants in our group set out to experiment with the TVS model. Over the next eight months, only 11 companies committed themselves to a full and fair trial, but all 11 were successful. That is, they found the model did what they hoped it would: It gave them a way to measure and evaluate the quantitative value added — or not added — by their training interventions.

For Instance...

You can't really evaluate the success of "soft-skills" training? Don't tell that to Vicki Brown, Joan Shaughnessy and Priscilla Smith. Brown and Shaughnessy are training specialists and Smith is vice president of human resources at Prudential Insurance and Financial Co. in South Plainfield, NJ. They chose as their pilot project a course that taught "coaching skills" to middle managers.

They began with some in-depth questioning of higher-level Prudential managers — the bosses of the intended trainees. "What skills do you see as being essential in good coaches?" the trainers asked. The managers responded in general terms, talking about motivational skills, analytic skills, communication and listening. The trainers dutifully listed these things. But then they pressed on, addressing each skill individually, probing for the tangible value of applying the skill and the tangible

---

THE FALLACY OF THE BURDEN OF PROOF

One of the self-imposed barriers to seeking the concrete value of training programs is the mistaken notion that the trainer must present proof, with a capital "P," that training had a specific effect on the organization's bottom line. So many factors affect the human and financial performance of a company, it is said, that isolating the pure contribution of a training program is impossible.

In laboratory terms, this is true. In real-world terms, it's utter nonsense. Demonstrating causality of that type is impossible for everyone in business, not just for trainers. Practically speaking, in business there are almost no opportunities to prove causal relationships between given activities and specific effects. Proving causality demands control of all variables. In the real world there is no such phenomenon as control.

But many line functions have established "unspoken agreements" in which they assume some correlation between certain actions and subsequent results. This has been going on for so long that people speak of these connections as if they were provable. The most obvious example is sales. If a salesperson meets the quota, the assumption is that the person is a competent seller of the product. There is no proof of that. Buyers buy for many reasons that have absolutely nothing to do with the salesperson. Salespeople do not control customers.

Likewise, manufacturing managers do not control suppliers of material and equipment or even their own employees. The chief financial officer does not control the cost of capital. Control is a concept, not a reality.

All of us struggle to influence our environment, but none of us control anything. Only in the laboratory can control be demonstrated, and then only within a very small field of investigation.

"Statistical proof" is a misconception. Statistics only try to show that the null hypothesis was probable, not that the stated hypothesis was proven.

So before trainers hang their heads in futility they should understand the fact that when we talk about business, the word proof has no place.

The objective of a valid and reliable evaluation effort that assigns a specific value to the outcome of a training program is simply this: To demonstrate that there is a probable correlation between the training event and a subsequent change in quality, productivity, sales or service. The methodology should imply the following:

"Given the conditions as stated, and assuming other things being equal, the observed effect quite probably is the result of the training."

Before you jump all over that as a disclaimer, please note that the principle of ceteris paribus (other things being equal) is the foundation for all attempts at proof. And it is precisely the assumption that underlies all business planning and subsequent evaluation. As business managers we prepare budgets for the coming year making exactly the same assumption. After the budget year has passed we will know what the results are, but we often won't know and seldom can "prove" what caused us to be over or under our projections.

The old argument has it that trainers shouldn't try to determine the dollar value of their programs to a company because they can't prove that training — and nothing but training — produced a particular business result. That argument is a hollow sham.

— *Beverly Geber*

consequences of failing to apply it. For instance, managers agreed that "poor listening" might result in rework or missed assignments. The trainers pressed further, asking for specific examples of rework and missed assignments: How often do these things happen? What's the cost when they do happen? From there, hourly pay rates could be used to arrive at a plausible estimate of the dollar value of "good coaching."

Then, by tracking rework, missed assignments and so on after the training course, managers themselves could collect the data that would confirm or contradict the initial estimates of the coaching program's value.

This approach relied on planned, specific questions and a structured questioning technique (more about that in a moment). The questions focused initially on the work process, not on training. As the conversation evolved from the general to the detailed, tight connections were established between processes and outcomes. This eventually led to descriptions of expected value. When the program was actually conducted and results obtained, the customer-managers would see for themselves the effects of training.

The critical difference between this and typical questioning methods occurs at two levels. First is the connection drawn between specific acts and specific outcomes. All too often when trainers question managers in the course of a needs assessment, they settle for vague, undemonstrable connections between certain behaviors and certain business results. When this happens, any hope of assigning a concrete value to a performance problem — or to the training course that solves it — is lost.

Second is the projection and later verification of the tangible, dollar value that comes from those specific results. Throughout the process the underlying question is: "What difference would that make?" If a supervisor were a better listener — so what? If production workers were better team players — so what? The manager's answers are continuously probed until some visible, tangible outcome is revealed — an outcome having to do with quality, productivity, sales or service. Once this outcome is uncovered, it is usually easy to put a dollar value on its effects.

It is as important to identify the reason for failures as it is to evaluate successes, and a reliable evaluation methodology ought to do both. This was, in fact, the case with Prudential's effort. The initial study concluded that if trainees acquired the coaching skills taught in the workshop and demonstrated these skills on the job, the value added would be three times the worth of the investment. Post-training assessments determined that the workshop wasn't meeting expectations. Only 55 percent of the members of the pilot group were found to be using the new skills successfully on the job, while 45 percent were not. Working with the unit manager, the

All too often trainers' questions during needs assessments are hopelessly vague.

trainers reviewed the data (which was clear, specific and plentiful, thanks to the preparatory work) and were able to identify the problem. They are now moving to correct it.

If behaviors taught in a course aren't transferring to the job, that's good to know. The key point there, however, is not that the coaching course failed to hit its target. It's that this soft-skills program had a target, one expressed in monetary terms: It would repay the company's investment three times over in traceable dollars.

A process that can assign a value to training can also be used to discover the cost of not training. As part of a downsizing and cost-cutting program, Alberta General Telephone Ltd. (AGT) of Edmonton, Alberta, Canada, decided to save training expenses by shortening the entry-level training program for customer service reps from two weeks to one week. Rudy Nieuwendyk, manager of HR education and development, decided to track the effect of that decision.

By using performance measures already in place, and tracking the variables other than training that have an impact on performance, he found that reps who completed two weeks of training were able to complete a call in an average of 11.4 minutes, whereas those completing only one week of training took 14.5 minutes.

The bottom line of this analysis was that the extra time required to complete calls cost the company more than $50,000 in lost productivity in the first six weeks. In addition, the cost of lost quality due to increased errors, increased collectibles, and service-order error rates exceeded the amount lost due to decreased productivity. So the cost to AGT of cutting back on training amounted to more than $100,000. Management decided to restore the two-week training program. The company is thinking about expanding it even more.

Nieuwendyk's next goal is to apply the TVs approach to the company's quality-training efforts. "We delivered a lot of quality training over a four-year period," he says. "It would have been heresy to question the value of quality training. [But] after the training was done, we came to understand that we hadn't clearly identified what it was that the training was to affect. We had no reliable method to determine who needed training in what to affect what behavior to obtain what measurable result. What we are beginning to do now is to determine the what, who, why and how before we invest the training dollars."

The Model

The TVS approach breaks down into four basic steps.

Step 1: Situation.

The "situation" is the business problem or opportunity with which we're concerned; that is, it's the pre-training status of somebody's (or some group's) performance. We analyze the situation by asking managers a series of questions that uncover and clarify the source of value within the function and the key processes for obtaining that value. In other words, what do these people do that is important to the organization, and how do they do it? Once we know that, we can settle upon definitions of acceptable and current levels of performance. Finally, we establish the value of the gain we would achieve if the current level of performance were brought up to an acceptable level.

The situation analysis shows what the issue looks like strategically, how it works tactically, how it affects the organization, and what it costs. This is the most important step in the process. It requires considerable detail and precision. It begins and ends with a focus on value. When done properly, the potential measurable value of training (or some other intervention) becomes clear.

Step 2: Intervention.

This step has two components: problem diagnosis and training description. In diagnosing the problem, we study the performance shortfall to find its source and a likely solution. The solution may or may not be training. A checklist, based on the seminal work of Bob Mager on analyzing performance problems, points to the true source of the problem.

Following Mager's lead, we ask a series of branching questions: Is there a performance discrepancy? If yes, is it important? If so, could the person do the job if her life depended on it? If not, is it because she lacks certain skills? If so, can training help? If it isn't a skill issue, what is it? And so on.

Based on the outcome of this diagnosis, we decide whether to attack the problem with training or to seek a different solution. If we decide to train, we naturally want to develop a course that builds the specific skills people will need in order to close the gap between the current level of performance and the acceptable level.

Step 3: Impact.

Suppose we've decided that training is the remedy. We have designed and delivered the training. Now the question becomes, what difference do we observe in the trainees' behavior and performance after they have completed the course? An impact statement describes:

• The variables that might have caused the difference in performance.
• The relative effect of each of the variables.
• How employee behavior, as a result of the training, changed and affected performance (as in the AGT example).
• Why training did or did not affect performance (as in the Prudential case).

Step 4: Value.

Value is the monetary worth of the effects of changed performance. It is a measure of differences in quality, productivity, service or sales, all of which can be expressed in terms of dollars. Sometimes the dollar value is imme-

---

This approach can help forge a stronger partnership between trainer and client.

---

diately evident, as with increases in market share or margin on sales. Other desirable outcomes, such as a reduction in time to market or an increase in customer satisfaction, can be converted to dollars.

One company in our group, a pharmacy chain, developed a 240-hour, state-approved course to certify pharmacy technicians to expand their role to include counting and pouring prescriptions. A change in state regulations, which previously had reserved these tasks for registered pharmacists, made this expanded role for technicians possible. Since technicians are paid less than pharmacists, the company saves money every time a prescription is processed by a technician. With some uncomplicated math, the company determined that the value added by the certification program — its payback after expenses — amounts to $318,422 per year.

Typically, the "impact" and "value" steps are the missing links in attempts to determine the concrete worth of training programs. This is where the disclaimers crop up and everyone starts backpedaling from definitive statements of value added. But when the link is strongly forged right at the start, in the situation phase, the impact and value become relatively easy to determine. Sometimes they're quite obvious.

Partners

Training veterans may say they don't see anything new in this process. All it does, after all, is identify a business problem, suggest a solution, and estimate the value of the result. But I would argue that two factors make this approach noteworthy.

The first is methodological. Right from the beginning, in the situation phase, the trainer employs a focused analytic method with a set of directed questions. These help managers dig answers out of their operating results — answers to questions about what good performance looks like and why skills matter.

Second, the approach forges a strong partnership between the trainer/performance analyst and the client/manager. And since a very tight focus on value is maintained throughout the process, the partnership is based on the manager's core concern: performance. Tangible values are identified for each skill to be taught. There is no vagueness or backing off from visible, quantitative evidence. The result can be a powerful bonding of trainer and customer — a bond that exists all too rarely in organizations today.

It is clear, at least to everyone involved in this project, that the door is open to objective training evaluation. All we have to do is walk through it.

Notes:

Simplifying ROI

Elaborate studies of return on training investments are terrific if you've got the time and money. Here's an alternative if you don't.

BY JAMES HASSETT

Everyone can always use more training. Every single person in your organization could probably benefit from learning new job skills. On the other hand, everyone could also use a week off, another $10,000 in the bank and fresh mints on their pillows each night.

On any given day, managers would rather see their employees working on the job rather than in a classroom or training center learning how to become more efficient. The costs of training are always easier to see than the costs of not training. Therefore, the question of whether employees need more training inevitably comes down to time and money. Will the time and money you invest today in training be repaid — with interest — in the next week, month, year or decade?

How do you measure a particular training program's contribution to the bottom line? Several state-of-the-art cost studies prescribe exacting methods for tracking return on training investments. These methods are certainly worth considering. However, a more modest four-step procedure called training investment analysis can be an attractive alternative. This procedure can help you obtain a simple, straightforward estimate of the impact of any training program on your organization's bottom line.

ROI Research

There's a long, rich history of research on the effects of training — both economic and noneconomic. From anthologies such as Lakewood Publications' *Evaluating Training's Impact* to Donald Kirkpatrick's classic 1975 article "Evaluating Training Programs" in *Training & Development* magazine, innumerable researchers and practitioners have offered models and words of wisdom on evaluating training.

Kirkpatrick delineated four levels of training evaluation: *reaction* ("How did you like the training?"), *learning*

If you look at everything that happens after a training program as the result of the training program, you are falling into a classic fallacy.

("What do you know now that you didn't know before?"), *behavior* ("What do you do differently?"), and *results* ("How did the training affect your organization?"). Each succeeding level of evaluation is a bit more difficult to perform and less frequently done than the one before it.

Measuring results does not necessarily mean measuring a monetary return. For example, for the last several years, our company has worked on a series of training programs regarding new computer systems used by flight standards inspectors in the Federal Aviation Administration. The primary mission of the FAA is to increase aviation safety. In this context, a results study would focus on using the computer systems or on the effectiveness of inspection programs for aircraft and personnel, not on profit and loss.

Even profit-making institutions have training programs that are not designed to increase profits. In the banking industry, for example, employees are trained to comply with government regulations.

However, in any organization that seeks to make a profit, one of the most compelling demonstrations of a training program's effectiveness will be its effect on the bottom line, or what is often called return on investment (ROI).

In 1990, *Training and Development* published "Return on Investment: Accounting for Training," a special report by Anthony P. Carnevale and Eric R. Schulz that summarized the American Society for Training and Development's research on this issue. In that survey, two out of three training managers reported they felt increasing pressure to show that programs affect the bottom line. However, only 20 percent of these same organizations did ROI studies, in part because they felt this type of evaluation "takes too much time or is too costly."

Another review (published in TRAINING, August 1991) cited a Federal Express analysis as a good example of the state of the art in measuring ROI. The study focused on 20 employees who went through the company's two-week training program soon after being hired to drive FedEx vans. Their performance was compared with a control group of 20 other new hires whose managers were told to do no more (nor less) on-the-job training than normal.

Performance was tracked for the two groups for 90 days in categories such as accidents, injuries, time-card errors and domestic air-bill errors. The 10 performance categories had dollar values assigned by experts from engineering, finance and other groups. The cost of each accident, for example, was placed at $1,600.

The basic math for computing the ROI was straightforward. The annual cost of errors for untrained couriers was estimated at $4,833, vs. $2,492 for trained couriers. That works out to a training-produced difference of $2,341 per person per year. This is $451 more than the cost of the $1,890 training course (a price tag that includes instructors' and trainees' salaries, as well as the costs of hotel, meals, airfare and covering couriers' duties during training). When this savings of $451 for one courier is multiplied by the 1,097 new employees who went through the program in a recent year, the ROI for that year was $494,747. This represents a very healthy 23.9 percent return on investment. The study itself cost about $10,000 and took five months.

This kind of rigorous evaluation doesn't make sense for every training program, however. Would you spend $10,000 to evaluate a $5,000 program? Even if you can afford the cost, can you afford the time? The ASTD report cites the case of a $40,000 study conducted by New England Telephone to measure the effectiveness of a technician training program. Trouble was, by the time the report was completed, "everyone familiar with the evaluation had left the department that financed it." The need for a more modest approach, at least in some cases, is obvious.

Meanwhile, Back in the Real World

Many people seem to believe that corporate bottom lines provide an objective measure that can be used as the basis for a harsh brand of frontier justice: A manager makes a decision, it increases profits or it doesn't, and the manager gets a raise or is fired as a result. In the real world, managers and accountants know that nothing is ever that cut-and-dried.

Anyone who has ever written and enacted a business plan knows that financial predictions often fail to match reality. It would be nice to have a simple, inexpensive and unambiguous system for deciding what actually caused a business venture to succeed or fail. But in practice, this is somewhere between prohibitively expensive and impossible. This leads directly to a key fact underlying the rationale for training investment analysis:

Fact 1: Many interrelated factors affect profit and loss; training is just one.

This seems painfully obvious. Training, by itself, almost never determines the bottom line. But it is easy to lose sight of this fact when you are doing a study that focuses on training's ROI.

Intuitively we know that, under some conditions, training does increase efficiency and profits. If you want people to sell a complex product, they must know what it is. If clerks are to enter orders on a form, they must be trained to fill out forms accurately. For those who distrust such intuitions, the Federal Express study is just one in a long series of studies that supports this conclusion.

However, it also follows that, under other conditions, even the best training will not increase profits.

Suppose an eccentric entrepreneur believes that 8-inch floppy disks are going to make a comeback due to a ground swell of support for used computers. He believes that training his sales force is crucial, and he hires the best trainers in the business. But his prediction is wrong: Nobody buys the used computers or the disks.

Does that mean that the training was at fault? Of course not.

Or suppose that a full-service brokerage firm is concerned about losing clients to discount brokers. It decides that training its employees in customer support will reverse this trend. The firm invests in a customer service training program for all of its brokers and support personnel.

Unfortunately, the company also decides to continue charging an 8 percent front-end load to cover sales commissions and 4 percent per year for marketing expenses. The week that the training is completed, the cover of Money magazine gives the firm an award for the all-time-worst buy in mutual funds. Again, in profit-and-loss terms, the training likely will have no impact. But the reasons customers go to the competition have nothing to do with the training.

External factors (such as the state of the economy and the world) are difficult to analyze and nearly impossible to control. If you look at everything that happens after a training program as the result of the training, you are falling into a classic fallacy. Logicians even have a special name for this error in thinking: "post hoc ergo propter hoc," which means "after this, therefore because of this," which is not logically correct.

Whenever possible, judgment calls that quantify the effects of training should be made by decision makers or management.

Thus, a definitive analysis of a training program's ROI is impossible until enough time — months or years — passes and the impact becomes clear. Even then, the results are never entirely unambiguous because it is so difficult to unravel the effects of training from other variables.

All of this leads, indirectly, to a second fact underlying training investment analysis:

Fact 2: The most important analysis of training's return on investment occurs before a training program is offered — not after it is over.

A year after the training is over, your company will move on to new challenges. If the training worked, it may be no longer relevant. And if the training failed, it may no longer matter.

According to an old Chinese proverb: To prophesize is very difficult — especially with respect to the future. Yet that is precisely what we do with each new business decision and each new training program. It follows that training investment analyses that are performed after the fact are mostly for the record book. They have a place in long-term corporate policy, but the most important training to evaluate is not last year's, it is next year's. That's the program you will go ahead with or cancel. And that's the program that will affect the bottom lines you care about most: this year's and next year's.

ROI Focus

Before you begin a training investment analysis, ask: Will (or did) this training program give employees knowledge or skills needed to meet organizational objectives that are not directly measured by short-term profit and loss? If the answer is "Yes," then a single-minded focus on the bottom line is misplaced. Instead, you should consider analyzing noneconomic results of the program, such as improved compliance with regulations or safety procedures.

If the training is aimed at increasing profits, assess how profit is measured in your organization and whether it is necessary to show how profit is linked to training. Seek out the views of key decision makers, and talk to them first about their expectations and needs.

For example, in a December 1991 article about Federal Express in *Training & Development*, founder and chairman Frederick W. Smith says:

"You could never cost justify the cost of our FXTV network or our interactive video training system. But if you ask me, those would be among the top 10 highest payoff projects we've ever done at Federal Express. Maybe even in the top three." As the article explains, Smith believes it's important for the company's leadership to support things like quality and learning "that cut across the organization and don't have a clear ROI." This strong corporate belief would make a study of training investment analysis at best redundant, and at worst subversive.

The KISS Rule

It is hard to go wrong following the KISS rule — Keep It Simple, Stupid. Training investment analysis explicitly recognizes that in many situations, the best available information is an informed estimate. That being the case, the accompanying work sheet is designed to simplify the process so that these informed estimates can be reached as efficiently as possible and then put into action.

Note that training investment analysis represents a small retreat from more formal evaluations with control groups, before and after tests, and complex methodology. But also note that an easier analysis procedure makes it more practical for you to focus on the bottom line when it matters most: as you plan your training.

Here are the four steps to a training investment analysis:

1 Determine the information your organization needs. A training investment analysis should always use the same financial procedures and terminology that other departments in your company use when they evaluate a potential investment in equipment or software. If another department has produced a report, get a copy. You may find that others avoid the term return on investment, and use an alternative accounting concept such as the payback approach or the net present value approach or the rate of return approach. If so, you should do the same. Learn to speak the same language as your financial people, and calculate costs the same way they do.

If your organization requires a sophisticated analysis, you may be able to apply models developed in previous studies of training ROI, such as:

• Ives and Forman's multilevel ROI model, including cash in-flow benefits and depreciated costs (*CBT Directions*, June 1991).

• Spencer's step-by-step model for calculating the costs and benefits of an HRD program (*TRAINING*, July 1984).

• Godkewitch's examples of financial utility equations (*TRAINING*, May 1987).

• Schneider, Monetta and Wright's innovative use of a management inventory to measure the ROI of a supervisory course (*Performance and Instruction*, March 1992).

However, if your organization does not demand this level of analy-

---

Focus on bottom-line measures when it matters most: when you're designing training.

---

sis, these methods may be overkill. This leads to the second step in training investment analysis.

2 Use the simplest and least-expensive method possible for finding the information you need.

In many settings, the Training Investment Analysis Work Sheet will provide all the structure that you need to calculate the returns from your training program. You can use it to predict the effects of a new training program or to study the effects of an old one. It also can be used to generate the best guess or a range of possible effects — from the lowest return to the highest possible return.

At the top of the work sheet, record the overall objective of the training program, its audience and the time period in which you expect the training to produce significant economic results. For most organizations, one year is a good place to start.

If your company is known for its fiscal patience and its emphasis on long-term results, you may want to look at effects over two or three years, since longer periods will generally show greater effects. At the other extreme, if your company's stockholders prefer instant gratification, and anything beyond the next quarter or two is considered the distant future, you may be forced to analyze the return over three to six months, even if this underestimates the total value of the training.

Part 1 of the work sheet calculates the revenue produced by training. Two options are provided. Option A, itemized analysis, provides a list of ways in which training may increase revenue: increased sales, higher productivity, reduced errors (for example, in manufacturing or billing), client retention, employee retention, and other. For example, let's say a sales training program for computer networks results in five additional sales per person per year. If each sale produces a marginal profit of $10,000, and there are 20 salespeople in the department, the total revenue produced by training is five times $10,000 times 20 or $1 million.

Some of the figures requested here are unambiguous, such as the number of employees and revenues per sale. However, in each category, at least one of the figures requires an informed estimate of training's effects, such as the additional sales per employee, the percent increase in productivity or the number of errors per employee avoided as a result of training.

This leads to one of the most important elements of training investment analysis: Whenever possible, judgment calls that quantify the effects of training should be made by decision makers or management. Admittedly, these figures will be informed estimates rather than unassailable truths. However, if decision makers are responsible for making the estimates, they will be far more likely to accept your final conclusions. Their participation in your estimating process is likely to increase their support of training investment analysis. At the least, this process will make it clear that the training department is sensitive to bottom-line issues and is doing as much as possible to tailor its training programs to increase profits.

After all of these judgments have been made and the calculations have been performed, the total revenue produced by training is the sum of the estimates from all categories.

In complex situations in which it's difficult to assign the effects of training to distinct categories, the only practical way to calculate training's effects will be to use Option B, the summary analysis. Very simply, this calculates the difference in revenues with and without training. Suppose,

TABLE 1
TRAINING INVESTMENT ANALYSIS WORK SHEET

Objective: _____

_____

Audience: _____

Returns measured over: _____ One year _____ Other _____

PART 1: CALCULATING THE REVENUE PRODUCED BY TRAINING

OPTION A — ITEMIZED ANALYSIS

Increased sales:
- _____ Additional sales per employee
- x _____ Revenues (or margin) per sale
- x _____ Number of employees
- = _____ Revenue Produced by Training

Higher productivity:
- _____ Percent increase in productivity
- x _____ Cost per employee (salary plus benefits plus overhead)
- x _____ Number of employees
- = _____ Revenue Produced by Training

Reduced errors:
- _____ Average cost per error
- x _____ Number of errors avoided per employee
- x _____ Number of employees
- = _____ Revenue Produced by Training

Client retention:
- _____ Average revenue per client
- x _____ Number of clients retained
- = _____ Revenue Produced by Training

Employee retention:
- _____ Average cost of a new employee (training plus lost productivity)
- x _____ Number of employees retained
- = _____ Revenue Produced by Training

Other: _____ _____

TOTAL Revenue Produced by Training: $ _____

OPTION B — SUMMARY ANALYSIS

| Revenue After Training | − | Revenue Without Training | = | Revenue Produced by Training |

PART 2: CALCULATING THE RETURN

| Revenue Produced by Training | − | Cost of Training | = | Total Return on Training Investment |

© 1992 Brattle Systems, Inc.

---

for example, the current sales forecast for next year is $4 million in profit. But key decision makers believe that with the added boost of a sales training program, this figure can be increased to $5 million. The revenue produced by training is then $5 million minus $4 million, or $1 million.

Once Part 1 is completed, Part 2 calculates the return by subtracting the cost of training from the revenue it produced. In the case of our mythical sales department, if it spent $200,000 on a custom-designed training program, the return would be $1 million minus $200,000, or $800,000.

3 Perform the analysis as quickly as possible. There is always a trade-off between the rigor of a study and the time it takes to perform. Clearly, training investment analysis sacrifices rigor for simplicity and immediacy.

There are many times when a rigorous study of ROI is justified and possible. But remember the New England Telephone study, which was out-of-date by the time it was completed. The training investment analysis approach is designed for situations in which time and money are severely limited. The work sheet focuses attention on the elements of a training program most likely to have an impact on the bottom line and then makes an educated guess. This can improve the accountability of the training department in a way that is visible throughout your organization.

4 Publish and circulate the results. Ideally, summary of the results should be a desktop publication with the quality one would expect of any important corporate document. It should reinforce the idea that training is an investment and could include information on training expenses in other companies.

If you find that a particular training program will cost more than it will produce, publish and circulate the results just as quickly as you would with a positive study. It will increase your credibility as someone who is willing to face harsh bottom-line realities and adjust to them.

With any luck, your study will provide irrefutable evidence of what trainers have known all along: Many training programs pay for themselves by increasing profits and/or reducing costs.

How to Escape Corporate America's Basement

There's just one way to earn respect in business: Contribute to the bottom line. You can demonstrate the dollar value of training without spending all of your time on elaborate evaluations.

BY JOHN V. NOONAN

I often tell colleagues that I can find the training department in any corporation within 10 minutes. It's easy. Go to the basement and walk around. When you get close to the loading dock, you're almost there.

There is one exception to this rule. If the corporation has multiple buildings, go to the structure farthest from the executive offices. Then look in the basement.

All right, that's hyperbole. But it's a fact that training is at the bottom of the pecking order in most companies. The problem is that training is seen as a staff function that doesn't really contribute to the bottom line.

If you're a trainer who wants to move out of the basement and increase your political status, I have succinct advice for you: Use bottom-line evaluation to show the value added by training.

The prime formula in the business world is really quite simple: Revenue minus cost equals profit. Departments and individuals who show how their activities relate to this formula do well. They are better positioned in the organization and have higher status than those that don't. Think about it.

The language of business is revenue, profit, market share, stockholder's equity and operating income.

What is the language of training? Left-brain/right-brain dominance. Metacognitive strategies. Myers-Briggs personality-type testing. And, my personal favorite, neurolinguistic programming. That one always makes me reach for the little airplane bag.

Is it any wonder "businesspeople" don't buy into the value of training?

This may sound harsh, and my guess is that many of you are think-

Businesspeople aren't looking for experimental "proof." If you want to publish in a refereed journal, get a job at a university.

ing, "Noonan, you're just another blood-sucking capitalist like those other idiots I have to deal with every day." Fine, be outraged. But your indignation isn't going to change line managers' low opinions of training.

Evaluation

Why do trainers have such a hard time justifying their existence? The language problem is one reason, but there are others.

First, the data you need in order to document the financial value of what you do is hard to get. It's not just lying around waiting for you to pick up. No one hands it to you. You have to come up with creative ways to get it.

Second, management is not going to give you any clear directions or expectations about how to prove your value. Top managers rarely will give you feedback on your programs. And when they do, it's usually too late.

When is it too late? Here's one clue: Your boss calls you into the office and says, "The executive board is very pleased with the training programs. But they notice that we have spent a lot of money on training, and they think it's time to evaluate the programs [read "department" and "you"] to see which ones are working well and which ones aren't."

Your first reaction might be, "Good. It's about time upper management showed some interest in training." Let me offer another interpretation: These executives have already made up their minds. They are offering you a "courtesy" chance to justify your existence because they want this to look like a business decision, but your department is about to go down the tubes. If management asks for an evaluation, it's generally too late.

A third difficulty is that most trainers lack skill and knowledge in the whole area of measurement, statistics, research and evaluation. They roll their eyes backward when they see numbers, which always conjure up images of the C's they received in Algebra I.

But that's only half of the problem. Actually, the distribution of mathematical skills in the training community is bipolar: Trainers either know nothing or they have advanced degrees in measurement and evaluation. This brings up a related issue. The people who do understand measurement and statistics carry all kinds of academic baggage. You'll hear "...not experimentally sound... Campbell and Stanley's experimental and quasi-experimental research designs... separation of variables... can't randomly assign control groups... can't control independent variables."

Get a grip, folks. Businesspeople aren't looking for experimental "proof." They only want reasonable evidence — a plausible business case. Persuasion on the value of training is more a matter of organizational positioning than of airtight experimental research. If you want to publish in a refereed journal, get a job at a university.

Fourth, evaluation is often thwarted by a lack of resources. Good evaluations take time. Lots of it. I often hear trainers say, "If I had that much

TABLE 1
SUMMARY SPREADSHEET

Course: Two-day session on consulting skills
Vendor Cost: $6,000

	A Salary+Benefits	B Time	C Component Pay (A x B)	D Productivity Before	E Productivity After	F Productivity Gain (%) (E − D)	G Value Added (F x C)
1	$50,000	10%	$5,000	50%	70%	20%	$1,000
2	$50,000	80%	$40,000	50%	80%	30%	$12,000
3	$50,000	70%	$35,000	50%	80%	30%	$10,500
4	$50,000	40%	$20,000	30%	70%	40%	$8,000
5	$50,000	40%	$20,000	40%	80%	40%	$8,000
6	$50,000	70%	$35,000	60%	90%	30%	$10,500
					Total	190%	$50,000
					Average	32%	$8,333

time, I would rather spend it putting together and offering another training program." This is a lot like a marksman saying, "If I had 10 more minutes, I'd rather shoot at the target than look to see if the first 20 shots got close." Yes, good evaluations are time-consuming. But it is time well spent.

Finally, trainers are usually in lowly staff positions without access to the data they need to do the best evaluations. They lack the authority to look at the most valuable information: productivity data relating to the performance of trained and untrained people on the job. (This is assuming such information exists at all in a usable form, which it often doesn't.) What do you do? For starters, you can simply ask those with access to supply you with the data. This may or may not require some persuading. If you can't do that, then you have to come up with your own creative productivity measures.

Levels of Evaluation

You can evaluate training on several different levels. At what we might call Level 0, you can keep records of "who took what courses when." This is very easy to do with a desktop computer, but it really doesn't show how you are adding value. Some people call this data "rump hours" or "bic hours" (for "butts-in-chairs"). If you are not already evaluating at this level, then put down this article and start typing your résumé. There's no hope for you.

As for determining the quality of a training program, Donald Kirkpatrick's time-honored model proposes that there are four levels of evaluation. Each level gets harder to do, but gives you better data. The theme: Easier techniques have less value; harder techniques give greater value. (Isn't life like that?)

Level 1: Reaction. Did students like the course? This is what you find out with those evaluation forms you pass around at the end of a class. The data you gather this way is nice to know, but you wouldn't want to walk into a meeting of the executive team and say: "See? We know that training is adding value because the students give our courses high ratings."

Level 2: Learning. What did students actually learn in the course? Can they do something now that they couldn't do before the training? Learning is usually measured with pre- and post-tests, but sometimes with a post-test only. You're getting closer, but top management is cautious because you are still confining evaluation to the training event. They'll ask, "What impact has this learning had on the job?"

Level 3: Transfer. Are students applying what they learned to their jobs? Follow-up surveys of participants and supervisors or on-the-job observation are the usual methods for determining if training transferred. Finally, you have taken evaluation out of the training event to demonstrate some impact on the organization. With this data, you are going to get management's ear.

Level 4: Results. What is the impact on the organization of this change in behavior on the job? Are sales up? Costs down? Cycle time reduced? Is time saved? Usually this level of evaluation requires you to look at actual job performance and productivity. When you present this data to top management, you'll hit a home run. Why? Because you're talking dollars, cost savings, the bottom line — the language of business.

A Better Way

If we could, perhaps we'd do a Level 4 evaluation for every course we run. But face it, we can't. There's no time.

Or is there? Allow me to illustrate a technique that we use at Kraft General Foods to compute a dollar value for every course we run. Our monthly report to management includes a spreadsheet that shows the value added to the business by each course.

In one year, the grand total was over $3.1 million. Not bad for a two-person training department!

How do we do this? We cheat! We use a Level 1 technique to collect Level 4 data. (Our apologies to Dr. Kirkpatrick.)

Before you gasp in horror, however, remember that we're looking for plausible evidence of training's value, not experimental proof.

Here's the rationale. Assume that I'm paying Fred $50,000 (in salary and benefits) to do a job. Suppose I can isolate a set of job tasks — Tasks A, B and C — on which Fred spends 20 percent of his time. This means that I am paying Fred $10,000 a year to do Tasks A, B and C. Suppose that I can measure Fred's productivity on Tasks A, B and C before the training, and suppose I find that his productivity is 60 percent that of an experienced, high-performing individual at the same salary level.

This means that before the training,

Fred's value to the organization, for Tasks A, B and C, is $6,000 (60 percent of $10,000). Forget for a moment that I am actually paying him $10,000 to do Tasks A, B and C. Now suppose that I take a post-training measure of Fred's productivity and find that he is now 80 percent as productive as an experienced, high-performing individual. Fred's new value for Tasks A, B and C is $8,000 (80 percent of $10,000). I have added $2,000 of value by training him!

Ready for the mathematical formula? Here it is.

Value Added = (S x T) (P2 – P1), where:
S = Salary.
T = Time (percent of total).
P2 = Post-training Productivity (percent of master performer).
P1 = Pre-training Productivity (percent of master performer).

This technique is based upon the seminal and underappreciated work of Lyle M. Spencer Jr. (see the *Handbook of Human Resource Development*, American Managment Association, 1985). Table 1 shows a typical spreadsheet applying these computations to all the students in a class. (For simplicity, we assumed a common annual compensation.)

Last year we averaged $6,000 of value-added per student per course. Multiply that times your number of student days!

Getting the Data

I can hear it now: "Sure, but how do you get these productivity measures?" Answer: We use a well-known but little-used technique. We ask the people involved.

Table 2 shows the questions we ask on the end-of-course evaluation form. (Yes, I said the end-of-course form, not a survey sent out a few months after the course, when graduates presumably would have a far better handle on the actual impact of the training on their job performance. I know it sounds fishy, and we'll return to this point in a moment.)

The data from Question 1 goes into Column B on the spreadsheet; Question 2 into Column D; and Question 3 into Column E. The numbers add up quickly. People won't believe how much value — dollars — your training really provides. You'll need to walk them through the rationale and spreadsheet.

Then the objections will come. Don't worry, you can handle them.

**TABLE 2
END-OF-COURSE QUESTIONS**

1. What percent of your total working time will you be spending on tasks that require the skill/knowledge presented in the course? (Circle one.)
   0 10 20 30 40 50 60 70 80 90 100

2. Rate your productivity, **before training**, on your job tasks that require the skill/knowledge presented in the course (100 percent represents the productivity of an exemplary employee; 50 percent means that you could complete the tasks half as well or half as fast).
   0 10 20 30 40 50 60 70 80 90 100

3. Rate your productivity, **after training**, on your job tasks that require the skill/knowledge presented in the course (100 percent represents the productivity of an exemplary employee; 50 percent means that you could complete the tasks half as well or half as fast).
   0 10 20 30 40 50 60 70 80 90 100

Objections

First off, skeptics will say, "This isn't real productivity data, it's just people's perceptions!" They're right; it is just participants' impressions. Suppose they only improve half as much as they think they will. Believe me, you will still have some very impressive numbers. Or, you could use this objection as an entree to collecting on-the-job data. ("You're right. It would be a stronger case if I had objective performance data. Can you help me get it?")

Next objection: "If you want accu-

> You'll need to walk through your computations to quell their skepticism.

rate data, you need to ask the bosses. People always think they're better than they really are." When I hear this one at a presentation, I usually ask the audience for a show of hands: "Hands up for all of you who think that your boss can give a better estimate of your productivity than you can." I haven't had anyone raise a hand yet.

Next, the most obvious one: "Wait a minute! You ask these questions at the end of the course, when everyone is all pumped up from it. What do you expect? Of course they'll inflate their estimates."

This one actually called for some follow-up study. We tested the stability of the ratings. We surveyed a sample of participants and their managers three to six months after several courses. We asked the same questions, altering them slightly so that they asked about actual productivity on the job since the training.

We got data back on 26 participants across 13 classes. (Yes, that's a pretty lousy response, and it explains precisely why we'd rather pass out the surveys at the end of the course, when we have a captive audience.) The participant ratings were fairly consistent. They had overestimated by 17 percent (24 percent vs. 41 percent) the amount of time they spent on job tasks that required the skill taught in the course. They showed roughly the same pre-training estimate of productivity (50 percent vs.52 percent), but overestimated their post-training productivity by 8 percent. That is, three to six months later they said that they were 8 percent less productive than they thought they would be — roughly 73 percent of an experienced, high-performing person vs. 81 percent.

The managers' estimates of time spent on the job tasks were 27 percent less than the participants' estimates, and the managers rated participants' pre- and post-training productivity lower. But managers' and participants' estimates of pre- to post-training productivity gain were the same — roughly 30 percent higher. Our formula uses productivity gain to compute value added, so the fact that the managers supplied lower pre- and post-training ratings doesn't affect our computation.

What does this all mean? It shows that there is error in the rating process. But with our study, we made a reasonable attempt to measure the error and, consequently, we can adjust for it. The net effect is that we routinely reduce our estimate of value-added by 27 percent. That is, we compute the value on the spreadsheets, then multiply by .73 to arrive at an adjusted value. The numbers are still not too shabby. A $4 million estimate is reduced to about $3 million? So what? I'll take it.

Next objection: "I'm not convinced. You admit there is error. You still have nothing but people's opinions. You don't have any hard data!" Response: "We're building a business case, not trying to publish in an academic journal. Why don't you go get a job at a university?"

I'm not claiming that executives will take one look at numbers like these, swallow them whole, and sit back delighted with the meal. When you start presenting millions of dollars of value, they are likely to be skeptical. You'll need to walk them through the rationale and computations carefully to change their skepticism to understanding.

We trainers have claimed for years that a solid training program adds tremendous value to an organization. And we're right. This simple evaluation technique helps to bear us out. It also has great intuitive appeal. You maximize the value added by training when you have courses that (1) teach skills that people use a lot on the job, and (2) produce the greatest gain in productivity — regardless of the initial productivity level.

If you're still with me, your action items are obvious.

1. Stop speaking in training jargon.
2. Talk as if you're in business. (You are.)
3. Think strategically about how you demonstrate your value to your organization.
4. Keep your eyes on the productivity of real people in real jobs.
5. Use some kind of technique to compute how many dollars of value you're bringing into the organization. (If you don't like the model described here, use a different one.)

Notes:

Training for Impact

Is your training department judged by the number of bodies it runs through classrooms or by the results it achieves? Here's a step-by-step process to help you create a more valuable role for HRD

BY DANA GAINES ROBINSON

Ever hear of "training for activity?" You may not call it that, but undoubtedly its characteristics will sound familiar: Trainers spend most of their time in the classroom delivering programs; accountability focuses on activity — the number of programs conducted, the number of participants and so on; the training function is *valued* for the same things for which the department is held accountable — the number and variety of its programs; having a large course catalog becomes a real barometer of success.

Those characteristics are common among training departments. It also is common for trainers in such departments to "burn out" from all the stand-up training and begin to wonder about the value of their efforts: Are people really using the skills being taught?

There is an alternative. A human resources development department may have:

• Trainers who spend less than half of their time in the classroom.

• Accountability that focuses upon *results achieved*, both in terms of on-the-job behavior change and the organizational impact of the training,

• A function valued for assisting management in resolving business problems and/or maximizing business opportunities.

This second set of characteristics describes a results-oriented training department that is "training for impact," and while they may not be the norm at present, they certainly are part of HRD's future. Neal Chalofsky, national vice president for professional development of the American Society for Training and Development, reinforced that notion plainly enough in his editorial comments on ASTD's competency study for trainers. In the future, Chalofsky says, "Trainers will be responsible not only for learning, but also for making sure that learning is applied on the job. Trainers will be responsible not only for identifying training needs, but also for evaluating whether those needs are met."

Line management is demanding increased accountability from all functions, particularly staff areas which traditionally have been the most difficult to evaluate. The HRD profession, as evidenced by the competency study, is moving toward results-oriented training as a standard. There can be no doubt that HRD departments which demonstrate a track record of results meaningful to management will be those most able to gain additional resources. The movement away from activity and toward impact appears irreversible. Where to begin?

The "training for impact" model in Figure 1 (on p. 22) suggests one approach. Developed over the past six years, it has been validated through its use in determining the results of sales training, supervisory and managerial training, customer relations training and technical skills training.

In order to illustrate the steps involved in the model, let's use a fictitious organization known as Nu-Karparts, Inc. Nu-Karparts, we'll say, is a wholesale company that supplies automobile parts to retail stores throughout the United States.

Step 1. Symptom or request for training

Training needs surface in many ways: Sometimes a line manager calls with a request; sometimes training is "mandated" from top management; often the HRD department itself uncovers a potential problem.

At Nu-Karparts, the director of distribution called the corporate training director to indicate concern over the growing number of customer complaints coming into his office from the retail stores. These complaints suggested an increase in customer dissatisfaction and required a great deal of senior-level management time to resolve. The distribution director was certain that a training program he had heard about — one which instructed customer service representatives in how to handle people — would be appropriate. He wanted to pilot-test the program in two distribution centers; granted positive results there, he would implement it in the other two centers.

Step 2. Identify client

Once a need has surfaced, the HRD department must determine the key decision maker for the project — the highest-level individual (or group of individuals) who has the power to make a go/no-go decision *and* has a need to be actively involved. This person or group becomes, in effect, the "client."

Generally, clients are people who (a) are two or more levels above the learner, (b) are in the learner's chain of command, (c) approve any significant action regarding the training project and (d) have the most to gain or lose from the success or failure of this effort.

Rarely is the client either the learner himself or the learner's immediate manager. It is also unusual for the client to be the company's training director. Together, the client and the trainer will be making many critical decisions regarding the training project. Ideally, they will arrive at these decisions in a collaborative, consensus manner.

At Nu-Karparts, the trainer assigned to the customer relations project determined that the appropriate client group would be the director of distribution and the two distribution center managers involved in the pilot. These were the people who had the most to gain or lose. After the training director discussed the advantages of a client team with the director of distribution, they decided to move forward with these three people as that team.

Step 3. Learner needs: Assessment #1

It is almost always unwise to respond to a training request based upon the input and perspective of just one person; the probability of an accurate diagnosis is very low. At best, the training department may wind up addressing some part of the true problem with modest results. At worst, the diagnosis may have been completely inaccurate, resulting in misplaced use of training resources and damage to the credibility of the training function.

A basic axiom of HRD is that before training resources can be appropriated effectively, a problem's *cause* must be determined. Only then can a decision be made as to whether the problem is something training can address. Information from multiple sources is critical to needs assessment to ensure that all relevant perspectives are included. Possible sources for data gathering might be:

Clients — Key decision makers already identified.

Learners — People who will participate in any training effort which results. Involving the prospective learners helps foster "buy-in" should training be identified as a solution to the problem

Other interested parties — People who interact with the learners. They could be the direct managers or the employees of the learner. They also could be other staff or line personnel outside the chain of command of the learners. Finally, they might be customers or clients. Each situation determines what categories of people should be included.

State-of-the-art — If someone requests a program in influencing skills, it is the responsibility of the HRD professional to research the field and identify the validated behaviors and skills required to become an effective influencer. We are not in the business of training others according to precepts and programs someone happens to *think* will work. We are in the business of identifying, building and delivering programs that produce behavioral skills which have been *proven* to work (below).

As Figure 1 illustrates, once information about the learners has been collected it must be analyzed, interpreted and readied for reporting to the client. During this meeting, the trainer and client must draw conclusions from the information. From these conclusions, implications must be determined: "Here's what we have concluded. So what?" The end result of the meeting should be an agreement between trainer and client as to what skills and knowledge, if any, will be taught to which groups of people within the organization.

At Nu-Karparts, the trainer conducted a needs assessment and reported back to the director of distribution and the two center manager. The data indicated the following:

1. Customer service representatives (CSRs in the company's jargon) in the distribution centers were gathering information from customers in a variety of ways; there was no standard method.

2. About 12% of the calls taken each day were complaints. In a typical month, 22 of these complaint calls were escalated to the director and vice president levels.

3. Most CSRs were not skilled in asking questions of customers and, therefore, were not getting complete and accurate information when they filled out complaint forms; 50% of the forms were filled out incompletely.

4. Seventy-five percent of the customers interviewed by the trainer during the needs assessment indicated that the CSRs seemed defensive when a complaint was made.

Based on this information, the clients and the training director agreed that CSRs should receive training in both telephone fact-finding skills and the use of empathy.

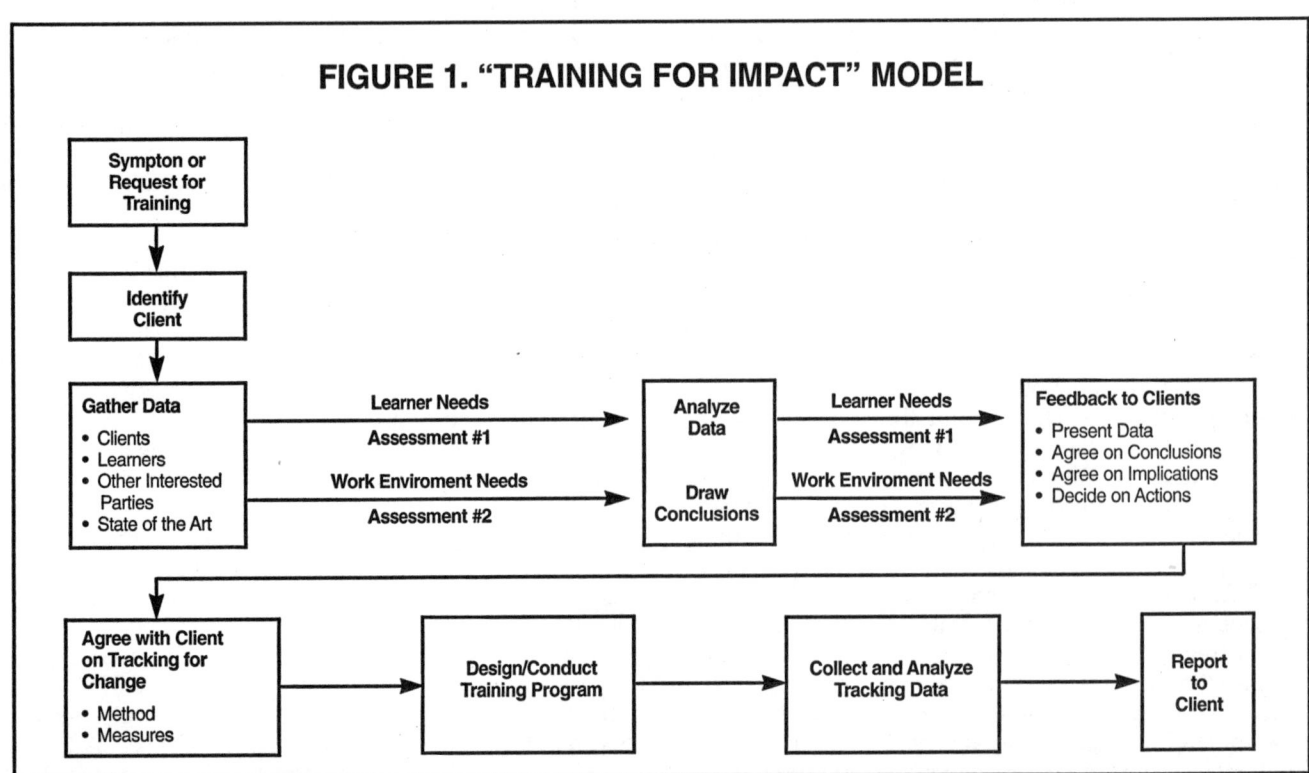

FIGURE 1. "TRAINING FOR IMPACT" MODEL

Work environment needs: Assessment #2

Once the client and the HRD professional have agreed upon specific training objectives, a second diagnostic effort is required if the goal is to produce long-lasting results on the job. Why? Because such results occur only as the product of a learning experience that is on-target and well-delivered, and a work environment that is *supportive* of the new skills. A zero on either side of the equation means long-term results will be impossible to achieve.

While the training department has a great deal of control over the learning experience, it has virtually no control over the work environment. This is where the client/trainer partnership becomes most critical and can really pay off. In order to ensure that skills will transfer to the work environment and persist over time, an analysis of that environment is necessary. In essence, the HRD professional will be attempting to answer these questions:

• What, if anything, about the learners themselves will inhibit or enhance the use of these new skills on the job?

• What, if anything about the learners' managers will inhibit or enhance the use of these new skills on the job?

• What, if anything, about the organization will inhibit or enhance the use of these new skills on the job?

Once collected, this information again must be analyzed, interpreted and reported to the client. By painting this type of picture, the trainer shows management what will happen if the work environment does not support the new skills — the results management desires will not occur.

At Nu-Karparts, the trainer succeeded in convincing management of the benefits of a work environment assessment. Even if CSRs had the skills to fact-find on the telephone and to use empathy, they might not use those skills for reasons relating to the organization: The problem would remain and the time and money spent on training would be flushed down the drain. Therefore, the trainer conducted a second assessment to determine whether anything *may* prevent CSRs who completed the training program from using the fact-finding and empathy skills they learned.

The study indicated that there were, indeed, organizational barriers. CSRs pointed out that their primary accountability involved the number of calls they took in a day; the effective handling of complaints was not a performance criterion. Obviously, it would require more time to handle a complaint well, meaning that fewer calls could be taken; in effect, a CSR

FIGURE 3. RESULTS FROM NU-KARPARTS TRACKING STUDY*

Behaviors	Prior to Training	After Training
1. CSRs will acknowledge the feelings of customers by labeling the feeling.	2.83	4.02
2. CSRs will rephrase what a customer has said before responding.	2.94	4.16
Scale: 1 = Behavior never used 2 = Behavior used about 25% of the time 3 = Behavior used about 50% of the time 4 = Behavior used about 75% of the time 5 = Behavior used 100% of the time		
Organizational Results Complaints per month escalated to director manager level of the organization.	22	5

*In a typical tracking study, dozens of behaviors may be observed. Only two are selected here for illustration.

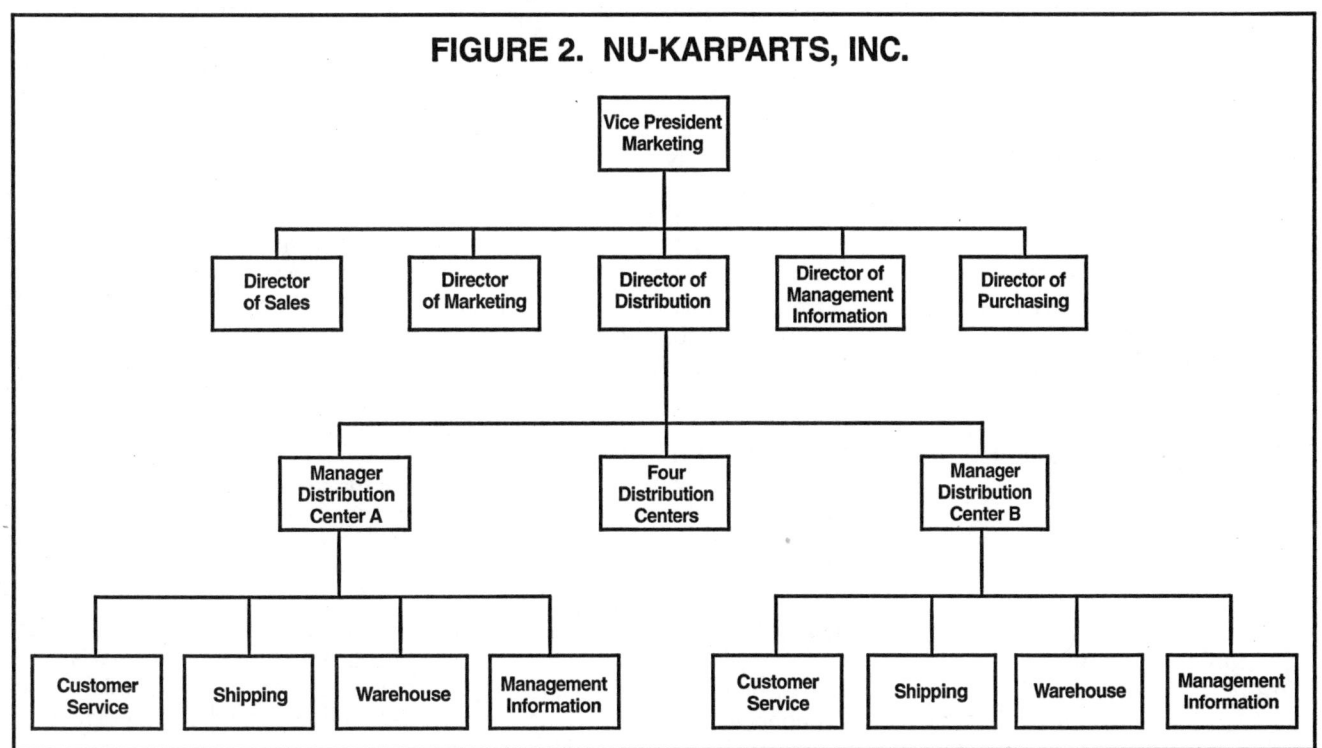

FIGURE 2. NU-KARPARTS, INC.

could be punished for taking more time to handle complaints.

Management agreed to set up a new accountability system for CSRs that would evaluate the handling of complaints as well as the quantity of calls handled.

Agree with Client on Tracking for Change

Once the program's outcomes have been clearly delineated, it is important to design a system that will monitor the results achieved both in qualitative and quantitative terms. The system must track both the behavior change which has occurred on the job and any resulting bottom-line impact to the organization. In order to accomplish this, the client and the trainer must agree on specific outcomes to be tracked.

The HRD professional must create the necessary survey process to gather the information. This usually requires collecting information about behavior both prior to training and at some point following the training. It also may be appropriate to compare the performance of people trained in the program against the performance of a similar group of people who have not received training.

At Nu-Karparts, the clients wanted to know if the CSRs were displaying behaviors such as "acknowledging the feelings of customers" and "rephrasing what the customer has said before responding." They also wanted to know if the number of complaints escalated to top management decreased over time. If complaints were being handled at the lowest level, avoiding the need for management involvement, customer satisfaction probably would increase — and that was another major goal of the training effort.

Information about CSR's behavior was gathered prior to the training program and again four months later. In order to determine if the new behaviors were being used effectively, questionnaires were sent to the CSRs, to their supervisors and to customers. In this manner, information from the CSRs' self-assessments could be verified from other perspectives.

Information about escalated complaints also was collected.

Design and Conduct Training Program

With the front-end work completed, the training department designs and delivers — or selects and buys — the program. Whether designed internally or purchased outside, the program should address the identified learner needs and proceed with an eye toward any work environment barriers which might be present.

At Nu-Karparts, the training department designed a two-day program for the CSRs. Their supervisors were provided with an overview of this program and some skill-building in reinforcement behaviors.

Collect Tracking Data and Report Results to Client

When the specified period has elapsed, post-training information is collected, tabulated, analyzed and reported to the client. This is truly where the "rubber meets the road" for the training department and the client team, for now we are looking at *results*. At this point, management and HRD either congratulate themselves on the program's success or decide on any actions to encourage results which have not yet appeared.

It is critical that the data which the HRD professional brings to this meeting paint an accurate picture so that appropriate decisions can be agreed upon. While HRD reports on the results, HRD *and* the client must determine the "So what?" and agree upon any required actions. If a study has been well constructed and presented, questions such as the following can be addressed:

• What behaviors are people using or not using on the job?
• What bottom-line impact, if any, did we have?
• If we have not achieved the desired results, why not?
• Should the training program be changed? If so, in what ways?
• Is additional training required?
• What must management do to create a work environment that will continue to support these new skills?

At Nu-Karparts, results indicated that behaviors *had* changed. As shown in Figure 3, CSRs who had been through the training program were using the behavior of "acknowledging feelings" at a mean frequency of 4.02 up from a mean frequency of 2.83; they were using the behavior of "rephrasing" at about the same frequency. The average number of escalated complaints dropped from 22 to five per month, providing a real organizational benefit. Most complaints were being handled at the lowest level possible. Because CSRs now were being evaluated on their use of the new skills in handling customer complaints, a reward system was in place to reinforce their *continued* use. All in all, the program appeared to be a success; the training had *impact*.

Can It Really Be Done?

This description of "training for impact" may imply that an enormous — perhaps a prohibitive — amount of time is required. That is not the case. Knowledgeable trainers typically conduct some front-end work to clarify learner needs before launching their programs. The unusual parts of this process are the addition of a work environment assessment and the design and implementation of a tracking system. Combined, these two activities require an additional five to seven days spread over the lifespan of the training project.

What *is* demanded here is skill: The HRD professional must be able to design good diagnostic systems; consulting skills are necessary both to forge the critical partnership with the client and to make that partnership work. Also required is a revised accountability system for the HRD department. Rather than being evaluated according to how many programs it offers in a year, the training department must be judged in light of the results it helps to achieve. Most HRD professionals probably will have to initiate this change by convincing management that significant benefits can derive from it.

And the benefits *are* significant, not only to management but to the training department: increased credibility in the eyes of management; the intrinsic reward that comes from knowing people are *really* using the skills learned in the classroom; allocation of limited training resources to assignments where results are relatively assured; creation of a work environment which supports these results; the education that management receives as to what training can and cannot do. With management viewing the training department as a partner in moving the organization forward, support for budgets and staffing becomes more probable.

The "training for impact" model is not appropriate for *every* training effort; but it is essential that at least some of your training projects each year follow this type of model.

Measuring the 'Goodness' of Training

Evaluation. Measurement. Return on investment.
They all mean the same thing: Mass confusion

BY JACK GORDON

Dip into your company's training curriculum and pick a course. Any course. Got it? Fine. Now, how good is that course? Ten points if you object that this is a meaningless question until I define what I mean by "good." Ten more if you catch yourself reaching about instinctively for a heavy stick, because we are headed into the subject of instructional evaluation here, and that, you know, is a snake pit.

Right off the bat, for instance, we run into conceptual distinctions between "training" and "education." As retired George Washington University professor and HRD (human resources development) Hall of Fame member Len Nadler proposed 21 years ago, it is one thing to teach employees skills that will help them do their present jobs better (he suggested we call this training). It is something else to expose them to information or situations that we hope will enable them to perform better down the road in a variety of possible jobs (education or "development," depending on the time frames involved). In the first case, we're expecting an immediate payoff of some sort: The person will go straight back to the job and begin doing something differently, and this difference will be a good thing for the organization. In the second case — if, for example, we send a promising young manager to Belgium or Venezuela for a few years of international seasoning before bringing her back to corporate headquarters in Houston — we can't necessarily define the specific new behaviors we want to see when she returns. Nor can we say exactly what benefits we believe will accrue to the organization or precisely when we expect to reap them. Still, we believe this international exposure to be worthwhile.

If we think in those terms, measuring the quality of a training program obviously is a different proposition from evaluating an educational or developmental initiative.

Swell. So how good is a training program? That question has gotten snakier over the past few years

---

**If training is good
by definition, your course
is good. If you want to
make it even better,
add a week.**

---

because there is a diminishing amount of common ground for framing a discussion about goodness.

In what we might call the classic performance technology view, advanced by people like HRD Hall of Famers Robert F. Mager and Thomas F. Gilbert, a good training program is one that contributes the maximum concrete benefit to the organization in the least possible time.

The point of training, Gilbert said in his 1978 book Human Competence, is to equip people for "worthy performance." His "First Leisurely Theorem" states that the worth of human performance is equal to the value of a person's accomplishments (on the job) divided by the cost of the behavior that goes into producing these accomplishments (W = A/B). Similarly, training is worthwhile to the degree that the accomplishments it enables people to achieve outweigh the cost of the training. In Gilbert's terms, it's impossible to talk about training without measuring a return on the investment. Evaluation is built in. You train to cure a performance discrepancy, and you figure out in the beginning how much that discrepancy is costing the organization. So does the training cure the problem or not?

To Gilbert — and Mager — less is more. An excellent way to increase the goodness of a five-day training program would be to redesign it as a two-day program that enabled trainees to accomplish the same results, or better ones, back on the job.

Contrast that view of goodness with the American Society for Training and Development's call for all companies to spend at least 2 percent of their annual payroll (and preferably 4 percent) on training. Or compare it with management consultant Tom Peters' advice in a recent syndicated column that companies should "train without limits. Pick up the tab for training unrelated to work — keep everyone engaged, period."

In this conception, training is good by definition, and more training is always better.

At a conference, Mager told a group of training directors about two priests who asked him to design a program that would increase the reverence of their parishioners. The project stalled when the priests were unable to agree on what sort of behaviors they would accept as evidence that reverence had, in fact, increased. The point of the story was that if you can't define what successful performance would look like, you can't design a coherent training program at all, let alone measure its efficiency or effectiveness.

If the program you pulled out of your curriculum back there at the start is a six-week, state-of-the-art course intended to turn employees into global-team-leadership-creative-ninja-risk takers, you probably ought to stop reading right here. The program may be delivering a multitude of priceless blessings to your organization — who knows? But your chances of documenting those benefits to the satisfaction of a skeptical party are likely nil. If training is good by definition, your course is good. If you want to make it even better, add a week.

Levels

Still here? Well then, assuming we are not satisfied with the premise that training is good by definition (suppose, for instance, we fear that premise is a formula for a few years of high times and fat budgets in the training world,m= followed by a vicious backlash that will make "training" a dirty word for a decade, the accelerating pace of change notwithstanding), how might we determine the goodness of a job-related training program?

The most convenient way yet devised to talk about that question was outlined in 1959 by Donald L. Kirkpatrick, a former professor at the University of Wisconsin and now a training consultant in Elm Grove, WI. Kirkpatrick proposed ("noticed" might be more accurate, he suggests) that there are four main "levels" at which you can gauge the quality — the efficiency and/or effectiveness — of a training course.

At the first (and easiest) level, you can measure trainees' reactions to the course. Did they like it? When they walked out, did they feel their time had been well spent? Did the material make sense to them? Was the instructor knowledgeable and helpful? Do they believe the things they learned will be helpful to them back on the job? Were the donuts fresh and tasty? Chairs comfy? Slides and overheads readable from the back of the room?

Level 1 data is gathered most often with questionnaires handed out at the end of a session. These "happiness sheets"are often sneered at by people who insist that they measure only the entertainment value of a course and not its quality. Kirkpatrick, however, defends trainee-reaction data. What you're measuring with a happiness sheet, he says, is initial customer satisfaction with the training experience. What's so shameful about that? A happiness sheet can help you improve the design and delivery of the instruction in perfectly valid ways. The sheet only becomes sneer worthy if you pretend it's telling you what's happening at higher levels of evaluation.

At Level 2 you measure learning. Did they, in fact, acquire the skills or knowledge you intended to teach them? Depending on the course objectives, this can involve anything from a pencil-and-paper test (Can they recall and describe three techniques for reducing stress?) to a simulation or a full-fledged skill demonstration (Presented with a variety of malfunctions on a mainframe computer system, can course graduates diagnose and repair the various problems within a certain time frame?).

At Level 3 you want to know whether the trainees are using their new skills and knowledge back on the job. Since you tested them at Level 2, you know that they can load the truck correctly, but are they loading the truck correctly out there in the real

---

Sometimes the view from Level 4 will reveal that 'success' at Level 3 is actually failure.

---

world? Three months after the training course,say, you might hide behind a crate on the shipping dock and watch them load some trucks. Or you might interview them, interview their supervisors, survey the customers to whom the loaded trucks are sent, etc.

At Level 4 you're looking for business results. Assuming these people are doing things the way you taught them to, what difference does it make to the organization? What impact does their new behavior have on the company's performance, health and welfare? Are the trained factory workers producing more widgets per hour, with fewer defects, than untrained workers? Have widget sales increased because the salespeople are using the new prospecting techniques you taught them? Has turnover decreased among hourly workers since supervisors started using the methods from the "positive coaching" course? Are customers shopping here more often because of the new treatment they're getting from employees at the service counter? If the answer to any of these questions is yes, how much is the result worth to the organization in dollars and cents? How does that compare to the total cost of the training program? At Level 4, you're asking about the company's return on its training investment. You're measuring ROI.

Sometimes the view from a Level 4 perspective will reveal that "success" at Level 3 is actually failure. *TRAINING* knows of one case in which a bank conducted some market research that showed that its customers liked to be treated with great respect by loan officers, especially young ones. A checklist of respectful behaviors ensued — smile, shake hands, always apologize for any delay longer than five minutes. The checklist became the foundation of a training program. Back on the job, trainees were reinforced for using the checklist behaviors by "mystery shoppers" who would "catch them doing something right" and give them $20 bills. Up through Level 3, everything looked swell.

Then it occurred to somebody to interview some customers. "Why are your loan officers acting so weird?" the customers complained. "I just walked in the door and one of them rushed up and said, 'Sorry to keep you waiting.' " The loan officers, coveting the $20 prizes, were overdoing the checklist behaviors. All that smiling and handshaking and apologizing struck customers as robotic and phony. It made them jumpy. It made them wish they'd gone to a different bank.

At any of the four levels, evaluation can be done well or poorly, convincingly or laughably. At any level you can gather evidence that will help you improve a course in some way. But as the bank found out, tracking efficiency at one level doesn't necessarily tell you about effectiveness at the next. It's probably fair to say that the bulk of all employee training programs conducted in the United States are evaluated only at Level 1, if at all. Of the rest, the majority are measured only at Level 2.

"We don't do as much evaluation as we'd like, mostly due to the expense, lack of time and lack of client interest," says Edward J. Zobeck, manager of employee development for AAA Michigan in Livonia, the state branch of the American Automobile Association. He speaks, undoubtedly, for a great many training directors. Clients, meaning line managers, are generally loath to add the expense of rigorous evaluation to an expense they already regret — that of training. "We do Level 1 routinely," says Zobeck. "In many courses we go to Level 2, and we get some anecdotal evidence at Level 3. That's about it."

When training directors say they wish they could do more rigorous evaluations, their concern often is to protect themselves against a rainy day: the day when a new management team comes in or some executive gets a burr under his saddle, and suddenly everybody wants to know about the payback for the organization's investment in training. If the answers aren't there, heads may roll and programs may get the ax.

Zobeck's concerns are different. In the first place, he says: "A lot of the technical training we do is for entry-level people. We know they can't perform the job when they come in the door." There is little chance, in other words, that some manager will suggest the organization could get along perfectly well without programs that teach insurance-product knowledge, claims adjusting, how to use the computer system and so on.

No, if Zobeck had the time, the money and his druthers, his first Level 4 evaluation efforts would be aimed at programs he himself distrusts. "We've got a few courses we offer 'just because,' " he says — usually because they were requested at some point by a manager with clout.

Kirkpatrick argues that with ``soft-skills'' training, in particular, there often are good reasons (besides lack of time and money) not to carry an evaluation beyond Levels 1 or 2. For instance, a technique like "management by walking around" won't necessarily work well for every manager; some supervisors just create suspicion when they start showing up for casual chats with subordinates. Therefore, if you're teaching MBWA, you may not want every trainee to use the learned behaviors on the job: "If this doesn't seem to be working for you, don't force it. It's just something to try."

A related consideration: When an organization teaches certain interpersonal communication methods or uses training to promote particular attitudes or values, employees sometimes complain that the company is trying to tamper with their personalities or force them to fit some homogeneous mold. The trainer's common response is that trainees are merely being "offered some new behaviors" to try out. If they find that these behaviors don't work well for them, they are perfectly free to reject them. This explanation springs a big leak if the trainees are later pressured or "judged" (at Level 3) on the basis of whether they are behaving in the recommended manner back on the job.

Then there's Nadler's distinction between training and education. With management and soft-skills courses, far more often than with technical programs, companies simply figure they're doing education. Direct, measurable results are beside the point. Granted, this just ducks the question of whether last week's leadership seminar was worth the bother, but let's let that one lie for now.

Hissing

It's at Level 4 that you want to start watching your ankles in earnest, ladies and gentlemen, because here's

---

"If you do a good needs analysis up front, evaluation will take care of itself."

---

where we run straight into those snakes.

The hissing begins as soon as somebody mentions the word proof. Can you prove that some particular training course, and nothing else, is solely responsible for a $500,000 increase in sales revenue? For a 75 percent drop in the reject rate for a production process? For a 50 percent reduction in turnover among hourly workers? Are you trying to claim that the advertising department had nothing to do with that sales increase? Do managers get no credit at all for introducing and enforcing the new production procedures that you trained those workers to perform? Might not some fluctuation in the economy or the job market have something to do with the fact that hourly workers are hanging onto their jobs longer now than they did last year?

No? It was just your training program and nothing else, eh? Well then, Bucko, if quarterly sales ever happen to drop after you run a sales-training course, we suppose you'll accept full blame for the loss, too, right?

To some observers, the most notable feature of this argument is that it is able to pass in the training world as political savvy. "Hey, when sales go down, nobody accepts the blame, sweetheart," says consultant Jerry Peloquin in a 1987 *TRAINING* article. "Everybody explains why it's not their fault."

True, some punctiliousness about the propriety of laying claim to "bottom-line results" is understandable as a reaction by responsible training professionals to the outlandish claims of some yahoos in their midst: A motivational speaker gives one after-dinner pep talk in conjunction with Acme Widget's national sales campaign, and six months later his publicist is awarding him credit for generating $30 million in new revenue for Acme Widget.

Nevertheless, insists one consultant and former training director who asked not to be named, bickering about whether it is ever justifiable to claim a specific dollars-and-cents business result as the product of a training program is a silly waste of time.

Suppose, he says, outlining the standard case against making such a claim, that management wants to sell more cans of peaches. "They call in people from advertising, marketing, operations and training. Advertising runs a big ad campaign urging people to eat canned peaches. Marketing pressures grocery stores to give more shelf space to the peaches. Operations tightens up canning and distribution to make sure peaches are never out of stock. Training runs a program on selling canned peaches. Sales of canned peaches go up 412 percent."

If, in a situation like that, you stood up in a meeting and declared that the training course was solely responsible for the 412-percent increase in sales, this consultant says: "Of course you'd get laughed out of the building! Of course a lot of factors besides training go into producing an economic result. This is supposed to be some deep insight?"

The expert in question refers to himself as "an embittered former evaluator who has been through a 12-step withdrawal program." Arguments about whether you can absolutely, positively isolate the impact of an instructional program on something like a change in sales revenue are beside the point in the business world, he insists. The debate about "proof" arises from the same academic mind-set that invents some of the torturously elaborate evaluation techniques you can read about in education textbooks. For example, he cites the Solomon 4 Group Design, in which one group of students is pre-tested (for existing knowledge), trained and post-tested; the second group is pre- and post-tested but not trained; the third group is trained and post-tested but not pretested; and the fourth is just post-tested.

"Things like that aren't designed by people looking to see whether anything useful got done," the Embittered One declares. "They're designed so that academics can argue with other academics — and government-grant overseers — about the air-tightness of their evaluations."

No, you generally can't get iron-clad proof, says Embittered. But you often can collect awfully good evidence that a training course is or is not contributing mightily to a particular economic gain.

Kirkpatrick echoes that sentiment and adds that evidence is all anybody really wants to see anyhow. "Top management isn't going to ask, 'Can you prove it?'" he says. "They'll ask for evidence. And evidence is not all that hard to come by."

Indeed it isn't, agrees Embittered. And the way to come by good evidence is to know what you're looking for before you ever conduct the training. "If you do a good needs analysis up front, evaluation takes care of itself," he says. The reason many people think evaluations at Levels 3 and 4 are so difficult and expensive and time-consuming is because "they're coming in after the fact to fish for results: 'We didn't know what we were doing, so now let's find out if anything happened.' If you don't taste your cooking until after you've served it, of course you'll run into trouble."

According to Dana Gaines Robinson, a consultant with Partners in Change of Pittsburgh and coauthor of the 1989 book, *Training for Impact: How to Link Training to Business Needs and Measure the Results*, the key to good evaluation — and to good training — is to establish a "causal link" between a skill deficiency and a specific business problem, preferably a problem to which a dollar sign can be attached. Again, you do this before you run the course. It's called needs analysis.

Is wastage a problem on the manufacturing floor? How much does the current scrap/waste rate cost the company? Does a significant percentage of that waste occur because workers don't know how to do the job properly? If so, there's your causal link. Now, what does that percentage represent in terms of dollars and cents? If you train the workers and the waste rate drops as predicted, that's pretty good evidence that the program returned X dollars on the training investment.

On the other hand, suppose your needs analysis consists of a questionnaire that asks people how they feel about "interpersonal communication on the inter- and intradepartmental levels" ("Please rate on a 1-5 scale.") The average rating turns out to be 3.0 (Actual translation: "Huh?"). You then run these people through a generic communication-skills program, because obviously there are

---

If an executive suggests a course be cut, "I shouldn't have to say a word. Some line manager should be up there raising hell."

---

two whole numbers worth of room for improvement here. In this situation, you probably will find it time consuming, expensive and difficult to come back later and gather persuasive evidence that this program had some specific effect on business operations.

Part of a System

According to Thomas Gilbert, evaluation is only meaningful if it's conducted within the broader context of a coherent performance improvement system.

Those who agree, and structure their training departments accordingly, sometimes have little patience for the training world's ubiquitous talk about the need to "sell line management on the value of training."

"If I have to 'sell' my programs to line managers, I'm doing something wrong," says Walt Thurn, manager of employee development for Florida Power Corp. in St. Petersburg, the person in charge of technical training for the utility. "Developing subordinates is managers' responsibility, not the training department's. We don't take responsibility for doing their job."

Here is Thurn's definition of a successful training course: If a senior executive suggests that the course be cut, "I shouldn't have to say a word. Some line manager should be up there banging on [that executive's] desk and raising hell."

This is no fantasy, Thurn maintains. In 1984 Florida Power launched a preemployment training program for candidates applying to become line workers — the people who mend powerlines, set poles, hang transformers, string wires and so on. The program is designed to give applicants a realistic picture of the job — to let them know exactly what they are getting themselves into. Turnover among first-year line employees promptly dropped from 48.6 percent to 9.4 percent. And there the figure has remained, with slight variations, ever since.

In the late '80s, top management proposed to cut the program as a cost-saving measure. "There was a major revolt by the line managers," Thurn says. "For a while there, I was expecting gunfire to start." The preemployment program is still running. To date, it has saved the company more than $2 million.

How does Thurn know that? Because he knew how much the 48.6 percent turnover rate was costing the company before he ever designed the preemployment program. And how did he know that? Because line managers figured out the costs and told him.

At Florida Power, all technical training not mandated by government regulations works like this: Any manager requesting training for his subordinates completes a "performance analysis work sheet." The work sheet requires the manager to specify the performance problem he wants to solve, calculate the cost of the problem, explain what he thinks is causing it (i.e., What makes you think they're performing poorly because they don't know how to perform well?), and explain why formal training might be a more efficient and effective solution than alternatives such as job aids, work reassignments or on-the-job training. The manager sends this work sheet to Thurn's department, which then does a training analysis: Assuming this problem looks as if it could be fixed by training, how much would it cost in development time, trainer salaries, travel costs, trainee time (i.e., the value of employees' salaries while they're off the job in the training course) and so on? The performance work sheet and the training analysis are passed on to a committee of operational managers (power plant managers and others, including Thurn), which meets once a month. If the proposed training program appears to have a significant payoff — that is, if the problem is considerably more expensive than the solution — the proposal goes onto the list of training projects to be considered when the annual training budget is hammered out.

For instance, Thurn says, pulling two proposals out of a file, here's a request for a program for distribution dispatchers, the people who send line employees to respond to reports of power outages and so on. The requesting manager calculates that inefficiencies due to performance problems are costing about $25,000 a year. The training analysis says an instructional solution would cost about $18,000. That's not a terrible return on investment, but the training committee won't assign it as high a priority as the second proposal, which requests a new program to teach 56 power plant workers how to operate and maintain certain equipment in a plant.

In this one, the manager has documented $1.8 million in costs due to equipment damage, material costs, lost work hours, the need to repeat tasks that were botched the first time and so on. For instance, the work sheet explains, this year at least 27 employees have had to go back and re-do jobs (for example, repair a pump with the right gasket), and the time wasted was worth $109,000.

The training analysis says the project can be tackled by developing new software for a mobile technical-training simulator the company already owns. The total cost of development and delivery (including vendor-developer's fees, trainer time, salaries paid to the 56 employees while they are using the simulator, etc.) will be $78,232, or $1,397 per trainee. A $78,000 solution to a $1.8 million problem will grab the training committee's attention.

Under this system, Level 4 evaluation becomes a simple matter of determining whether or to what degree the trained workers have overcome the performance problems the course was supposed to address. All anybody has to do is track the same indicators they were tracking before the program began, and they know what the payoff was.

There is no great mystery to any of this, Thurn points out. It's essentially just refried Bob Mager.

Many trainers, however, might smell a political problem here. Is a line manager whose people aren't performing up to snuff really going to put himself through all this rigmarole and then wait months for a committee to decide if maybe he couldn't have a little training? (As a matter of fact, Thurn has four years' worth of proposals sitting on his desk right now.) Why wouldn't the manager just say: "To hell with it. I'll reach into my own budget and go find a training supplier who wants the work."

Thurn admits that it takes an average of seven to nine months for a request for training to turn into a program. In emergencies, of course — a fire in a power plant shows that workers don't know how to use the fire systems very well, for example — the training department drops lower-pri-

---

"Training can be a bottomless pit. You can drown yourself in swill if you don't control it."

---

ority projects and jumps on the new problem. But barring emergencies, considerable time lags are standard.

"If a manager with a $25,000 problem has the money in his budget to [hire an outside training supplier], we'll give him a list of vendors who would do a good job for him," Thurn says. "The committee process is a guideline. You've got to use common sense, as well."

But Thurn makes no apologies for the delays built into Florida Power's process. He insists that the cure would be far worse than the disease. "Under any system you've got limited resources," he says. The question is, how are you going to apportion them? "A lot of training departments eat themselves up trying to help every Jack, Sally and Joe. They lose track of the big picture. Training can be a bottomless pit. You can wind up drowning yourself in swill if you don't control it."

"The hardest thing for trainers to do is say no [to a request for training]," Thurn continues. "It goes against the very grain of what a trainer is." But if you want to do training that contributes in real and demonstrable ways to the performance of the business, "'No' is probably the most important word to learn to say."

The Quality Factor

From the perspective of those interested in tracking the results of any instructional program, there is still a fly in Thurn's ointment. He's talking only about technical training. Florida Power's management and soft-skills curricula do not operate under this system. To the best of TRAINING's knowledge, no company's soft-skills training is nearly that cut-and-dried.

Will there ever be more rigor in the evaluation of soft-skills training? Dana Robinson thinks so. She's betting that the "total quality" movement sweeping the country will provide the catalyst.

"In almost any quality effort, one of the steps is to evaluate results," she explains. "The quality model is: Measure and identify needs; change; evaluate the results." To the extent that training teaches skills and principles attached to a quality campaign, "it must not only teach the skills but also model the process. As the quality movement takes root, training can't be an exception. It will have to be an example of the principles involved."

Indeed, top management at AAA Michigan just approved a plan for a major quality-improvement initiative (4,000 employees will go through the initial orientation programs), and Zobeck says a chunk of training-evaluation money is included in the budget. As this issue went to press, he didn't know yet how far he'd take his measurement efforts, but he had his eyes on Level 3. As for Level 4, "That's more or less built into the quality process. It won't tie directly to training, but both performance and business results will be measured."

Robinson reasons that pressure to "model the quality model" will come to apply not only to technical-skills training, but to many of the soft-skills courses frequently taught in conjunction with quality drives: teamwork, problem solving, decision making, negotiating, effective listening and so on. Not that she thinks tomorrow's typical soft-skills course will be evaluated at Level 4. But she has seen a marked increase in interest in both Level 2 (testing) and Level 3 (evaluation). If nothing else, management may start asking for evidence that workers learned the skills in question and are using them on the job.

Notice anything hauntingly familiar about the quality model Robinson outlined: Measure needs, change, evaluate results? Does it remind you of anything? Like maybe: "Do a good needs analysis up front and evaluation will take care of itself?"

Yes! In fact, as Robinson would be first to tell you, if we substituted "train" for "change" in that quality model, the result would look remarkably like the good old "systems approach" to training. That's the very thing we've really been talking about for a good bit of this article.

If the total quality movement does spur a change to a more rigorous training environment, trainers who have read their HRD Hall of Famers — their Mager, their Gilbert, their Joe Harless, their Geary Rummler — ought to feel pretty much at home in their "new" surroundings.

For Further Reading

Calculating Human Resource Costs and Benefits, Lyle M. Spencer Jr. John Wiley & Sons, New York, 1986. (Work sheets and financial formulas galore for measuring ROI.)

Handbook of Training Evaluation and Measurement Methods, Jack J. Phillips. Gulf Publishing Co., Houston, 1983. (Gathering data, calculating ROI.)

Training for Impact: How to Link Training to Business Needs and Measure the Results, Dana Gaines Robinson and James C. Robinson. Jossey-Bass, San Francisco, 1989. (Documenting behavior changes and measuring their effect on productivity.)

Human Competence: Engineering Worthy Performance, Thomas F. Gilbert. McGraw-Hill, New York, 1978. (Classic statement of the "performance engineering" approach to training.)

Measuring Instructional Results, Second Edition, Robert F. Mager. David S. Lake Publishers, Belmont, CA, 1984. (Focuses on Level 2 evaluation — how to design a good test of skills or knowledge.)

Notes:

How to Calculate The Costs and Benefits of an HRD Program

This one's exactly what it sounds like: A step-by-step method for figuring out the real cost of training and the dollar value of its impact

BY LYLE M. SPENCER JR.

You don't really need an introduction, do you? For years thebiggest boogeyman in the human resources development community has been the legendary difficulty of expressing the impact of HRD programs in cost-benefit terms: *What can we tell top management about the "bottom-line" results of our efforts?*

This article presents simple methods for calculating the costs and benefits of training, consulting and other HRD interventions in a variety of settings. So let's just get started.

PART I: CALCULATING COSTS

Two kinds of expenses are involved in any training effort: (a) labor costs and (b) direct costs, such as travel, per diem, materials, purchased services (e.g., consultants), equipment, facilities, (e.g., room rentals), and opportunity costs (e.g., the expense of hiring temporary workers or paying overtime to people attending a training program).

Labor costs — the value of the time spent by both HRD people and program participants — usually make up the largest part of the cost of any training program. Expenses in this category can be calculated in two ways: direct labor cost or full labor cost.

Direct labor cost is each person's salary divided by the number of days he or she works in a year (the U.S. average is 230 days). For example, a trainer earning $25,000 a year and working 230 days would have a direct cost of $25,000 ÷ 230 = $108.69 per day.

Full labor cost is a person's salary plus fringe benefits (e.g., holidays, vacation, health benefits, pension costs), plus overhead (e.g., occupancy costs, support-staff salaries, equipment rental, etc.) and, if the person works in a profit center, the profit percentage the center is expected to earn — all of this divided by the number of days for which the person is *paid* (counting paid vacations, holidays and sick time, the U.S. average is 260 days). Figure 1 shows the calculation of the full cost of a person's time. (The worksheet below allows you to calculate your own full cost per day.)

Full costs provide the best estimate of how much it actually costs an organization to deliver an HRD service. A good estimate of the full cost of a person's time is roughly three times his or her direct salary cost. This figure, called a "full-cost multiplier," provides a useful rule of thumb for estimating program costs. As we'll see, the full costing of people's time is the key to calculating the costs and benefits of training efforts.

Here's how to calculate the *labor costs* of an HRD project:

1. Identify all the steps of the project (e.g., curriculum development, trainer-training, delivery, evaluation).
2. Determine who is involved in each step, including both HRD people and the program participants, and how much of each person's time is involved.
3. Calculate the full cost of each person's time per day (or per hour, if appropriate). If several people with approximately equal salaries are involved, you can use averages.
4. To find the total cost of labor for each step, multiply the number of people involved times their cost per day (or hours) times the number of days they will spend on the project.

Follow these steps to determine the project's *direct costs:*

1. Identify the type of cost (e.g., materials, travel, per diem, computer time) involved in each step.
2. Determine the cost per unit (e.g., one workbook, one trip, one day's per diem).
3. Determine the total number of units involved.
4. Multiply the cost per unit times the number of units to find the full

---

FIGURE 1
Calculating the Full Costs of a Trainer's Time

The full cost of a person making the current HRD specialist's average salary of $25,000 and paid on the basis of a 260-day (2,080-hour) year is calculated as follows:

Expense	Calculation Formula	Amount
1. Salary	S	$25,000
2. Plus: fringe benefits @ 35% of salary	.35 x S = .35S	8,750
3. Subtotal	1.35S	33,750
4. Plus: overhead @ 125% of salary and fringe	1.25 x 1.35S = 1.69S	42,188
5. Total full cost/year	3.04S	$75,938
6. Total full cost/day	$75,938 (direct cost/year) ÷ 260 (days worked/year)	$292.07
7. Total full cost/hour	(direct cost/day) ÷ 8 (hours worked/day)	$ 36.51

cost for each direct expense.

Add full labor costs to direct costs to find the *total cost* for each step of the project. Add the step totals, and you have a project total.

This procedure is illustrated in Figure 2 (below), which is a calculation of the cost of a management-training program for plant supervisors conducted by the training department of a large manufacturing concern.

Here's what's going on in Figure 2.

Step 1: Course Development. Trainer Smith spent 10 days developing a 16-hour course on basic supervisory principles for plant managers. The course was delivered in eight, two-hour segments. Smith's salary was $30,000 a year, so his full cost per day was $30,000 x 3 ÷ 260 = $346. Therefore, the full cost of his time for Step 1 was $3,460 ($346, day x 10 days). Direct expenses for this step were $260 for off-the-shelf training materials purchased from vendors. (Note that at five development days for each day of training delivered, this was particularly efficient course development. Industry norms range from 10 to 75 development days for each day of training. Note also that some common "steps" were not involved: discussion with "clients," needs assessment, etc.).

Step 2: Training Trainers. Next, Smith conducted a five-day training session to teach plant supervisors from eight factories to deliver the program at their locations. The full labor costs for this step were the five days of Smith's time at $346/day, plus five days each of the plant supervisors' time at $288/day. Direct costs included Smith's per diem (consisting of meals at a local restaurant), materials for the eight trainees at $50 per course manual, travel to the training site for each of the trainees at $350 average per person, $75 per person a day per diem for eight people for five days, and $150 a day for the room in which the training was conducted. Total labor costs for Step 2 came to $13,250. Direct costs amounted to $7,050.

Step 3: Training Delivery. The eight plant supervisors trained 10 foremen in each of their factories. The full labor costs for the supervisors were their full costs of $2,88/day apiece times three days (16 hours of training, plus one hour of preparation for each of the eight sessions) for a total of $6,912. Full labor costs for the 80 trainees were their full costs of $231/day times two days for a total of $36,960. The direct costs for this step were $50 per person for course manuals times 80 participants for a total of $4,000.

Step 4. Evaluation. Smith subsequently spent three days contacting the eight supervisors and analyzing a reaction questionnaire given to each of the 80 foremen. Full labor costs for this step were Smith's three days times $346/day for a total of $1,038. The direct costs were $100 for telephone charges and computer time.

This plant-management training program cost a total of $73,030. It was a fairly typical case in that 85% of the cost was in people's time. Note that in Steps 2 and 3 the cost of participants' time was much greater than the cost of the trainer's time. *This is true in most HRD interventions: The real cost of a training program is the participants' time.*

This simple procedure (despite all

**FIGURE 2
COSTING WORKSHEET**

Analysis Step	Labor ("Who?")	(1) #	Full Cost/ Time	(2)	(3) Time	(4) Cost (1)x(2)x(3)	Expense	(5) Cost/Unit	x	(6) # Units	=	(7) Cost (5)x(6)	Totals (8) = (4)+(7)
1. Development of course	Smith (HR person)	1	S $30K x M 3 T 260	= $346/day	x 10 days	= $3,460	Materials	$260	x	1	=	$260	$3,720
Step 1 Total						**$3,460**						**$260**	**$3,720**
2. Trainer training	Smith (Trainer)	1	S $30K x M 3 T 260	= $346/day	x 5 days	= $1,730	Per diem	$20	x	5 days	=	$100	$1,830
	Plant Supervisors	8	S $25K x M 3 T 260	= $288/day	x 5 days	= $11,520	Materials	$50/person	x	8 people	=	$400	$11,920
			S x M T	=	x	=	Travel to training site	$350/person	x	8 people	=	$2,800	$2,800
			S x M T	=	x	=	Per diem	$75/person/ day	x	5 days x 8 people = 40	=	$3,000	$3,000
			S x M T	=	x	=	Training room	$150/day	x	5	=	$750	$750
Step 2 Total						**$13,250**						**$7,050**	**$20,300**
3. Delivery of training	Plant Supervisors (Trainers)	8	S $25K x M 3 T 260	= $288/day	x 3 days (16 hrs delivery, 8 hrs prep)	= $6,912			x		=		$6,912
	Head Foreman	80	S $20K x M 3 T 260	= $231/day	x 2 days	= $36,960	Materials	$50/person	x	80 people	=	$4,000	$40,960
Step 3 Total						**$43,872**						**$4,000**	**$47,872**
4. Evaluation	Smith (HR Person)	1	S $30K x M 3 T 260	= $346/day	x 3 days	= $1,038	Telephone & computer time	$100	x	1	=	$100	$1,138
Step 4 Total						**$1,038**						**$100**	**$1,138**
					Total Labor Cost	**$61,620**				**Total Direct Costs**		**$11,410**	**$73,030 Total**

the multiplying and dividing, it's not really any more difficult than preparing a budget) can be used to cost virtually any HRD project or program. The figures involved are not complex, but because people may not have kept accurate track of their time, calculating costs for a training program may require a probing inquiry strategy: What steps were involved? And for each step, who was involved? How much does each person make? For how much time (how many hours, days) was each involved? Finally, were any direct costs such as materials, travel and per diem involved in the step?

Most people, if asked the right questions, can readily come up with these figures. People know their salaries and can at least estimate the salaries of others. Your controller can tell you your organization's actual full-cost multiplier (it may not be "3") and the number of days paid. "Best guesstimates" of time spent in various activities turn out to be surprisingly accurate — within 3 percent of actual time spent as monitored by time sheets, in most cases I've experienced.

PART II: CALCULATING BENEFITS

There are only two ways to demonstrate benefits or increased profits in business: one can either increase revenues (by raising prices or by increasing volume or sales) and/or one can decrease expenses.

Rarely do HRD efforts affect pricing decisions. Training and consulting efforts have been shown to expand volume by increasing production or sales, but most "dollar" benefits which derive from training and development programs involve cost avoidance — such as reducing the cost of time, people, materials, equipment downtime, turnover, or various expensive "people problem events" such as grievances, accidents, disabilities and so on.

Time

Reducing the person hours or days needed to perform any organizational function (e.g., time wasted in useless meetings) is the easiest way to show dollar benefits from HRD efforts. Simply multiply the time saved (hours or days) times the full cost per hour or day. For example, if 10 people making $30,000 a year (each having a full cost per day of $346, or per hour of $43.25) can avoid a single one-hour meeting, it saves the organization $432.50. Is it a weekly meeting? Estimate it for 50 weeks in a year, and you've saved the organization $21,625.

You may argue that this isn't a real savings because these people are still being paid. But if their time is freed from unproductive activities, they can either spend it performing more useful activities, which may increase revenues, or the organization may find it needs fewer people. The current

---

WORKSHEET
Calculating Your Full Cost Per Day

Direct Rate
1. Your yearly salary = _____
2. Divided by the number of days you work a year _____
3. Your *direct cost/day* = _____

Full Cost Rate x3
4. Multiplied by 3 is your *full cost/day*[1] = _____

Applied Rate
5. The number of days a month (e.g., use last month) you work on specific projects (be honest!) _____
6. Divided by 20 (days/month) ÷20
7. Your *applied rate* = _____

Cost per applied person day
8. Divide your *full cost/day* (4) _____
9. By your *applied rate* (7) _____
10. Equals your *cost/applied person day* = _____

This is how much you cost your organization/clients for each day of service.

---

[1] A more precise calculation of your full cost can be obtained by:

(1) Your yearly salary (1a _____) divided by the number of days you are paid per year = (1b _____) (American Industry standard = 260 days) = your direct cost per day (1a ÷ 1b) _____ (1)

(2) Multiply (1) by your organization's *fringe-benefits rate* (American industry average = 35%) _____ (2)

(3) Fringe cost in dollars: (1) x (2) _____ (3)

(4) Subtotal: total compensation = (1) + (3) _____ (4)

(5) Multiply (4) by your organization's overhead rate (professional-service firm average = 125%) _____ (5)

(6) Overhead in dollars = (4) x (5) _____ (6)

(7) Subtotal: total labor cost = (4) + (6) _____ (7)

OPTIONAL: if your organization breaks general and administrative (G&A) out separately

(8) Multiply (7) by your organization's *G&A rate* if calculated separately from overhead; _____ (8)

(9) G&A in dollars = (7) x (8) _____ (9)

(10) Subtotal: total cost with G&A = (7) + (9) _____ (10)

OPTIONAL: if you are an external consultant

(11) Multiply subtotal (10) by your organization's *pretax profit rate* (American industry average = 10%): _____ (11)

(12) Profit in dollars needed/day on your efforts if organization is to meet its goal = (10) x (11) _____ (12)

(13) TOTAL: (7) + (10) + (12) _____ (13)

(14) Calculate your applied rate (see instructions (5) through (7) above). _____ (14)

(15) Calculate your *cost/applied person-day: (13) ÷ (14)* = _____ (15)

This is how much you cost/must return to your organization each day if it is to meet its profit goal.

FIGURE 3
Costing a Grievance

(1) Step (What happens 1st, 2nd, etc.?)	(2) Who is involved?	(3) How long? (hours)	(4) Salary/year of each person involved	Full cost calculation (5) Cost/person/hour (4) x 3 (OHD factor) / 260 days ÷ 8 hours	(6) = (3) x (5) Total Cost Per Step	Total
1. The worker complains to the foreman.	Worker	.25	$15K	$21.64	$5.41	
	Foreman	.25	$20K	$28.85	$7.21	$12.62
2. Worker complains to shop steward.	Worker	.50	$15K	$21.64	$10.82	$10.82
	(Steward)	.50	(Paid by union)			
3. Local union rep. tells hourly how to write grievance.	Worker	.50	$15K	$21.64	$10.82	
	Union rep.	.50	$15K	$21.64	$10.82	$21.64
4. Hourly writes up grievance.	Worker	.50	$15K	$21.64	$10.82	$10.82
5. Union-plant mgmt. meeting.	Worker	.75	$15K	$21.64	$16.23	
	Union Pres.	.75	$16K	$23.08	$17.31	
	Plant personnel rep.	.75	$25K	$36.06	$27.05	$60.59
6. International union rep. writes division personnel; division staff calls plant, researches and writes response, decides whether or not to go to arbitration.	Div. staff	8	$32K	$46.15	$369.20	$369.20

If no arbitration

7. Trip to meet with International rep. to deal with four grievances.	Div. staff	16	$32K	$46.15	$738.40	
	Trip direct cost		$400		$400.00	
					$1,138.40 ÷ 4 = 284.60 per grievance	
8. Implement agreement*	Plant personnel rep.	2	$25K	$36.06	$72.12	72.12
TOTAL PER GRIEVANCE IF NO ARBITRATION						$842.41

If arbitration (5% of grievances go to arbitration).

9. Legal preparation	Corp. staff lawyer	16	$45K	$64.90	$1,038.40	
	Div. staff	6	$32K	$46.15	$276.90	
	Plant pers. director	4	$25K	$36.06	$144.24	
	Labor lawyer	4	$60K	$86.54	$346.16	$1,805.70
10. Arbitration meeting	Corp. staff lawyer	4	$45K	$64.90	$259.60	
	Div. staff	4	$32K	$46.15	$184.60	
	Plant pers. director	4	$25K	$36.06	$144.24	
	Labor lawyer (arbitration fee)	4	$60K	$86.54	$346.16	$934.60
						$2,740.30

*There is additional cost per grievance due to the expected value of arbitration:
- Expected value (E(v)) = probability (5%) of occurrence x cost ($2,740.30) per grievance = $137.02
- Total cost of grievance = $842.41 (no arbitration) + $137.02 (5% probability of arbitration) = $979.43

---

reduction in middle management and staff personnel (who spend most of their time in meetings) to cut costs is one example of this trend. Time savings always add up to people savings, and the full cost of people's time is the best way to estimate where these savings can be made.

Materials

Benefits from savings on materials include reduced waste of inventory due to more efficient scheduling or better quality-control procedures.

These savings are very easy to calculate. Multiply the number of units saved per day, week or month, times the cost per unit, times the number of days, weeks or months that the savings occurs. (A year is a good standard for extrapolating savings.)

Equipment Downtime

Significant benefits can be shown from increasing the use or preventing the downtime of expensive capital equipment — computers, for example. The dollar value of an hour of equipment time is calculated by dividing the equipment's cost by the number of hours it is expected to be used. For example, a $3 million computer system with a useful life of five years has an amortization value of $600,000 a year. If the system is expected to be used 20 hours a week or 1,040 hours a year, the dollar value of each hour is at minimum $600,000 ÷ 1,040 hours = $577 an hour. (Operator labor, maintenance and other overhead costs-occupancy and electricity, for example will add to the equipment's value per hour.)

Anything HRD people can do to increase equipment utilization — conducting workshops that improve scheduling or maintenance of expensive equipment, recruiting or training key operators, teaching or helping people to "market" use of the equipment — enables them to claim the dollar benefits of each hour of increased usage or each hour of downtime saved.

Retention Turnover Costs

The costs of recruiting and training new people to replace those who quit or are fired are, at minimum, equal to the direct salary of the people who leave. Recruitment, whether done in-house or by a search firm, usually costs one-third of the first-year salary for the job involved; training costs about 10% of the first-year salary; and "learning-curve" costs, which account for the fact that people take some time on the job before they become fully productive, amount to 50% of first-year salary.

Any training program or consulting intervention which reduces turnover can claim the dollar value of each person saved. Retention benefits can be estimated on an organizationwide basis by multiplying the turnover rate times the total number of people in a given salary category to find the dollar value of reducing turnover by, say, 1 percent.

People Problems

The dollar value of any "people problem event" (grievances, strikes, accidents, disability days) can be calculated using the same costing inquiry technique explained earlier. Figure 3 "Costing a Grievance," shows a case in which each grievance was found to cost the organization an average of $979. (*See note on p. 36.)

This same procedure can be used to cost accidents: What's the first (second, third) thing that happens? Who is involved? How much does each make? For how long is each involved? Are there any direct costs (e.g., disability claim costs) involved in the step?

Strategies for Showing Benefits

The opportunities are virtually unlimited for calculating benefits from interventions that save people's time, materials and equipment downtime, or that reduce turnover and "problem events." A simple strategy for calculating benefits in any training intervention is shown in Figure 4, a standard problem-solving sequence with three cost-benefit steps added.

First, always "value the problem" at the beginning of an intervention, when someone first requests your services. State in dollar figures what existing practices cost the organization. Go through the costing strategy with the "clients" to help them identify the dollar value of their problem, and hence the benefits of any training program or consulting you can offer them.

For example, if someone approaches you for a first-level management-training program, you might ask, "Why do you think this training is needed? What problems are the first-level managers' lack of ability currently causing?" The answer might be something like, "Poor morale, leading

---

RED FLAG: WHAT SHOULD TRAINING TAKE CREDIT FOR?

BY JACK GORDON

Experienced HRD people will point to a hole in this argument for calculating the benefits of a training program and "claiming" those benefits as a direct result of training. In many cases, they will say, things such as job-turnover rates, improved sales figures, etc. are affected by any number of factors that have little or nothing to do with the training program.

Perhaps the economy has gone sour and jobs are harder to come by — therefore workers are staying longer whether they're satisfied or not. Perhaps sales improved simply because the economy *picked up* — or because sales managers realized that top management wanted to stress a particular product line and lit fires under their people independently of the training program.

Individual managers or superintendents may want to claim their own efforts were partly responsible for the improvement you are crediting to your intervention, critics will say, and you will create enemies by trying to chalk up every dollar saved as a direct result of your program.

These concerns sometimes are valid and they cannot be dismissed lightly. But the fact remains that your intervention was a response to a *problem*. Turnover was too high, regardless of economic conditions. Your training program was not the first indication sale managers got that the CEO wanted those widgets to move faster: If their "fire lighting" deserves the credit, why was there so little improvement in sales between the time they got the word and the time your program was delivered? And if the sharp upturn in office morale has indeed occurred not because of your participative-management seminars but simply because somebody painted the restrooms, you either did an extremely poor needs analysis or somebody gave you extremely bad information about the problem to begin with.

Obviously, this is another reason why it's better to "cost" the problem, the solution and the benefits *before* you launch the intervention. If somebody has a better, cheaper or more effective solution to the problem, let him speak now; otherwise, it's your solution and you deserve to claim its benefits — or at least the lion's share of them.

FIGURE 4

Adding Cost-Benefit Calculations to Problem-Solving Consulting

- **PROBLEM IDENTIFICATION:** Prioritization, selection
    1. "Value the Problem": State in dollar terms what it costs the organization now.
- **ANALYSIS:** Diagnosis, data collection, "root-cause analysis"
- **ALTERNATIVES:** Generate solution options
- **DECISION-MAKING:** Select best alternative
- **IMPLEMENTATION PLANNING/ GOAL SETTING**
    2. "Value the Solution": State in dollar terms what the solution/program could save the organization.
- **IMPLEMENTATION**
- **FOLLOW-UP WITH:** Technical assistance, trouble-shooting, reinforcement.

---

to high turnover." At this point you could ask, "How many people, at what salary level, are leaving?" This will give you a baseline cost of turnover against which you can show benefits if your training program results in decreased turnover.

Consider the costs and benefits of a training intervention *before* you begin. Valuing the problem will help you focus your efforts on those specific aspects which are most likely to pay off in dollar terms. For example, you can focus a management-training program on time management (directly translatable into the dollar value of time saved), retention of key people (translatable to the dollar value of reduced turnover), or reduced downtime of expensive equipment (directly translatable to the dollar value of equipment cost per hour).

Second, always "value the solution." Put a dollar figure on your program's benefit to the organization. You often can present this data in a way that makes the case for your program absolutely compelling. For example, $73,000 seems a lot to pay for the plant management training program described in Figure 2, and cost-conscious executives might refuse to fund it. You could point out, however, that if turnover is reduced by just one $12,000 worker a year in each of the eight factories involved, the program would save $96,000 — and not only pay for itself, but return 30% on investment.

Finally, always "value the result." Follow up and evaluate the results of the intervention, and state in dollar terms (in a one-page final report, for instance) what the solution or program actually saved the organization. Circulate this memorandum widely — to your boss, to your peers and to other members of the organization.

Adding these three cost-benefit steps to any proposed intervention should also be considered as a means to market, as well as to justify, HRD services. You'll find that this simple calculation will quickly change the perception of the value of your HRD function.

---

*Note that a technique called "expected value" calculation is used to account for arbitration, an event that was quite expensive (it cost an additional $2,740) but occurred only once in a while (5% of grievances went to arbitration). An expected value, E(V), is the probability or percentage (P) of an outcome multiplied by the amount (A) of the outcome. E(V) = P x A, where A is the cost (e.g., of an accident or a strike).

In Figure 3, the expected value of arbitration is .05 (one in 20 grievances go to arbitration) times the cost of arbitration ($2,740) = $137 per grievance.

Expected-value calculations are particularly useful in dealing with the probability of lawsuits, affirmative action complaints and the like. Obviously, anything an HRD person can do to reduce this probability will show an expected-value benefit.

The Dollars and Sense of Corporate Training

At last, there just might be a way to answer the question, "What is training worth?"

BY MICHAEL GODKEWITSCH

Sick and tired of waging an annual uphill battle for training budgets because you can't demonstrate a return on investment in strict, monetary terms? Discouraged by the age-old truth that training and development activities are the first to go when profits are down? Depressed because you have no hard numbers to back up the claim that training pays off?

Well, take heart. Just about everyone concerned with managing people cost-effectively has suffered from the same maladies. And there is at least a partial cure.

Most organizations invest in training because they are convinced that higher profits will result. And usually, this is what happens. Training improves workers' skills and often boosts their motivation, leading to better productivity and increased profitability. But to be certain and to be accurate about this causal relationship is seldom easy: How much profitability results from how many dollars invested in what kind of training?

One of the toughest challenges facing managers who are responsible for developing and training people is to clearly demonstrate the financial value of training. Trainers might nurse gut feelings that funding for corporate training will translate into a healthy return. But that's not enough. In accounting language the question is: Does investing in corporate training add enough value to our human resources asset to make it a priority investment? In cost-accounting lingo: Does capital spent on training have a high return on investment and a short payback period, coupled with high present value? In lay person's terms: Do we get our money's worth out of corporate training?

A Question of Financial Utility

In the last decade quite a few economists and management and social scientists have tried to answer this basic question. One general and intuitively simple measure of the financial value of an intervention (e.g., a training program) is the resulting gain minus its cost. In turn, gain can be defined as the effect of the intervention times the monetary value of that effect. The complete equation, then, for calculating the financial utility of an intervention would look like this:

$$F = N[(E \times M) - C], \text{ where}$$

F = financial utility
N = number of people affected
E = effect of the intervention
M = monetary value of the effect
C = cost of the intervention/person

If we could only quantify these terms, we could evaluate any intervention (in this case, training courses) in financial accounting terms such as direct profit, present value, discounted cash flow and payback period. While costs and numbers of people affected are usually well known, the other two terms (effect of an intervention and monetary value of the effect) are much harder to pin down. But recent advances in industrial/organizational psychology have given us a way of quantifying these terms and thereby solving the equation.

To understand how these terms can be quantified, it is important to grasp the notion that any skill, attitude, etc., can be "measured" and will show some distribution of scores. Even fairly unquantified skills such as "overall managerial skills" are "measured," when, for example, a group of senior executives rate that ability in a subordinate group of managers. So-called "normal" distributions of skills show a lot of scores at and near the middle, and fewer at the extremes. Just as every distribution has an average or mean, it also has a standard deviation (SD), a measure of dispersion that describes how "bunched" the distribution is. In a normal distribution, about 70% of all scores fall within one SD from the mean.

To quantify the effect of a training course, we compare the distribution of a given skill among the participants before the training with the distribution after training. The shift, expressed in SDs, is the effect of that training course. Unfortunately, most organizations do not bother to or cannot measure skills before training, much less after, and so do not really know the impact of their training.

The good news is that Michael Burke of New York University's department of management, and Russell Day of the Illinois Institute of Technology and Chicago and North-Western Transportation Co., published "A Cumulative Study of the Effectiveness of Managerial Training" in the *Journal of Applied Psychology* (April-June 1986). Using a novel technique called meta-analysis, they summarized the effects of 70 published and unpublished studies on the effectiveness of corporate training. Burke and Day based their summary of the effectiveness of training content and methods on four criteria: subjective learning (judgments of course participants or trainers); objective learning (results on standardized tests); subjective behavior (changes in on-the-job behavior, as perceived by course participants, peers or supervisors); and objective results (tangible, bottom-line indicators such as reduced costs, improved quality or quantity of output).

The researchers provide hard data on the effects of different management training programs and teaching methods. Figure 1 shows some of Burke and Day's findings on the effects of corporate training,

While training often can be quantified objectively, the notion of value is by definition tied into what stakeholders feel and think. Several industrial psychologists, including Wayne Cascio (University of Colorado at Denver), Flank Schmidt (UC Office of

Personnel Management), and Jeff Weekly (University of Texas at Dallas), have come up with a practical way to quantify job performance. They frame the definition in terms of the standard deviation of job performance, which they agree is equivalent to roughly 40% of annual salary. In practical terms this means that for a given job or level of responsibility, a worker who performs one SD below the average worker (or at the 15th percentile) is seen to be worth 40% less than the average salary paid by that job. The reverse also holds: A worker who performs one SD above the average (or at the 85th percentile) is seen to be worth 40% more. This does not mean that workers who perform at different levels actually get paid (or even should be paid) such radically different salaries or wages; this political point is not at issue here.

How Much Is Training Worth?

Since the kinds of managerial training and the training techniques that Burke and Day reviewed are from a range of corporations, the findings can be generalized. This means that any given organization can calculate the financial utility of a given training course by plugging the appropriate numbers into the above formula — even if that organization has not done the internal research on the effect of specific course. By using this formula, of course, you're assuming course content, method and culture are comparable between the "norm group" and the one your organization wants to evaluate for financial utility, and your company's trainers and trainees are not radically different from the norm group. On the whole, these assumptions will usually be safe.

In order to determine the overall worth of a corporate training course in — let's say — human relations for middle managers, you must first figure out the cost of the training per person. If, for each student, tuition costs $1,300, travel and living expenses amount to another $1,300, and prorated salary plus benefits for the eight-day course come to $2,700, then the total cost per student (C) equals $5,300.

Next, assume that the size of the effect of the training on behavior on-the-job (E) is .44 SD, as judged by senior management. With the average annual salary of middle managers in this case at $60,000, the monetary value (M) of one SD of job performance (which, you recall, we're defining as 40% of annual salary) is 40% of $60,000 or $24,000. One final piece of information: 150 middle managers received the training.

By plugging in the appropriate numbers, you find that the financial utility of this training course is $789,000 in total, or $5,260 per person.

F = N [(E x M) - C]
$789,000 = 150 [(.44 x $24,000) - $5,300]

Now, if you want to calculate the payback period in terms of years, simply divide the per-person cost of the training(C) by the gain (E x M):

$5,300 / .44 x $24,000 = .5 years or 6 months

And to get a figure for return on investment, just subtract cost from gain and divide by cost:

(.44 x $24,000) - $5,300 / $5,300 = approx. 100%

An example calculating the financial utility of a company's overall training effort is worked out in Figure 2.

Now that it is feasible to report the reaped profits from dollars spent on nontechnical training in corporations, human resource professionals have hard answers to the question that used to stop them in their tracks: What is training worth?

FIGURE 1
EXAMPLES OF EFFECTS OF TRAINING CONTENT AND METHOD

	Effect	No. of Effects Studied	No. of People Measured	Effect Size in Standard Deviations
CONTENT				
General managerial programs	On-the-job behavior	88	11,707	.40
Human relations leadership/ supervision communications managing people	On-the-job behavior	118	6,537	.44
Problem-solving and decision-making	Objective tests	11	605	.17
Performance appraisal	Bottom-line results	46	1,326	.64
Overall corporate managerial training	Bottom-line results	60	2,298	.67
METHOD				
Lecture plus group discussion and role playing	Objective tests On-the-job behavior	20 21	1,708 1,117	.37 .34
Self-paced workbooks	On-the-job behavior	69	3,081	.40
Behavior modeling	On-the-job behavior	17	446	.78
Multiple techniques	On-the-job behavior	76	5,169	.51

FIGURE 2
FINANCIAL UTILITY OF TRAINING

Overall corporate business education in Company X:
F = N [(E x M) - C]
N, number of persons trained in 1996 = 2,500
E, effect size (in standard deviations) = .67
M, monetary value of one standard deviation = .4 x $62,500 (average salary)
C, average cost per person = $3,000 (across all courses)
F, financial utility = $2,500 [.67 x .4 x $62,500 - $3,000] = $34,375,000

ROI: What Should Training Take Credit For?

When calculating the return-on-investment for a training program, take the bows and accept the boos only for things you can control

BY JAMES R. COOK
AND CAROL M. PANZA

Statistics can be manipulated and used to prove almost anything. That disturbing little axiom comes to mind often these days as we follow the ubiquitous debate about the ultimate question: "Is training really paying off for our organization?" The reason it comes to mind is that the question often takes this form: "How do we get hard statistical data to prove that gains in organizational performance outweigh and justify dollars we invest?"

It seems to us that there are some dangerous assumptions underlying this whole line of thought. The question of return-on-investment (ROI) for employee training should be approached cautiously and judiciously. Otherwise, advocates of strong employee-development programs may be giving themselves "just enough rope," and wind up hanging from it.

That training should prove its worth is not to be argued. What training should take credit for and how to document its impact are the key issues.

Consider this scene:
Sales manager: "Welcome back. Did you have a good time in Atlanta?"
Life insurance agent: "Actually, we didn't get around the city too much. They kept us pretty busy with the training program. But it was terrific. We learned a lot about the company's target markets and using telemarketing to reach them. And I feel a lot more confident about getting leads because we did role plays and even practiced scripts with live calls."
Sales manager: "That's super! I knew you'd get a lot out of New Agent Orientation Week. But now that you're back here in the real world, I'll show you some unique things we do in this agency. Don't forget all that stuff you learned in Atlanta though. It may come in handy someday."
Agent: "Oh...okay. Uh...thanks, boss."

Let's say you're the corporate vice president who fought to establish New Agent Orientation Week, or the training director whose people built the program. Would you want to be

---

If you take credit for post-training performance, can you also take the heat if performance plummets after training?

---

responsible for the sales gain resulting in that manager's territory from the fact that his agents attended your course? Probably not. Unless you were looking for a quick way to get some quantifiable negatives on your track record, target-market sales increases for new agents wouldn't be *your* choice as a measure of ROI for training.

That's not to say that measurement of results isn't important. For very sound business reasons most of us would argue for looking at results as a function of the investment required to produce them. The trouble comes in determining which results a given organizational unit is really responsible for. What does each ultimately control?

Take a look at the diagram of ABC Insurance in Figure 1. We have highlighted the training department and agency operations. The labeled arrows tell us what is "flowing" between training and agency operations, and between operations and the market. That is, they describe the basic inputs and outputs that link the functions together and to the external market. In ABC's scheme of things there is no direct link between the training department and the market; there is no way to *make* sales happen except through the direct actions of agency operations.

The figure does show, of course, that you can trace a connection from the market (and sales revenue) *through* agency operations to the training department. Training does play a role in sales performance. It helps line departments determine training needs, develops and delivers programs that cause learning, and suggests follow-up activities to ensure better performance. All of these are important outputs with a single bottom line: to support salespeople by influencing their skills and knowledge. Training is clearly a resource for improving or maintaining agency performance.

But don't warm up your calculator yet. The relevant term here is "resource." Training's outputs are inputs that contribute to line results. They do not determine line results. They do not make sales happen.

Certainly the results or outputs of a support function like training must link up with line results — in this case, sales dollars from the target market. But taking all the credit for a change in line performance is risky business. What, after all, can the training department control? Can it control the amount of time, if any, spent on telemarketing? The number of sales calls completed per week? The on-the-spot feedback (and consequences) delivered by a sales manager? No. Training can no more control these factors than agency operations can control product pricing, product features and benefits, agent sales commission schedules or conditions in the general economy and the financial markets.

So what about claiming the value of the change in line performance as a return for dollars invested in training? Willing to go for it now? What does that kind of ROI computation

---

The New Training Library ———————————————————————— *Evaluating Training's Impact* **39**

really say? It says that training, or the addition of specific skills and knowledge, is the only contribution to the changed results. How do you suppose the line organization is going to feel about that? What is the value of their management?

Further, are you willing to take the heat for the same ROI measurement in a case where performance does not improve or perhaps even gets worse in the months following your training program? More likely, your answer in such a situation would be something along these lines:

- "The skills weren't applied properly on the job, or they weren't reinforced."
- "Consequences weren't in place to reward desired behavior or even to discourage undesirable behavior."
- "Resources weren't available to permit the salespeople to do their jobs properly."
- "The market went sour."

In other words, if a training program that you had designed or championed failed to produce the sort of bottom-line ROI we're talking about, you'd stand up and howl that skills and knowledge are only one component of the performance system. No fair-minded, rational person could hold training solely responsible for lackluster market results. After all, "we" did our part. We provided our deliverables.

Care to wager on how far you get with that response if you've tried to grab all the glory for a change that *was* in the right direction? Think you might hear something about having your cake and eating it too?

Another Route

Where does this leave training? If it can't take credit for results produced by line operations, how does it prove its contribution and justify its existence?

To begin, a company must define the results for which its training function is accountable, and then substantiate that the function produced quality outputs in those areas. In the cycle presented in Figure 2, accountabilities fall into two broad categories. One category, represented by the dotted lines, identifies the traditional staff role of advice, recommendations and support. The category represented by the solid line is the only "end result" that belongs entirely to the training department. The only result in this cycle for which training should have absolute accountability is the design and delivery of a training product that meets the goals established by management. We feel that the training function should improve documentation of the outputs for which it *is* accountable, and take credit for both successes and failures in those areas. Trainers should not look to the concrete results of line departments to prove their worth as a staff function. As Peter Block put it in his book, *Flawless Consulting*, "If consultants really believe that they should be responsible for implementing their recommendations, they should immediately get jobs as line managers and stop calling themselves consultants."

Those dotted lines in Figure 2 represent the training department's "consulting" role. These are very important but different contributions that must be measured and substantiated differently.

The first step in the training cycle is to understand management's goals. The direction in which the organization is moving is the context for a needs analysis to determine if training is required to meet established goals. Training's accountability is to provide as much advice and support (including tools and resources) as necessary to help management make an informed decision on the need for training. When appropriate, that advice should include recommendations *not* to use training as a solution, plus viable alternatives to help produce the desired outcome. This advice function may require a strong and determined voice that must be heard above the din of quick-fix solutions. But like it or not, the final decision rests with the client, not the consultant.

Training must document its efforts, however, and prove that it provided quality service. This documentation should be in the form of memos to management, written reports of activities, examples of tools and instruments appropriate for the type of analysis to be conducted and any other documentation that could prove training provided quality output in helping line management determine its needs.

Once the decision to train some group of employees has been made, the content and training population must be determined. In the content area, the training department may

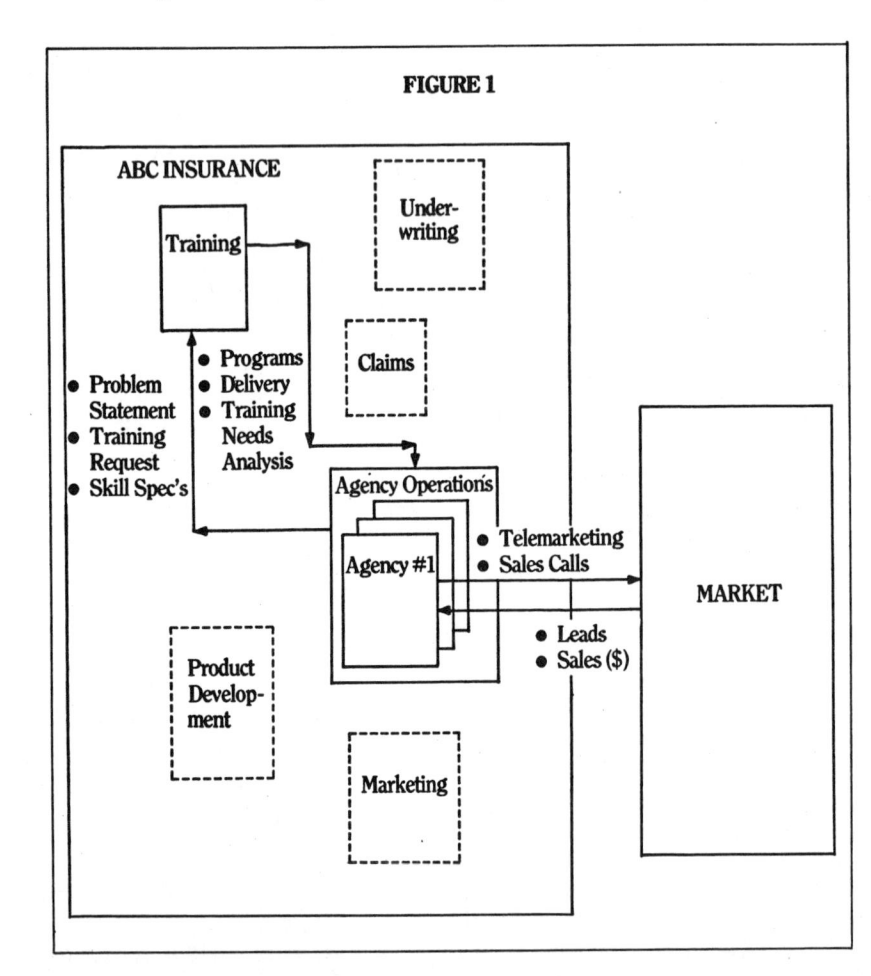

FIGURE 1

find some of its most difficult work. This may include task analysis, pouring over job descriptions, looking at skills inventories and endless interviews with bosses, incumbents and subordinates. Again, the final decision on what will be taught belongs to line management. "But they don't understand what's needed!" trainers will cry. Well convince them. But before you conduct any training, be sure that line management, not the training department, owns the content.

What does the training department use to show its contribution to the content decision? Documentation would include a description of the content-analysis process, along with the recommendations provided to management. Recommendations should be accompanied by all the supporting evidence the training department can muster.

To select trainees, repeat the process. The decision belongs to line managers. The training department must advise, recommend and provide data uncovered in the content analysis which would help the decision process. And again, it must document the fact that it has done so.

Results

All of this "soft" supporting evidence is getting a bit much? You're yearning for something more tangible? Don't despair. We come now to the part of the training cycle that *belongs* to the training department: the design and delivery of training that produces desired learning. The question that must be answered and documented is: "Did they learn what we intended?" Learning is the product of good training, and the training function must be able to show that the desired product was produced.

If we're talking about New Agent Orientation Week, some documentation should exist to prove that each trainee learned the techniques of telemarketing, in this case, taped recordings of the live calls or video records of the role plays would suffice. If neither of these is feasible in a given program, there at least should be a record of instructor observations regarding the performance of each student. Proof of effectiveness involves some recorded performance response or activity that shows that training produced its desired output learning.

In addition to documenting the fact that students learned what they were supposed to, the training function must be able to answer two other questions: "If they did not learn, why not?" and "Did they learn efficiently?" Both of these questions require proof that the content analysis was done correctly, that the program design followed acceptable industry

---

Trainers: Be very cautious of taking credit for results that belong to others.

---

standards and that the product was produced as efficiently as possible in terms of time and cost. That it's difficult to "prove" all this, we don't deny. But the importance cannot be overestimated that trainers often are accused of taking too much time to deliver their product; if they can't prove otherwise, perhaps they deserve the criticism.

Traditional student evaluation sheets are only secondary documentation of good training. Have we stumbled on a fly in the ointment? Could it be that in some cases trainers don't have clear standards against which to measure whether or not they have delivered quality instruction? If the answer is yes, then this is an area in which training as a discipline needs work to better prove its worth. The same logic holds for the programs produced. If you can't show how your products meet established standards of quality, you should expect criticism of those products.

Payoffs

Assuming you *can* document that the trainees learned, the next question is whether the learning transferred to the workplace — that is, are the trainees using the new skills on the job? Here again, the training department is accountable for advice and recommendations to line management on how to ensure this learning transfer. But it is the line manager, not trainers, who must *cause* new skills to be applied. Trainers are in the "can-do" business. Line managers are in the "will-do" business. Training professionals should provide trainees'

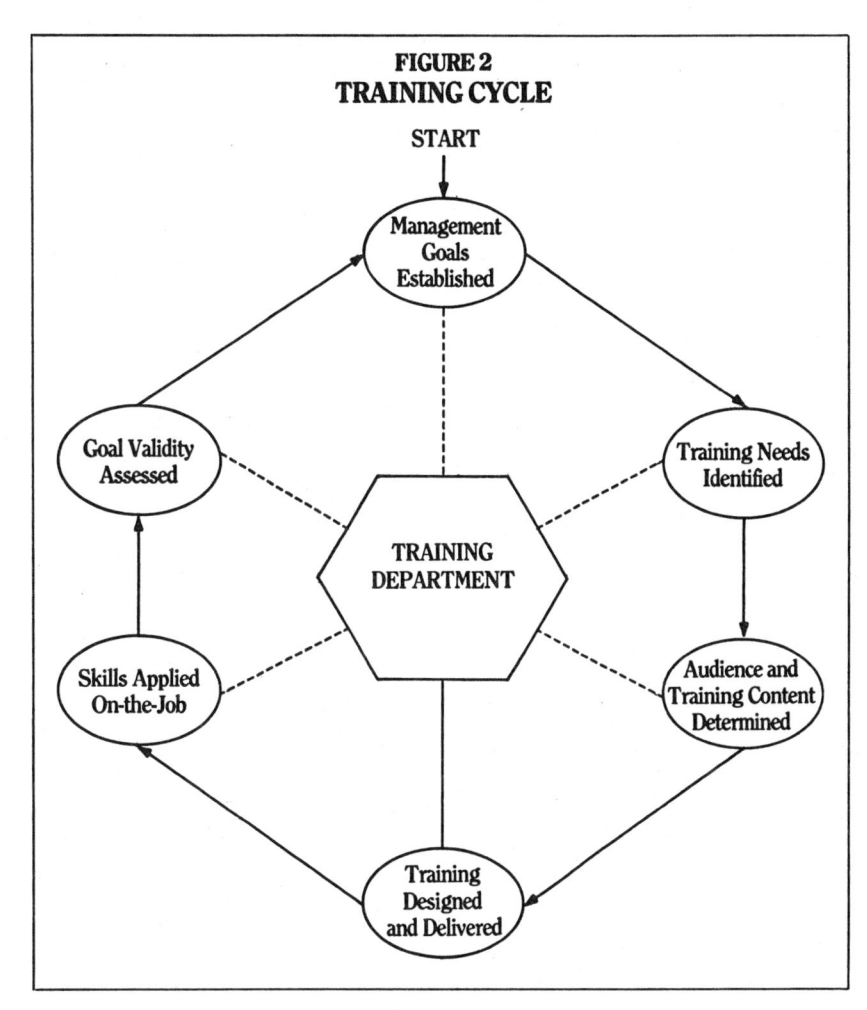

**FIGURE 2
TRAINING CYCLE**

START → Management Goals Established → Training Needs Identified → Audience and Training Content Determined → Training Designed and Delivered → Skills Applied On-the-Job → Goal Validity Assessed → (TRAINING DEPARTMENT) bosses with specific techniques on how to follow through on training. But they should not assume responsibility for the application of those recommendations.

To complete the training cycle, there must be a way for line management to determine if the training provided was worth the return. "Validation," in this sense, means substantiating that the instruction accomplished its original intent. The data that must be gathered will depend on that intent.

If training was done to improve performance in some specific job, then data must be gathered to see if performance gains have occurred. The training department, using interviews, observation, questionnaires and the like, may gather this information and provide a report for line management. Management must then decide on the value of the training. In their support role, trainers should help in interpreting the data and in suggesting ways to correct any problems that turn up in the performance study. The specific approach to data collection should be agreed upon before the training is conducted, with timetables and key people identified up front. Also, the training department's role should be clearly identified, with its "deliverables," if any, agreed upon beforehand. This way, the training department can prove that it met its responsibility by providing quality products.

This whole discussion assumes, of course, that training was done to improve specific performance. What about the validation of training that has no specific performance goals in mind? Here, management just has to determine whether the training met its original intent, whatever that may have been. The training department's accountability basically ends with good documentation that the desired learning occurred in the classroom. If a particular performance change is not an expected outcome, there is no need to collect performance data — unless, of course, you're experimenting.

To put things in perspective, let's drop the new agent orientation program into the context of the training cycle. Figure 3 shows some of the "results" that may be expected for a segment of that program.

The figure reiterates the theme that New Agent Orientation belongs to line managers. They are using it as one of the resources available to develop new agents. In the overall scheme of paying for this development, the formal training program is just one expense among many that constitute the total cost of creating topnotch agents. The return on the training investment is calculated in the total ROI for which agency operations is accountable. Training's exact contribution to that total ROI in terms of dollars and cents is unknown and it will remain unknown despite all the statistical manipulation in the world.

Even if the training department could prove that the performance of new agents was due only to the training experience, the result belongs solely to agency operations, not to the training department. The risk of taking credit for positive results is evident in view of the multitude of variables that can cause negative results even when the training produced quality learning.

The message, then, is to prove your worth in those areas you can control and be cautious of taking credit for results that belong to others.

FIGURE 3

Steps	Management Actions	Training Department Actions
Management Goals	Management decides that it wants to reach certain target markets using telemarketing techniques.	No decision making. Should actively pursue up-to-date knowledge of management direction and key goals.
Training Needs Identified	Makes a decision that a segment of the new agent orientation program should cover target markets and how to use telemarketing techniques to reach those markets.	Suggests and recommends ways that training might best be used. May identify areas that could best be learned on the job, recommend ways for line managers to support desired performance, etc.
Audience and Training Content Determined	Hires new agents. Determines training schedule. Provides key people for training department to interview to determine training content.	Conducts a content analysis using interview and observation data. Recommends training content. Makes suggestions on prerequisite skills.
Training Designed and Delivered	Communicates expectations to trainees prior to program, including on-the-job application of skills to be learned.	Provides advice on how to conduct pre-course discussions with trainees. Designs and delivers a program that enables students to use telemarketing techniques to reach certain target markets.
Skills Applied On-the-Job	Gives specific assignments for new agents to use telemarketing techniques to reach certain target markets. Gives rewards for effort and results in this area.	Provides suggestions on how to follow through on and support the skills learned in the program.
Goal Validity Assessed	Determines if new agents are using the telemarketing techniques and if their performance shows that the techniques are helping them reach target markets.	Gathers specific data on the application of new skills. Provides feedback to management on revisions to training content, audience, pre-course preparation and/or supervision for application on the job.

How to Decipher the Real Feedback on 'Smile Sheets'

BY RON ZEMKE

Using participant end-of-course reaction forms, sometimes facetiously referred to as "whoopie sheets," has been widely criticized as a method of evaluating training program effectiveness. The naysayers suggest that post-course reaction sheets are of dubious value because:

- Participants have difficulty making meaningful and unbiased assessments of the utility and effects of their participation.
- Participant-reaction forms invite overly generous ratings of the training experience.
- Reaction forms are usually administered to participants at the end of an exhausting training experience, when they'd rather go home than give thoughtful feedback.

But Dr. Kent Chabotar, a senior analyst with ABT Associates, Inc., and an associate professor of management at the University of Massachusetts, Boston, believes that reaction sheets can be effective evaluation tools. Chabotar accepts the fact that "...despite criticisms, the reaction form continues to be the evaluation instrument used most frequently." He points out that trainees and management *expect* rating sheets at the end of a program, and, for many trainers, the economics of a research design evaluation are insurmountable. "Where the choice is not between simple and sophisticated training evaluations but rather between simple evaluations and no evaluations at all, the reaction form is very attractive," Chabotar observes. "Since it seems likely that the participant-reaction form will survive, training evaluators must find ways to capitalize on its strengths and minimize its weaknesses."

Toward that end, Chabotar offers us five rules for the effective design and analysis:

1. **Reaction forms should cover both training process and impact.** Some people argue that only impact on trainees and the organization should be measured. Others insist that the organization and delivery of the training are the major concerns. Charbotar tries to split the difference by suggesting that both be addressed. He suggests measuring the following three factors:

- **Training objectives** — the extent to which participants feel they were able to achieve pre-specified objectives calling for improvements in knowledge, attitudes, skills or job performance.
- **Training sessions** — a rating of the content and delivery of each training session or instructional unit, possibly including ratings of individual faculty.
- **Training components** — the overall reactions to training scope and goals, organization and administration, and content and delivery.

2. **Reaction forms should permit both essay and scaled responses.** Asking trainees to rate specific items using a Likert-like scale of some sort (e.g., 1 = poor, 5 = excellent) is great for quantifying and comparing outcomes. But, Chabotar cautions, there's also much to be said for "...in-depth feedback not only on *what* happened during training but also *why* it happened, and *how* the program can be improved." This, of course, means that essay-type questions are invaluable. He goes on to suggest that such questions should focus on specifics and gives some examples:

- What were the stronger features of this training program?
- What were the weaker features? How would you improve them?
- Could you name two or three new ideas you gained from attending this program?

3. **Reliability of results can be increased by asking the participant's supervisor to complete similar reaction forms.** An abbreviated or slightly modified version of the reaction form can be used to measure the supervisor's impressions and observations of the extent to which participants from his or her unit have changed after the program.

4. **Results can be more meaningful if selected performance standards are used in interpreting data.** Interpretation of the data generated by the reaction form is often complicated by the lack of performance standards against which to compare the results of specific programs," says Chabotar. He suggests anchoring reaction questionnaires in either *norm-referenced* or *criterion-referenced* performance standards.

- **Criterion-referenced** standards define "success" as an absolute average score on a reaction form item or series of items. For example, it may be decided that each of the items relating to workshop components must have received an average score of at least four on a five-point scale in order for the program to be declared a success.
- **Norm-referenced** standards define "success" in relative, not absolute, terms. Scores on any item on a given program's reaction form can only be interpreted in comparison with scores on that same item achieved by other training programs. Comparisons are commonly made on a percentile basis. For example, training program X could achieve an average rating of 4.5 on the item: "The ideas and activities presented were (1 = dull, 5 = very interesting)." This might seem impressive until compared with how other training programs did on that same item.

5. **Comparisons can be facilitated by accumulating a reaction-form-result data base.** By compiling a running record or data base of results from trainee-reaction questionnaires, comparisons among different training programs can be

FEAR AND LOATHING ON THE EVALUATION TRAIL

You've just finished a training program. The sessions are over. The instructors — your own staffers or outside professionals of your choosing — are winding down. The evaluations are in. You go over the ratings and comments on each individual's effectiveness and notice that in and among the goods and acceptables, interwoven with the praise and plaudits, are some harsh words and critical reviews. How do you handle them?

It can be a tricky problem. You want to use the evaluations for their avowed purpose — as constructive feedback on what was done and how it might have been done better. But you also want to protect the professional pride, confidence and perhaps fragile personal egos of the people who've given their best on your behalf.

"If you ask for evaluations," says Bernadine Eve Bednarz, manager of organizational training and development programs in continuing education in mental health for the University of Wisconsin-Extension, Madison, "then I think you have to count them for what they are. When people put themselves out teaching, they also have to be prepared to take the brickbats with the roses."

That's not always as easy as it sounds, she points out, particularly when organizational politics are involved. In one case, Bednarz circulated the unedited evaluations on a training program considered successful overall. Among the comments on the faculty was this: "She is intelligent, yet has not found her own style — having become a poor carbon copy of the famous person who led the workshop." Another trainer on the program called to object to publication of such disparaging remarks, arguing that it would have been better to share the negative commentary with just the individual involved instead of opening her up to group scrutiny.

On another occasion, a participant wrote: "Due to (her) zero personality, I find it hard to concentrate on the information she has to offer from her apparently very effective program." That, says Bednarz, sparked three phone calls and one letter from members of the planning committee who felt the remark was impolitic, deadly and should have been edited (one suggestion — "zero personality" to "retiring personality").

"How do you handle it best?" Bednarz asks rhetorically. "How do you distinguish between criticism that may be personal and vituperative and an observation that is legitimately worthwhile? You might have 45 good comments and one lousy, but what will people pay attention to? The one lousy. All you can do is look at the positive stuff, too, to keep it in perspective."

Bednarz makes no distinctions between her own instructors and outsiders — both get a frank and unedited replay of all evaluations, with a cover letter or other suitable introduction pointing out the level of positive reactions overall. The only exception to her rule, says Bednarz, would be in the event a participant turned particularly hostile, using racist or sexist pejoratives obviously out of sync with the content of the training. In such a case, which has never yet arisen in her experience, Bednarz says she would edit out the remark completely rather than attempt to soften the wording.

"You know it can be demoralizing," she admits, "but I think you owe people the honesty and have to assume they will be professional enough to be able to put things in perspective."

— *Ron Zemke*

---

made. More importantly, though, historical trends can be tracked and future projections made. Using simple "eyeball projection," you can sense when classroom quality begins to deteriorate and take quality assurance measures before much damage is done. Specific program objectives can be tracked over time. And across-program quality can be assessed for instructors, *and* the efficacy of specific instructional strategies can be assessed across instructors.

Chabotar points out that this idea has become an actuality. As an example, he references the "workshop evaluation system," designed by Edward McCallon; the "system" has a national data base containing trainee reaction results from over 40,000 workshop participants. The results from any training program can be compared with the results of the programs represented in the data base in terms of organization, objectives, presenter, ideas and activities, scope, and overall effectiveness. A similar system can be developed fairly easily within a specific organization. It simply requires standardization of reaction forms and a central collection of reaction-form data.

Dr. Chabotar cautions that trainee reaction forms are not a be-all and end-all. Nor will behavioral and research designs be superseded by them as appropriate evaluation methodology. Rather, he concludes:

"These recommendations are not intended to elevate the reaction form to undeserved status as a fully validated and reliable instrument. Its subjectivity and other defects prevent that. But the five rules are meant to acknowledge the remarkable persistence of the 'whoopie sheet' as a principal assessment tool and the consequent need to improve it. The reaction form can provide valuable information about training process and impact for the ultimate consumers of training: participants and their employing organizations."

Sins of Omission

Want your HRD department to give more than lip service to your organization's strategic plan? Here's how

BY BARBARA BOWMAN

Your annual state-of-training report to management is a dazzler. You developed five new programs, attendance was up by 20% and trainees routinely rated sessions as "excellent." Your programs consistently met their objectives — you've documented the fact — and graduates are actually back on the job *applying* the skills they learned in class. All this and you're under budget, too.

What more could you ask for? It's a training director's dream...or is it? Your assessment of this human resources development (HRD) department, which happens to belong to a hospital, might change if you also knew that:

• The hospital plans to introduce a new pediatric-rehabilitation program early next year. All the necessary governmental approvals have been obtained, funding is in place and publicity materials are ready. But there are no plans yet to train the staff to work with these complex new patients.

• The hospital was cited recently by its accrediting agency for failing to provide required ongoing infection-control instruction.

• Due to market shortages, it has been impossible to fill vacant medical transcription positions. Several typists now employed by the hospital have expressed interest in the jobs, but no training is available to prepare them for the new assignments.

• An increase in the number of elderly, bedridden patients has resulted in more back injuries among the staff There have been no classes on body mechanics or proper lifting techniques.

In other words, the programs offered by the HRD department were excellent, but what about the programs *not* offered? How do we evaluate needs not met, classes not taught, opportunities not realized?

The answer is, we don't. These sins of omission are blissfully ignored in typical evaluations.

Paths Not Taken

When they set out to determine, for themselves and for top management, how good a job they're doing, training departments focus on three aspects of evaluation: Participant reaction (Were trainees satisfied with the session? Did it meet their needs?), achievement of objectives (Did trainees mas-

> **How do we evaluate training needs not met, classes not taught, opportunities not realized?**

ter the information the program was designed to teach? Can they perform the skills?) and impact evaluation (Has a chronic problem been corrected as a result of the training? Has performance improved back on the job?).

Our hypothetical hospital training department performed beautifully according to all these evaluation measures. Programs were well received, they were cost effective and they produced behavioral changes both in the classroom and on the job. But, obviously, important training needs went unmet.

Quite logically, standard evaluation methods assess programs that have, in fact, taken place. It is another matter to evaluate the impact of a program that never happened. A ground swell of voices is exhorting organizations to tie training to their strategic plans. But using our usual methods, how can we evaluate the effectiveness of this linkage?

When HRD fails to support the strategic plan, it is generally because our evaluations fail to address our sins of omission. We need to take a different approach to evaluation, one that looks at how effectively the HRD department is meeting the *strategic* training needs of the organization. In other words, we need a system of total program evaluation.

The Missing Link

Total program evaluation links evaluation to needs assessment — the process of figuring out what employees need to know — rather than to program objectives. This is a fundamental change: "Trainers customarily have been taught that when performance objectives are set, evaluation methods are automatically specified as well. We assume that the appropriate objectives have been established and that meeting those objectives will meet the needs of the organization. This approach fails to acknowledge those cases in which program objectives are met, but major needs are neglected. By linking needs assessment to the total program evaluation, however, we can avoid sins of omission — the programs that should have been offered but weren't.

Total program evaluation uses three major sources of data to identify missing programs and to evaluate the effectiveness of programs that did occur:

1. A review of needs identified through a comprehensive needs assessment. This implies, of course, that you have conducted a needs assessment and developed a prioritized list of training needs. Review these needs annually to determine which have been met and which have not. If the company's strategic plan calls for the launching of a new product line, for example, has training support for it been initiated? Is the accounting department ready for its new computers? Are managers prepared for the new performance appraisal system? Has training been completed to correct the safety violations on the factory floor?

2. An assessment of employee satisfaction with programming. No evaluation can afford to neglect the perceptions of trainees. Total program evaluation asks employees to consider the overall HRD effort, rather than just individual programs. Items from a questionnaire used in this year's needs assessment can help you determine people's satisfaction with last year's programming. If you have collected good demographic information, you can correlate measures of satisfaction with departments, job classifications, shifts, seniority and other variables. This data also yields valuable information about whose needs are being met and whose are not.

Usually only employees who attend training programs are involved in evaluating them. Assuming these people attended voluntarily, they apparently felt that the program at least had the potential to meet their needs. Therefore, the results of a participant evaluation are inevitably skewed. What about employees who, for whatever reason, choose *not* to attend the program? This is your chance to find out why, and to determine whether you are neglecting the needs of a part of the organization.

3. A comparison of the results of this year's needs assessment to those of last year's assessment. Does the assessment conducted this year reflect a change in needs? Were problems identified last year resolved? Some needs, of course, are ongoing, but others should decrease in significance as a result of training.

If training is conducted to meet an identified need, but that need continues to appear in assessments year after year, something is wrong with either the training or the assessment. Maybe the needs are stated in such general terms that they are useless as guides for programming or evaluation. Maybe you're using inappropriate methods to deal with these needs. In either case, further study is in order.

Also compare employee satisfaction with this year's programming to that of previous years. Have problem areas been corrected? Has satisfaction decreased among any employee groups?

The Fatal Flaw

The potential flaw in total program evaluation is obvious: If it is based on a faulty needs assessment, it will be worthless. If your assessment missed important needs, the evaluation will fail to flag your sins of omission just as completely as one that considers only isolated programs. Here are a few points to keep in mind during the needs assessment process.

Be sure to review the type of material you will need in order to project long-term training needs. Consider the organization's goals and objectives, its business plan and, of course, its strategic plans. And don't forget the department-level counterparts of these plans.

Of course, not all organizations have strategic plans or other materials that lend themselves to this kind of analysis. They are far more common in some industries than in others.

We need to start linking evaluation to needs assessments, not to our program objectives.

Even if your organization has a formal plan, you may find that changes are not reflected immediately in the written documents.

Fill in the gaps with more informal sources of information. Interviews with managers at various levels will help you see the big picture. Senior executives will be more knowledgeable about long-term plans, whereas middle managers probably will be more aware of the effect of these plans on the day-to-day operations of their departments.

Don't ask line managers to describe their training needs; line managers don't always recognize training implications. Instead, ask them what new projects they'll be introducing, what changes they're anticipating, what kinds of people they'll hire and what problems they're encountering. It's your job to infer training needs from this information and validate them with the manager. Conduct these interviews at budget time if possible. Not only does this allow you to prepare your own budget more effectively, but managers are usually attuned to these issues when they are working on their own budgets.

In addition to its future plans, consider how the organization is functioning now. Identify performance indicators and use them as assessment tools. For example, production statistics, turnover rates, on-the-job injuries, quality assurance studies, reports from regulatory agencies and client comments may all point out potential training needs.

The key word here is *potential*. You may identify problems that are due to any number of causes; don't assume they automatically translate to training needs. This is especially important if you want the HRD function to be held accountable for meeting needs rather than just for providing instruction. The training department that confuses a procedural problem with a training need will not fare well in total program evaluation.

Use the employee needs-assessment questionnaire to verify managers' perceptions of needs and your own hypotheses rather than to present a laundry list of possible training topics. If you find a major discrepancy between managers' and workers' opinions, there may be poor communication between various levels of the organization. Again, this may be evidence of a training need requiring further investigation.

Considering these issues during the design and implementation of a needs assessment should result in data that can serve as the basis for a valid evaluation that addresses programs omitted as well as those actually offered.

Total program evaluation supplements rather than replaces the other three types of evaluation. It's still important to evaluate individual programs to identify strengths and weaknesses.

Let's go back to our hypothetical HRD department. What effect would total program evaluation have on our appraisal of its performance? A comprehensive needs assessment that followed these guidelines would certainly have identified such needs as preparing for a major new program, complying with regulatory agency requirements, meeting manpower needs by providing promotional opportunities and correcting unsafe techniques. Total program evaluation would have pinpointed several sins of omission and held the department accountable for meeting these needs.

Total program evaluation presents a new perspective on evaluation. It is a valuable technique for HRD departments that are serious about tying training to their organizations' strategic plans.

Chapter 2
Building Better Pre- and Post-Training Tests

One More Time: Test Trainees Before You Train Them

Pre-tests can be valuable in several ways, not the least of which is their ability to save your job by validating your training's success

BY PAUL RAHN

We've all been enlightened by those trainers who advocate "testing trainees before training 'em." As another author wrote in the pages of TRAINING Magazine not long ago, all you have to do is sit everybody down before your show starts and ask each trainee some questions on the upcoming subject. Here's the rest of the scenario: Each participant probably feels that he already is an expert and will appreciate this little challenge, but, unfortunately for his ego, your test will succeed in pointing out his weaknesses. Then you give him the benefit of your years of experience — that is, your training session, which explains all of the important concepts. During this time, a red light pops on in the trainee's mind every time you mention one of his weak subjects. And finally, you repeat the test you gave at the beginning. This time, the trainee scores well because the few things he didn't already know are now clearly imprinted on his mind, thanks to those flashing red lights.

To validate the effectiveness of your training, you subtract scores of the pre-test from the scores of the post-test to determine the real learning experience. After all, the training session was the only stimulus experienced by the trainees between the tests. Or could it be that the increase in test scores is merely a measure of the efficiency of the trainee's red light?

You can answer that question yourself, but it does raise another interesting possibility. Can pre-tests improve training effectiveness by sensitizing participants to key concepts?

A comparison with the tried and true method — tell 'em what you're going to tell 'em, then tell 'em, and then tell 'em what you told 'em,

Well-designed pre-tests help you start training the right people at the right level.

uncovers an immediate similarity. Giving a pre-test is just like telling what you're going to say, with emphasis.

It's difficult, of course, to give a pre-test that covers all the subjects you feel are important but isn't so lengthy that the impact of individual items is diluted. Even the long test will help strengthen the learning experience for those concepts tested: If it's important enough to be in a question, it must be important enough to learn.

As frequent TRAINING contributor Joel Hochberger, a long-time advocate of "testing 'em before you train 'em" has correctly pointed out, another positive benefit of the pre-test is that it can identify the participant's knowledge of the concepts covered in the tests. Training programs are usually attended by two groups. Group I knows everything you are going to say and shouldn't be in the sessions.

Group II doesn't know enough to start at the level on which your program begins and shouldn't be there either. A third, but insignificantly small group, knows enough to follow you but not enough to be bored. They're the people you should be instructing.

Group I should be presented with more advanced material — if you aren't afraid of encouraging them to pursue your job. Group II should be started at a lower level. And you should tell your recruiting staff exactly what type of person you want.

Now, back to the original problem of validating the effectiveness of a training program. Hochberger has already told us about the problems of using only a final test. I also hope you see the bias introduced by using the same questions before and after on the same group. You can solve this problem without unnecessarily complicating your life simply by proving the statistical validity of the measured improvement in test scores. Any good statistician in your organization can do number crunching for you and provide more information on degrees of freedom, statistical significance, standard deviation, correlation and other equally undefinable sums than you would ever want to know. If you lack such talent in-house, the local college's business, statistics or psychology department will be happy to assist, expecially if you allow them to use the data as the basis for an article in a scholarly journal. If you still can't find someone with the skills, don't worry; if you can find an average, add and subtract, then you can do the number crunching yourself in the simple designs.

The problem originally caused by the pre-test testing bias may be eliminated or at least controlled by any of several increasingly expensive and consuming methods. Provided you have a large enough group, the simplest procedure is to divide your participants randomly into two groups, "A" and "B." Group A is given a pre-test. Group B, the control group, is not pre-tested. Recombine the two groups and put everyone through the training program. After the session is over, give everyone the test originally taken by Group A. The difference between the average of Group A's post-test scores and the average of the test scores of Group B results primarily because Group A was sensitized by taking the pre-test. Thus, the true

WAIT TO CORRECT TRAINEES' TESTS

Common sense says you don't scold your dog tomorrow for the surprise it left on the rug today. Not if your objective is to prevent future unpleasant surprises. Psychologists would justify an on-the-spot scolding thusly: The effectiveness of a reinforcing stimulus is contingent upon the immediacy of the temporal relationship between the emission of the subject behavior and the presentation of the reinforcing stimulus. Verbiage aside, though, the principles of reinforcement do have a common sense sort of validation to them.

Learning is more effective when a reinforcer, called feedback, immediately follows the presentation and answering of test-like events. This proposal, a by-product of behavior modification and animal learning research, does indeed indicate that efficiency in learning and retention decreases the longer reinforcement is delayed.

There is increasing evidence that, when one is learning meaningful material, delayed feedback (of up to 24 hours) is reliably superior to immediate feedback, particularly when measured by delayed retention testing. And as you might guess, there are explanatory fictions (Skinner's term for theories) for this phenomenon also.

The two major theories that explain this "feedback-is-not-reinforcement" phenomenon are the Rehearsal and the Interference theories. The Rehearsal theory says the delay gives the trainee time to reflect and ruminate on the question(s) and the possible answer(s). The Interference theory says that during the delay between the test and feedback, the strength of the answers weakens; by the time feedback is available, the strength of a wrong answer has diminished sufficiently for it to be replaced by a correct answer. The answers are learned or practiced anew at the time of feedback without the interference of the test-like event. Immediate feedback to incorrect answers is low in effectiveness because the wrong answer is strong and interferes with the learning of the correct response.

J.M. Sassenrath of the University of California at Davis decided to find out which theory is more viable. Rather than run yet another study, Sassenrath reanalyzed data from a number of the original studies done by supporters of both sides of the question. His goal: to determine which sort of feedback, immediate or delayed, caused the greatest change in errors over time and which caused the most preservation of error.

Sassenrath is, by the way, a proponent of the rehearsal theory. Yet his reanalysis came down on the side of the Interference-Preservation explanation of why delayed feedback to testlike events is more effective than immediate feedback in promoting superior performance on delayed recall tests. Translation: Delayed feedback of up to 24 hours is more effective than immediate feedback. This is most important if you are more concerned with long-term recall than with immediate performance. The delayed feedback situation is, in effect, another learning or practice opportunity.

(Reported in "Theory and Results on Feedback and Retention," *Journal of Educational Psychology*, Vol. 67, No. 6.)

---

measure of the effectiveness of your training can be determined by subtracting Group A's pre-test average from Group B's post-test average.

There is, unfortunately, a weakness to this approach. Groups A and B must be selected randomly from your participants. If your group is small, you will not be able to assume that random group assignment will ensure that the two groups are "statistically equal." With a small group, you must use the matching technique of pairing two people whom you think will react (learn) in a similar manner and placing them in opposite groups.

Randomness or matching should take care of the selection biases that decrease design validity. But a multitude of other problems may be introduced in the form of history, mortality, experimental setting and some other "interactions" that statisticians working in the behavioral sciences have uncovered and have yet to devise a method for controlling — short of using a Solomon 4 Group 6 Test Design.* For those training managers under pressure to validate their programs and who also have extravagant budgets, a good statistician using the Solomon design will be able to crank out enough numbers to satisfy anyone in your organization who is questioning your effectiveness.

There are, then, three valuable uses of pre-tests. They can make classes more enjoyable because, no matter how often you get off the subject, your students will still remember the concepts on which you pre-tested them. You can start training the right people at the right level. And, finally, you can save your job by validating your training's success.

Incidentally, all three uses are only as good as the test happens to be in measuring what you think it's measuring. But that's a different subject, one that demands an even deeper understanding of multiple instrument or concurrent validity (the name depends on which statistician is describing it).

---

*The Solomon four group experimental design has been described as the "ideal model for controlled experiments" because of its ability to control for all sources of experimental error except measurement timing and reactive error, which are not subject to control by designs. The design is composed of four groups (two treatment and two control) and six measurements (two pre-tests and four post-tests). Although this design has many advantages, few instances of its use in applied experimentation have been reported. This is obviously the result of the increased cost of securing two additional control groups.

An excellent treatment of this subject may be found in D.S. Tull and D.I. Hawkins, *Marketing Research: Meaning, Measurement, and Method* (New York: MacMillan Publishing Co., Inc., 1976), Chap. 12.

6 More Benefits of Pre-Testing Trainees

Traditional wisdom holds that pre-tests can help determine the benefit of your training program or discover that trainees already know what you intend to teach them. But that's not all

BY BOB MEZOFF

Are you willing to invest five or 10 minutes at the beginning of your training programs to get the most out of your training budget? If you adopt pre-testing as a key component of your training programs, you can:
- Dramatically increase your trainees' readiness to learn.
- Help them learn far more from the training programs you conduct.
- Get trainees to make a psychological investment in the training process.
- Sensitize them to the key concepts you will present.

A pre-test simply measures knowledge or attitudes related to the training session prior to the program. Traditionally, pre-testing has been administered to determine the benefit of a training program and to determine whether, in fact, it is necessary. By measuring the difference between pre-test and post-test scores, you can determine what trainees learned from the course. On the other hand, if the pre-test shows that trainees already know what you plan to teach them, you can all save your time and effort.

These traditional rationales for pre-testing are solidly based in learning theory and are reason enough to include it as a standard element in your training design. Yet the pre-test's value as a learning tool does not stop there: The benefits of the method accrue incrementally.

Benefit #1
Unfreeze your trainees

Unfreezing is the first phase of a three-step process of "change" (or learning) identified by Kurt Lewin in 1947. Following this phase comes "change" and then "refreezing." The unfreezing phase is an important, in fact essential, prelude to learning. In order for change (or learning) to occur, the individual must "let go" of his or her traditional perceptions, beliefs and behaviors. A properly constructed pre-test is an effective unfreezing technique that can be administered in a matter of minutes.

Adults need to identify a purpose or personal motivation that will actively engage them in the learning process — otherwise they will have little incentive to learn. While some learning is purely "growth-oriented" (personally enriching yet not functionally critical), most organizational training attempts to teach people skills or information the organization has determined they should acquire.

The trouble is that trainees often come to a training program without that sense of personal motivation. The question "What's in it for me?" needs an immediate answer if trainees are to be receptive to the program. If adult learners don't see a personal benefit to the instruction, they can maintain a complacent sense of "I'm doing just fine with what I already know" and the training program will have little impact.

A pre-test, however, stimulates motivation by increasing anxiety and decreasing complacency. In our society there is so much pressure and anxiety inherent in testing situations that trainees often feel apprehensive about taking a pre-test, despite your assurances that they are not expected to know the answers.

Although trainees cannot "fail" a pre-test (again, pre-testing simply determines their existing knowledge or attitudes), this anxiety can produce positive results. When trainees discover they do not know the answers, they can see for themselves how much they have to learn.

The unfreezing effect works better for some people than for others. Research indicates, for example, that a pre-test is likely to have a greater impact on people with a field-attentive [or field-dependent] cognitive style (basically, people who are more sensitive to the way others perceive and judge them) and a lesser impact on those with a field-independent cognitive style (people who tend to be less concerned with the opinions of others).

Yet for those who pre-testing does influence, it dramatically increases their readiness to learn. And for those it does not influence, it doesn't diminish their learning in any way, regardless of the differences in responses. A pre-test that involves cognitive knowledge (where facts and skills are to be demonstrated) is an excellent way to get trainees "psyched up" to learn.

Even when a pre-test takes the form of an attitude questionnaire, trainees may doubt their responses, asking themselves, "I wonder what the right answer is?" or "I wonder what the company thinks the proper attitude should be?" This uncertainty sets into motion an unfreezing process which, in turn, creates a readiness to learn.

A word of warning: Only a properly constructed pre-test can nurture the unfreezing process and increase the trainees' appetite for learning. Ill-conceived or poorly constructed pre-tests can create resistance to learning, so it is crucial to take the time and effort to develop an effective pre-test.

Benefit #2
Intrinsic value

In some cases, trainees may learn as much from taking a pre-test as they do from the training process itself. For example, in *The Assessment of Change in Training and Therapy* (McGraw-Hill, 1969), J.A. Belasco and H.M. Trice demonstrated that some participants changed their attitudes about alcoholism simply as a result of taking a pre-test. Using a sophisticated research design, they were able to determine the exact effects of the pre-test. Although this study didn't show that every participant was affected similarly, on average there was a significant impact.

The fact that a pre-test occasionally can produce as much of an impact as an entire training session dramatically illustrates its cost effectiveness.

Benefit #3
Ceremonial effects

Pre-testing creates a "ceremonial effect" for the trainees. The higher the initial cost to trainees — in other words, the more effort they must put into the learning process — the more they will tend to value the training.

A difficult pre-test (or a pre-test on which the trainees are unsure of the "correct" answers) represents an initiation ceremony. Once they invest energy and effort into taking a pre-test, trainees are motivated to find out what the answers really are. The pre-test thus encourages a psychological investment in the training process.

A few minutes of pre-testing pulls the trainees into the context and content of the training program — even before initial warm-up and introduction activities begin.

Benefit #4
Sensitizes trainees to key concepts

The pre-test sensitizes trainees to the objectives and content of the course by enabling them to anticipate key points. Paul Rahn recommends this technique and compares it to the tried-and-true method of training: "Tell 'em what you're going to tell 'em, tell 'em, then tell 'em what you told 'em."

The 20 or 30 items on a pre-test "flag" the most important concepts and help trainees establish a mental "checklist" to distinguish those key points from the other workshop materials. Don't include minor points in a pre-test (or for that matter, the post-test): use it to focus trainees on the most important concepts.

Benefit #5
Focuses the trainer

Writing a pre-test forces the trainer to conceptualize exactly what he or she intends to teach in the training session, a result similar to the effect of writing instructional objectives. In fact, it's only possible to develop an effective pre-test if your instructional objectives are clearly defined.

A pre-test can't include all the objectives and therefore helps the trainer establish priorities among the various learning goals. When the trainer focuses on the most important goals, trainees are more likely to attain them.

The first time I developed instructional objectives and pre-tests for my training programs, I was amazed at how much easier it was to teach when I had an explicit idea of exactly what the most important points were. And I was appalled at how fuzzy my course design was before I had developed and assigned priorities to my objectives. My training program benefited from the pre-tests I developed because I was clear on exactly how much effort and time I should be spending on the key learning points.

Benefit #6
Establishes a rigorous learning climate

The opening minutes (or even seconds) of any human interaction are critical to determining how the relationship develops. This is true in job interviews, counseling sessions, and certainly between trainer and trainees. At the beginning of a session, participants will be scouting for clues as to how to respond, how serious you are and what kind of expectations you have of them. The early signals you send will set the tone that determines the climate for the remainder of the session.

A pre-test immediately makes trainees aware that: (l) your expectations are rigorous and serious; (2) there is an explicit body of information for the training course; (3) they are being measured and evaluated on their efforts to learn (at least as a group, if not individually); and (4) the company has seen fit to put an effort into measuring the effectiveness of its training programs. Effective testing (pre- and post-) suggests a high-quality training program.

By setting a rigorous learning climate, pre-testing also helps overcome the problem of unmotivated trainees. Some trainees may be reluctant or hesitant about attending a training session. As a result, they arrive as passive, rather than active, learners. In some companies, simply filling a chair and keeping one's eyes open are the only requirements for passing. This is especially true if training activities have earned a reputation as being a time to socialize with coworkers.

However, when the trainees arrive on the first day and are greeted with a pre-test, they immediately get the message that you are serious.

Pre-tests provide an incentive to learn for both high and low achievers. The pressure of pre- and post-tests encourages reluctant or low-achieving trainees to search out the trainer for extra help, remedial work or at least individual coaching during the session. Achievement-oriented trainees want to learn even more because they know that they will have an opportunity to demonstrate their mastery on a competency test (if that is the case) at the end of the training program.

SOME TRAINEE REACTIONS TO A PRE-TEST

"This test brings out the realization that I am totally ignorant in this field. There is much to learn."

• "I feel inadequate and I hope I haven't started something I can't complete. I guess I'm frustrated!"

• "Trying to answer the questions on the pretest was frustrating, frightening and upsetting. Could the real purpose of this testing be to point out to us what we don't know so we'll be shocked into learning it?"

• "This test leaves me feeling apprehensive, as though I should know data I'm totally unfamiliar with. If a failing mark on this test means expulsion, then I will bid the reader a fond adieu."

• "This test has a tendency to be a little disconcerting."

• "I found this test to be very frustrating and ego-deflating. I was not competent to answer the majority of the questions."

These comments are from a group of Canadian school administrators who had just taken a pre-test for a course on leadership training.

I was surprised that so many of the comments referred to anxiety created by the test. Since all of the trainees were school administrators, I assumed they would understand the traditional purposes behind pre-testing and realize that the test was not administered to make them feel inadequate. But apparently, even people who are familiar with educational environments find taking a pre-test disconcerting.

How to Use Certification to Evaluate Training's Effectiveness

BY SCOTT HEIMES

Evaluating training's impact after a training event is a challenge for every training department, says Karen Kitchel, director of associate training services for Minneapolis-based BI Performance Services. BI knew its training sessions were well attended and day-of-training evaluations were glowing, but the performance consulting firm wasn't able to prove that training was hitting home or that performance back on the job was improving. To achieve this elusive Level 3 evaluation, BI built a certification process into each of its courses. The effort earned it a 1995 Training Directors' Forum Outstanding Performer Award in the category of evaluating training's impact. Here's how BI did it:

In January 1994, BI's two-person training department did a companywide needs analysis to determine how training efforts could be tied more directly to the individual performance of BI's 950 associates. After surveying both managers and employees through focus groups, Kitchel determined that two areas should be "certified" — company processes and individual skills.

Process Certification Needs Manager Involvement

The first step in developing certification tests for company processes, says Kitchel, was organizing another focus group of the company's vice presidents and department managers to identify key company processes and brainstorm on how to best certify employees without adding wasteful bureaucracy to training courses.

The exercise helped Kitchel focus her early efforts on what was most important to managers and was a means of getting all-important top-level support for changes.

Once the company's key processes were determined, Kitchel added a certification test to existing training courses. Each test asks associates to demonstrate mastery of the process they were just trained to do, while being evaluated by a peer who completes an evaluation form created by the training department.

Asking peers, or teams of peers, to

When experienced peers administer certification tests, trainees often are more relaxed and perform better.

do the actual certification evaluations was a key decision, says Kitchel. "The goal with our certification tests is to verify knowledge and support success, not cause fear of failure or put additional pressure on trainees to pass. By having experienced peers do the evaluation, trainees are more relaxed and perform better," says Kitchel.

For example, once new phone operators complete training they must pass a certification test consisting of answering mock incoming calls, finding requested resources, routing calls, and performing other duties. During the test, an experienced phone operator monitors the call and fills out an evaluation form provided by the training department. If the peer "passes" the trainee, the trainee becomes certified. If the peer doesn't consider the performance up to par, Kitchel recommends additional training. Employees can take the certification test as many times as needed to pass.

Once a trainee passes the certification test, Kitchel issues an official certificate of completion with the individual's name and the process certified, which is signed by the president of the company. The certificate is then given to the vice president in charge of the trainee's division who presents it to the recipient during the next divisionwide quality meeting.

Recognizing employees' personal development in front of peers was a primary goal, says Kitchel. "Our certification program is a way upper management can recognize employees at all levels for training achievement. It has also helped raise the awareness of training's importance to the company's long-term performance improvement."

To date, over 500 process certifications have been awarded. Some departments have begun using certification as a way to document skills needed for advancement.

Get Employee Input for Skill Certification

To develop the skill certification tests, Kitchel did a second needs analysis using small focus groups of managers and employees from all levels of the company to identify skills needed to excel on the job. The first focus groups identified skills, then a manager-only focus group used an electronic voting machine called an *Analyst* to determine which topics were most important and demanded certification. (Kitchel says the voting machine can be obtained at many specialty game stores.) The voting machine forces focus group participants to organize topics in order of importance by assigning numbers to topics, eliminating gray areas and allowing the group to quickly come to consensus. "Pulling all the information together, it became very clear as to what we should work on first, second, third, and so on," she says.

In many cases, existing courses were revamped to focus more closely on those identified skills, and some new courses were introduced. A certification process was added to both old and new courses. Courses offered include: communication/listening, interviewing, delivering presentations, how to train new associates, problem-solving, and reinforcement and performance management.

For example, during the half-day communication/listening skills training workshop, trainees learned how to interpret body language, how to select words for clarity, and techniques for better listening. After the session, associates challenge themselves to improve in one of those areas and go through a role-playing exercise with a team or individual peer who then evaluates the trainee via a "Tell Me How I'm Doing" card. Again, the evaluating peer or team passes the trainee according to the certification criteria on the evaluation form.

Similar to process certification, the training department sends a certificate identifying skill mastery to the associate's division vice president, which is then presented at the next division quality meeting. Over 700 skill certificates have been awarded to date.

Notes:

Add 'Then' Testing to Prove Training's Effectiveness

How effective was your training program? Pre-post testing is a reliable measurement method, but it can skew your evaluation. Here's a simple way to increase the accuracy of your measurement

BY ROBERT G. PREZIOSI
AND LESLIE M. LEGG

Would you like to improve the accuracy of your training program evaluations? Would you like to increase your bargaining position when negotiating your training budget? Would it enhance your department's power base to reduce the cost of evaluating your training programs, while demonstrating their high impact? If so, you should consider the advantages of "pre-then-post" testing over pre-post testing.

Pre-post testing is a familiar technique to most trainers. Before training begins, participants rate their ability, knowledge or skill using a Likert-type scale (see Exhibit 1). Once the training concludes, participants rate themselves again on the same factor. The two sets of scores are compared to determine the changes in the participants' self-ratings as a result of the training. While low in cost and easy to administer, this type of self-reporting can create some problems.

First, there's the "glowing estimate" problem. If trainees overestimate their ability, knowledge or skill on the pre-test, score comparisons produce an inaccurate analysis of the effects of the training program

A more serious problem is the "response shift bias." This inaccuracy occurs, according to reseachers, because participants in a training program have a different frame of reference for a post-test than they did for the pre-test. The pre-post method does not take into account such changes in frame of reference.

For example, prior to training, a participant's self-rating on a scale of one (low) to 10 (high) is six in the area of recognizing nonverbal communication cues; after the training session, the same subject rates herself as a seven. But that "seven" rating reflects the trainee's new understanding that there is a great deal more to the subject than she thought; she realizes now that the pre-test score of six was an overestimation — a lower score would have been more realistic — but it's too late to change the pre-test rating. Thus, the response-shift bias produces an inaccurate measure of the learning that has taken place, and the trainer cannot fully document the benefits resulting from his program.

To obtain accurate comparisons, participants must rate themselves using the same frame of reference. Pre-then-post testing makes this possible. After the program has concluded, participants are asked to think back and rate their knowledge, skill or ability prior to training. This is the "then" measure. They are then asked to rate themselves in light of what they know now (the traditional post-test). The process eliminates response shift bias because participants use the same frame of reference on the then-test as on the post-test. In addition, a traditional pre-test measure is taken

---

EXHIBIT 1
Likert-type Scale

Using the following scale, rate yourself on the item listed below.

Low				Average					High
1	2	3	4	5	6	7	8	9	10

_____ My skill at listening to other people.

FIGURE 1
PRE-POST RESULTS (N = 20)
(Scale 1 -10)

Item	Pre-Test	Post-Test	Pre-Post % Increase
Leadership	4.42	7.75	75%
Motivation	6.08	7.95	31%
Communication	5.96	7.64	28%
Supervisor Responsibilities	7.04	7.85	12%
Personal Strength Awareness	5.90	7.92	34%

FIGURE 2
THEN-POST RESULTS (N = 20)
(Scale 1 -10)

Item	Pre	Then	Post	Then-Post % Increase
Leadership	4.42	4.00	7.75	94%
Motivation	6.08	4.93	7.95	61%
Communication	5.96	4.97	7.64	54%
Supervisor Responsibilities	7.04	5.37	7.85	46%
Personal Strength Awareness	5.90	4.62	7.92	71%

at the normal time

We can analyze the data from this testing approach in two ways: Pre-test and then-test scores can be compared so that the differences reflect the shift in frame of reference; the then- and post-test scores also can be compared and the differences analyzed based upon the same frame of reference. In our use of this testing technique, participants tend to overestimate their skills on the pre-test, and their "pre" scores are higher than their "then" scores.

Testing the Method

In one application of this approach, we used two groups of participants in a management development program. The experimental group consisted of 20 people being trained in two separate sessions; the control group consisted of 20 people who would receive the same training at a future time. Both groups were given the pre-test before the experimental group began its eight-week training program. The then- and post-tests were given to both groups at the conclusion of the experimental group's program. (The control group, in other words, took all three tests without receiving any training. As expected, the self-ratings did not change appreciably.)

FIGURE 3
CONTROL GROUP (N = 20)

Item	Pre	Then	Post
Leadership	5.42	5.41	5.42
Motivation	6.78	6.96	6.98
Communication	6.13	5.95	5.84
Supervisor Responsibilities	7.29	7.07	7.06
Personal Strength Awareness	6.90	6.97	6.78

The pre-then-post testing consisted of 22 statements covering the program content, such as "My ability to evaluate the most important factors in a leadership situation." Participants rated themselves on a Likert-type scale with values ranging from one to 10.

Figure 1 is a sample of the data collected from the experimental group, using pre- and post-test scores only. Figure 2 also reflects data from the experimental group, but includes the "then" scores. Scores from the control group are presented in Figure 3. The data in the first two figures speak for themselves: The response-shift bias is eliminated and a more accurate picture of learning changes is drawn.

The pre-then-post test scores also indicate that participants did indeed learn something as a result of the training program — significantly more than would have been documented by the traditional pre-post approach. This is a very important point when it comes to negotiating your training budget: You can precisely identify the impact your training is having. The percentage increases are significant enough to catch anyone's eye. (In a separate study of cross-selling training, the increases were even higher.)

Compared to direct observational techniques and other approaches, pre-then-post testing is an economical way to evaluate your training programs — an advantage that cannot be overemphasized at a time when costs and productivity are concerns of all organizations. HRD department resources used to implement this type of evaluation can certainly be justified by the benefits they produce.

Notes:

Constructing Tests that Work

Here's a refresher course on how to construct tests that measure whether trainees learned what they were supposed to learn from your training program

BY MARC J. ROSENBERG
AND WILLIAM SMITLEY

When the objectives of a training course demand a pencil-and-paper test of knowledge or appropriate job-like performance, the trainer confronts a deceptively difficult challenge: How do you write test items that effectively and accurately measure the extent to which trainees have learned the material you've been teaching them?

Like so many training tasks, this one looks easy until you try to do it. Constructing effective tests requires subject-matter expertise, clear and concise writing, and considerable time and effort. Above all, it requires that each test item be designed so that every student interprets it in exactly the way the designer intends.

The four most common types of written tests — multiple choice, dichotomous, matching, and short-answer completion — are all variations of the same basic, two-part format: first a stem, which is a statement or question that provides the stimulus to the student; then two or more alternatives, often called distracters, from which the correct response to the stem is selected. The alternatives may be provided directly, as in the case of multiple choice, dichotomous or matching items, or, as in the case of short answer-completion questions, they may be implied. In the latter case, the "distracters" are all of the imaginable answer choices the student must filter out in order to provide the correct response.

By looking at the four types of questions as variations of this universal format, our discussion of each type, including definitions, advantages and limitations can be simplified. We should note at the start, however, that the advantages and limitations of each format in a general sense will not indicate which is best for a given testing situation. The format you choose should reflect your analysis of the specific content you wish to test and the learning objectives of the training course.

Multiple Choice

A multiple-choice test item consists of a stem, in the form of a statement or question, followed by more than two distracters. A key point in the design of multiple-choice questions is that all distracters should be plausible. Here are three acceptable examples:

Question format: What cartoon character was Walt Disney's first commercial success?
 a. Donald Duck
 b. Goofy
 c. Jiminy Cricket
 d. Mickey Mouse

Incomplete statement format: Walt Disney's first commercially successful cartoon character was:
 a. Donald Duck
 b. Goofy
 c. Jiminy Cricket
 d. Mickey Mouse

Incomplete statement format 2: The cartoon character was Walt Disney's first commercial success.
 a. Donald Duck
 b. Goofy
 c. Jiminy Cricket
 d. Mickey Mouse

Major advantages of the multiple-choice format include:

1. Test scoring is simplified because possible bias by the test administrator cannot influence a student's score. And because all distracters are provided in the item, an answer key can be developed to allow anyone to grade the tests — you don't need a subject-matter expert to do the grading.
2. When more than two distracters are provided for each item, the trainees' chances of guessing the correct answer are reduced.
3. When enough plausible alternatives are available to be used as distracters, multiple-choice items are relatively easy to construct.

Major limitations of the multiple-choice format:

1. Since the answer is provided among the distracters, it can be guessed; you can't be certain that the student really knew the answer to a given question.
2. The format relies on recognition, rather than "production" of the answer by the student. It is generally agreed that recognition reflects a lower level of learning than does production.
3. When enough plausible distracters cannot be identified the development of quality multiple-choice items can become very difficult.
4. Since several distracters must be provided for each item, the format uses more space than some of the others.

Dichotomous Test Items

The stem of a dichotomous, or alternative-response, test item is typically a declarative statement but can be in the form of a question. The stem is followed by only two mutually exclusive distracters (yes/no, true/false, right/wrong, cold/warm).

Major advantages:

1. The dichotomous format is useful for distinguishing fact from opinion, right from wrong, or in any other situation where there are two, and only two, mutually exclusive alternatives.
2. As with multiple-choice items, scoring is simplified and unbiased.

Major limitations:

1. Since only two choices are provided, the student has a 50% chance of guessing the correct answer. Therefore, the dichotomous format usually requires more test items than

TEST ITEM CHECKLIST

_____   _____
Reviewer's Name   Date

Directions: Indicate whether *all* test items meet each criterion by placing a check mark [ ] in the appropriate box. Write the number of any items that did not meet the criterion in the space marked "REVISIONS." Use only those criteria which apply to each particular item or test type.

Revisions: If any test item receives a NO, revise that item as needed.

I. GENERAL CRITERIA

	YES	NO	REVISIONS
1. Is the item grammatically correct?	[ ]	[ ]	_____
2. Have ambiguous statements/terms been avoided?	[ ]	[ ]	_____
3. Is the item written at the trainee's language level?	[ ]	[ ]	_____
4. Does it avoid giving clues that can be used to answer another item?	[ ]	[ ]	_____
5. Does the item contain only a single idea?	[ ]	[ ]	_____
6. Is only relevant information included?	[ ]	[ ]	_____
7. Has the use of a correct answer from another item as part of the stem for this item been avoided?	[ ]	[ ]	_____
8. Is there only one correct answer for the item?	[ ]	[ ]	_____
9. Are all parts of the item on the same page?	[ ]	[ ]	_____

II. MULTIPLE CHOICE TEST ITEMS

	YES	NO	REVISIONS
10. Have negative and double negative stems been avoided?	[ ]	[ ]	_____
11. Have grammatical clues been avoided?	[ ]	[ ]	_____
12. Is as much of the wording as possible in the stem rather than in the distractor?	[ ]	[ ]	_____
13. Are all distractors approximately the same length?	[ ]	[ ]	_____
14. Are all distractors plausible?	[ ]	[ ]	_____
15. Are enough distractors present in each item (4-5) to reduce guessing?	[ ]	[ ]	_____
16. Are distractors arranged in an orderly manner (alphabetically, numerically, logically)?	[ ]	[ ]	_____
17. Have distractors such as "none of the above," "all of the above," "A & B only," etc., been avoided?	[ ]	[ ]	_____

III. DICHOTOMOUS TEST ITEMS

	YES	NO	REVISIONS
18. Is the statement worded so precisely that it can be judged unequivocally?	[ ]	[ ]	_____
19. Have negative and double negative stems been avoided?	[ ]	[ ]	_____
20. Have clues which tend to qualify the "absoluteness" of the stem been avoided?	[ ]	[ ]	_____

IV. MATCHING TEST ITEMS

	YES	NO	REVISIONS
21. Are there more distractors than premises?	[ ]	[ ]	_____
22. Is the premise list short?	[ ]	[ ]	_____
23. Are distractors more concise than premises so that reading load is reduced?	[ ]	[ ]	_____
24. Are the distractor and premise lists related to the same central theme, concept or idea?	[ ]	[ ]	_____
25. Are all premises, distractors and matching rationale on one page?	[ ]	[ ]	_____
26. Are premises and distractors arranged in an orderly manner (alphabetically, numerically, logically)?	[ ]	[ ]	_____
27. Is there only one answer match for each premise?	[ ]	[ ]	_____
28. Have grammatical clues been avoided?	[ ]	[ ]	_____

V. SHORT ANSWER/COMPLETION TEST ITEMS

	YES	NO	REVISIONS
29. Is the item constructed so that only one briefly written answer is possible?	[ ]	[ ]	_____
30. For incomplete sentence items, does enough of the statement remain to convey the intent to the trainee?	[ ]	[ ]	_____
31. Does the main idea of the incomplete sentence precede the blank?	[ ]	[ ]	_____
32. Is the only omission a significant word, symbol or number?	[ ]	[ ]	_____
33. For numerical answers, has the degree of precision been included in the stem?	[ ]	[ ]	_____
34. Have negative and double negative stems been avoided?	[ ]	[ ]	_____
35. Has a list of acceptable responses (variations of the answer that are acceptable as correct) been specified?	[ ]	[ ]	_____

---

other formats to measure the student's knowledge accurately.

2. Few important statements are absolutely right or wrong, true or false. Therefore, dichotomous test items can be difficult to construct. It usually is a mistake to try to "qualify" the stem with words such as "always," "usually," "never" and so forth; such qualifiers provide clues to the correct answer, as in these examples:

__T __F An open style of supervision is always the better way to deal with subordinates.

__T __F It never rains in California between the months of June and September.

If the test item doesn't fit the dichotomous format, don't force it; choose another format.

3. As with multiple-choice questions, the dichotomous format does not force the student to "produce" the correct answer.

Matching Test Items

In the matching format, a series of stems, usually called "premises," is listed in a single column, while the possible distracters are listed in a second column. All of the distracters in a matching series should be plausible answers for each stem or premise. All the premises and all the answer choices must be similar, or homogeneous.

In a matching exercise, stems should contain the majority of the information to be tested, while each distracter should be short, containing only a key word, number or phrase. This reduces the burden on the student of repeated reading of a long list of distracters.

Example of a matching format:
Match the type of frame joint with the correct method of nailing that should be used.

Frame Joint	Nailing Method
Soleplate to joist	a. Blind
Rafter to valley	b. Edge
Rafter to rafter	c. End
Header to joist	d. Face
	e. Toe

Major advantages:

1. Since the matching format allows all the distracters to be used as possible answers for all of the stems, a lot of test items can be covered on a single page. Matching tests also can be completed more quickly than tests using other formats.

2. The format measures factual knowledge and the student's ability to recognize relationships and make associations.

3. As with multiple-choice and dichotomous items, scoring is simplified and unbiased.

Major limitations:

1. As students complete the items they know to be correct, the possibility of making a correct guess increases through the process of elimination. This limitation can be reduced by providing more distracters than stems.

2. Stems and distracters in a matching group must be homogeneous. That is, they must relate to the

USING 'DAILIES' TO KEEP TRAINING ON TARGET

Our organization has sunk a lot of money into this training program — design time, material and logistical expenses, perhaps travel and lodging expenses for the trainees, not to mention lost work time. As with any investment, you want to know whether or not this one is working out, and you want to know soon enough to correct any mistakes.

To protect your investment, one instructional designer recommends borrowing a technique from another fast-paced, high-budget industry: the movies. Kenneth A. Lawrence, chief of instructional design at the Veterans' Administration Medical Center in Washington, DC, points out that the film industry avoids expensive return trips to remote locations by processing film samples each day, so that any necessary reshooting can be done immediately.

Those film samples are called "dailies." If Steven Spielberg were a corporate trainer, he might refer to dailies as a type of formative evaluation. That idea occurred to Lawrence a few years ago when the VA switched from local to centrally conducted training for its medical center procurement specialists nationwide. The new arrangement called for eight to 10 five-day training sessions a year. Each session would cost more than $10,000. No room for second chances there.

Lawrence and his associates decided that what they needed was an evaluation form they could pass out at the end of each day's training — a form that would give them results they could process and interpret overnight. They rejected a daily content quiz as cumbersome to create and administer. Instead, they settled on an instrument very much like your standard, end-of-session evaluation form. It asks trainees to rate the program on such dimensions as relevance to their jobs, clarity and pace. It also asks them to list the most important things they learned in the session, and to make any other comments they wish.

The difference is that instead of filling out the questionnaire only at the end of the course, trainees are asked to complete it at the end of each of the first three days and occasionally on the fourth day — "for example, when a new or revised course is being tested, or when a new instructor is presenting training," says Lawrence.

The form uses Likert-scale questions ("Rate this characteristic from 1 to 5"). After each class, an evaluator plots the response distribution for each question, and categorizes the write-in comments by frequency. Then the evaluator reviews the results with the instructor.

They're looking for the usual things. For example, the distribution on "relevance," (1 = all the material was highly relevant, 5 = little or no relevance) should be toward the left end of the continuum. For "pace," rated from 1 (too fast) to 5 (too slow), the responses should be grouped near the center, with outliers evenly balanced between the two extremes. Trainees' comments about the most important things they learned should bear a reasonable resemblance to the intended content of the course.

Not long ago, Lawrence says, the usefulness of gathering this sort of data daily instead of only at course's end was illustrated when an instructor got sick on the third day of a session and had to be replaced. The day's subject — analyzing bidders' projected overhead costs — was one that often gave participants trouble anyway.

The evaluation showed that one of the classes taught by the substitute instructor had a particularly hard time with the lesson. For example, the "clarity" item, which normally turned up a leftward distribution (meaning most of the day's instruction was understandable), showed a nearly flat distribution for this particular class. That night the trainers developed a review sequence. The instructor presented it first thing the next morning. According to Lawrence, that day's evaluation indicated that the problem had been resolved.

One additional benefit of dailies, Lawrence adds, is that their cumulative information can be very helpful in evaluating an entire course. It may not be as glamorous as a Hollywood screening, he concludes, but it does the job.

— *Marc J. Rosenberg and William Smitley*

same concept and must be phrased in basically the same way. If the designer isn't careful, students will be able to reduce the number of plausible distracters.

3. Again, the matching format relies on recognition rather than production of the answer by the student.

Short answer-completion:

Short-answer test items, also referred to as "completion" or "fill-in-the-blank" questions, have stems constructed in the same manner as multiple-choice items. But, instead of choosing from distracters supplied by the designer, students must come up with a specific word, number or symbol on their own.

Major advantages:
1. Short-answer items are relatively easy to construct since distracters do not have to be created.
2. They are very effective in measuring recall.
3. Unlike other formats, the short-answer item requires the student to produce the correct response rather than simply to recognize it. Thus, the possibility of guessing the correct answer is drastically reduced.

Major limitations:
1. The range of distracters depends upon the "mind-set" of the student at the time of testing. This mind-set may be different from the trainer's without being "wrong." Thus, the student might produce an unanticipated response which is arguably correct.
2. Scoring is more difficult due to potential subjectivity in the interpretation of responses. A subject-matter expert may be required to determine whether the response is correct.
3. A short-answer format should be used only when the correct response is, indeed, a significant word, number, symbol or short phrase. Here are two inappropriate items:
1. A telescope is_____
2. A tool used by astronomers to observe planets and ___ is a telescope.

Here is how the item might be improved:
3. A tool used by astronomers to observe planets and stars is a/an ___.
4. Short-answer items that are poorly developed may measure the wrong things — by asking the student to recall an insignificant aspect of some important concept, for example, organization.

Another important concern in the test-design process is that of layout. The organization of a written test centers around four major areas: (1) the cover page, (2) general test directions, (3) specific directions and (4) item groupings.

(1) The cover page: At least two matters should be addressed clearly and concisely on the cover page of any written test: the purpose of the test itself, and a reminder of the objectives of the lesson or course which the test covers.

(2) General test directions: These give the student any information necessary to complete the test. General directions should include: total time allowed; any resources the student is permitted to use during the test; whether any group work will be allowed; how to complete a separate answer sheet, if necessary; suggestions to help the student complete the test efficiently; scoring procedures and values for each test item; and instructions about what the student is to do at the conclusion of the test.

(3) Specific directions: Each set of test items, multiple-choice, matching, dichotomous or completion, requires specific directions as to how the student is to respond. It also may be appropriate to provide practice items. If the procedures by which students indicate answers vary throughout the test (e.g., circle the letter, write in a number or write in an answer), those procedures must be explained.

Whenever possible, however, construct tests in a manner that relies on as few differing procedures as possible. Don't forget to repeat your directions if the same types of questions appear in more than one place in the test or if a given format continues on following pages.

(4) Item groupings: The placement and grouping of test items is an important consideration. Some general recommendations:
1. If possible, group all items according to content.
2. Within each content area, group all items according to type (i.e., keep all multiple-choice items together, etc.).
3. Provide more space between items than within items.
4. Try to disperse the easier test items uniformly throughout the test.

Test Item Checklist

After your test has been constructed, a careful review by content and training specialists can identify potential problems, such as items that are ambiguous, poorly worded or incorrect. The accompanying checklist provides assistance in this process.

You also may save time and effort by reviewing the checklist before you begin writing test items. Remember, however, that the best "test of a test" is to try it out with typical students. Even the most knowledgeable reviewers cannot foresee all possible problems, since their "mind-sets" are inherently different from those of the students for whom the test is designed.

Notes:

CHAPTER 3
IMPROVING TRANSFER OF TRAINING TO THE JOB

28 Techniques for Transforming Training into Performance

This was going to be called "Things we know for sure about how to transfer classroom learning to on-the-job behavior." Guess what?

BY RON ZEMKE
AND JOHN GUNKLER

It happens all too often. The training program was a smashing success: The trainees raved about it, results from the written test told you that 90% of them had mastered 90% of the objectives, and they responded like old pros on the performance tests. But at a meeting over a new project a few months later, you are stunned when a regional field manager lances a verbal right cross off the side of your ego. "I don't know why you think you're so qualified to build training for the managers," he says, "when you haven't proved you can teach the service techs anything yet." That, of course, is the first word you get that repeat repairs, while down a little, are still high, misdiagnosis is still a problem and service managers now are up in arms about time standards.

In short, the operation was a success but the patient died. The training "worked" but the problem — whatever it was — didn't get solved. Somehow, what the trainees learned didn't transfer to the workplace and into their day-to-day performance repertoire.

Though much has been written, little has really been said about this perplexing problem. That may sound harsh, but we recently did a pretty thorough search of the literature and found that the most frequently recommended remedy is, "Do good training." This pronouncement usually comes in the guise of such seemingly sage advice as, "A thorough and properly done front-end analysis will differentiate between poor performance caused by a lack of skills or knowledge, and those performance problems that arise despite the fact that the individual performers are fully qualified, trained and motivated to perform," or, "To ensure that trainees will go back to the job and perform as well there as they did in

A thorough search of the literature on training transfer unearthed this refrain: "Do good training."

the training room, you must make a special effort to be sure that they see a payoff for exhibiting the new behaviors in the old setting," or, "Reinforcing the performance and providing feedback ensures that the new skills are adequately learned."

Boiled down, we are simply being told, "If you do it right in the first place, dummy..." and little more.

We certainly don't dispute the wisdom of the "Do good training" solutions scattered throughout the literature. It seems patently obvious that one must provide the very best, most job-relevant training possible if there is to be any hope that the skills and knowledge in question will be manifested in the trainee's on-the-job behavior.

Having sworn allegiance to the greater glory of doing good training, however, we must add that we see the "Do good training" admonition as begging the question. It also frustrates and tacitly insults the many trainers who have done all the good things they were supposed to do to deliver a good program but who, nonetheless, find themselves with a skill-transfer problem. We are reminded of the Little League father who, having given junior his best spiel about "eye on the ball, shoulders square and swing level," can only resort to repeating the lecture, volume up and nostrils flaring, when the kid proceeds to drop the shoulder and whiff the ball.

This brings us to the point where we are supposed to tell you either that we have just invented a miracle technique for overcoming the problem of learning transfer, or that we have discovered an abandoned cache of heretofore unpublished research by Gunneer Enslab, a mad Norwegian learning scientist who solved the whole thing once and for all in 1967, but who was run down by his estranged wife while waiting for a No. 2 bus on the first leg of his journey to visit the noted publisher/editor Ole Olsen.

Truth is, we haven't done either. We know of nothing you can rub on, administer, do or say to your trainees that is guaranteed to make transfer from training to the job a lead-pipe cinch — and that includes threatening to fire them if they don't go back and do it the way you just taught them to do it. Nor have our labors at literature review been that fruitful. In fact, relatively little research worthy of the name has been done on the problem. Are you listening, thesis-topic seekers?

The fact that there is only a modest amount of help to be gleaned from published research does not mean, however, that the cupboard is bare. For buried in the cracks and crevices of the training and development literature and related paper, there is quite a lot of practitioner-tested help, if not 100% scientifically validated formulas, for troubled training programs.

Our review kicked up 28 specific things trainers can do to increase the odds that skills, knowledge and behavior acquired in the training setting will be used back on the job. For conceptual clarity, we have lumped these suggestions into five broad, and not entirely exclusive, categories:
- Pre-training strategies.
- Good training strategies.
- Transfer-enhancing strategies.

TRANSFER OF LEARNING: THE LABORATORY PERSPECTIVE

"The empirical studies of transfer of training have provided a wealth of practical suggestions for enhancing the value of training in the world of work."

If you bought that, please consult the authors immediately for a once-in-a-lifetime opportunity to buy overwater real estate in a borough of New York City.

The truth is, as you cynics have guessed, that once again the laboratory has let us down. Not only is there little clearcut evidence that doing particular things will help transfer learning to the job environment, there isn't even much consistent theory behind why transfer does and doesn't occur. We can't even find agreement about how to define "transfer of training." Some researchers want to restrict its meaning to something akin to response generalization — the occurrence of a discriminated (trained) response to stimuli different from those to which the response was trained.

Others want "transfer" to refer only to the effects of prior learning on learning something new. And while it may make sense at times to measure transfer by measuring how readily something else is learned, it is the effects of training on performance that are of primary concern to trainers.

Given that prejudice, we define "transfer of training" as: the effects of training on the subsequent performance of an operational task.

By "operational task" we mean, simply, anything a person must do in the performance of his or her job.

There are a couple of things to note about this definition. First, because we specify "subsequent performance," the retention of what is learned in training will be a factor in transfer. And since retention depends, in part, on how well something is learned originally, the quality of original training will play a large role in how much transfer of training occurs.

This is one reason why much of the advice we find on improving transfer of training boils down to, "Do good training."

We would like to believe that "good training" means training that transfers to on-the-job performance. For many, however, the result of "doing good training" is simply improved end-of-training performance. At least, that is the implication of using end-of-training performance as the measure of training effectiveness.

In this article, we try to focus on things you can do to improve subsequent performance of an operational task. Many of these things (not all of them) also will tend to improve end-of-training performance, and so may also fall under the "do good training" rubric.

— *Ron Zemke*

- Post-training strategies.
- Finessing strategies.

Before we look at each of these "clusters" and the techniques that comprise them, there are a couple of caveats we need to deal with.

This five-part taxonomy is simply an attempt to take some of the sprawl out of the mass of ideas out there and impose some kind of order on them. You may decide, for example, that "job aids" are misplaced in the finessing category and are more properly considered part of post-training strategy. Okay by us. In fact, it is more than reasonable to consider a given idea or technique as useful in a multitude of transfer contexts. Since there is no great body of research to call upon for guidance, we pigeonholed the scientific techniques where they either seemed to make sense to us, or where someone else has suggested they belong.

To some extent, our classification scheme is arbitrary. We prefer to think of it as flexible. The only real point in explaining all this is to allay the remote possibility that someone might read our classifications as more authoritative than they are. So please be advised that when we classify a particular technique as, say, a pre-training strategy, we are not implying that there is some hidden reason why you should never consider the same technique for post-training use.

A final point before we get on to specifics concerns the exhaustiveness of this listing: It isn't. We are under no illusion that we have uncovered all the possible ways a trainer might go about increasing the probability that a skill learned in the classroom is used back on the job. This is not the ultimate "Everything you could ever want to know about transfer of learning" article. But it is a pretty good cut at the territory, even if we do say so ourselves.

PRE-TRAINING STRATEGIES

These are things you can do to or for trainees, before they begin the training, to help ensure they get the most out it and that the skills and knowledge they acquire in the training actually will have a chance of being supported back on the job. Some are things upper management can do to increase the probability of transfer. Others are things the trainees' supervisors can do. Some put the burden squarely on the trainees, while still others are things the trainer can do to prepare the trainees to make the most of the experience they are about to undertake. The common theme: All of these activities take place before the trainee ever steps into the training room or logs in on a computer terminal.

1 **"Hoopla": Making the training a "high-visibility" event.** The goal of "hoopla" is to convince (dare we say "sell"?) everyone who influences on-the-job use of the information and skills the training addresses that it is important to the organization that this training "takes." A situation that cries out for hoopla is the introduction of computerized executive workstations. People all around the organization are going to have to exchange old work habits for new and, regardless of how good the training is, there is going to be storm and strife aplenty before everyone settles into the new way of doing things.

The temptation will be to resist the change, or at least foot-drag on it, as long as possible. Introducing a new customer-relations strategy, bringing a new product on stream, or simply asking managers to begin to manage in a different way are all occasions that can produce the same tendency.

These are also situations where the

hoopla strategy — turning the spotlight of executive attention on the training — can help ensure that the training doesn't die or lie dormant after final papers are in and grades are passed out. Though specifics will vary from situation to situation, the thrust is the same: Someone "high up" in the organization champions the new way of doing things, sponsors the training to teach people how to do the new things in the new way, and insists on the importance of everyone pitching in and helping the newly trained people implement the new way of doing things. The laser beam of the high-up's attention has to be focused on two critical audiences: the trainees-to-be, and the supervisors and managers of the trainees-to-be.

There probably are a limitless number of ways to implement the hoopla strategy, but the simplest is the "executive memo." Be it from the chairman of the board, the president of the company, the chief operating officer, the head of the division or the manager of the department, someone the trainee and the trainee's supervisor fear and respect sits down and pens a semi-personalized missive that ac-knowledges the trainee is about to undertake an endeavor that has considerable·significance for the organization and the addressee personally.

The participant version of the executive entreaty is then sent to the trainee, timed to arrive prior to the beginning of training. Thanks to the wonders of modern word processing, the message can be as personalized as you deem appropriate.

As a fallback, the letter from the top can be day one, page one of the training materials. The preferred approach, however, seems to be to get the letter to the trainee before the program. Timing the letter to arrive a week prior to the training will give the recipient a sufficient period to verify that this training is indeed as important as your semi-personalized, word-processed letter claims, and to ponder the implications.

The supervisor version of the letter should cover the same ground as the trainee letter, with two additions. The supervisor should be encouraged to work closely with the trainee to see that he or she has all the support needed to apply the new knowledge and skills, and reminded to discuss the importance of the training to the trainee prior to the beginning of the program.

2 "How do you rate?": The trainee "self-assessment" strategy.

We seem never to tire of those little quizzes about sex, diet, happiness and health that appear in *Reader's Digest*, the Sunday paper and any number of consumer magazines. They touch that same streak of curiosity that has made Trivial Pursuit a runaway bestseller. Wouldn't you love it if people got that excited about your training? Can't promise that, but you can take a leaf out of the Blake and Mouton/Pheiffer and Jones Jay Hall bag of tricks and exploit this insistent little bit of human nature as a pretraining strategy.

The use of simple self-tests and self-assessment instruments prepares trainees for training by giving them a look at the content and some insight into what they do and do not already know about it. The hard part is developing a pre-training quiz that is meaningful, interesting and non-threatening — yet doesn't lead the trainees-to-be to think they know enough to skip the training if they do too well on it.

One approach is to make the instrument an obvious tease. The "tease" part has more to do with the way you position the questions and present the feedback. If you ask trick or deceptive questions, you run the risk of giving trainees the impression that your training, not to mention any subsequent testing you may do, is filled with "gotchas."

Consider this question: "Which of the following is always illegal to ask during an employment interview? (a) Are you married? (b) How old are you? (c) Have you ever been taken by an uncontrollable urge to sell life insurance? (d) Whoa! Nothing is illegal to ask a prospective employee, but some questions can put you at risk."

That's the sort of thing that might be appropriate on a self-administered pre-course quiz for a selection-interviewing course. The feedback could say something like: (b) "That's right! You really can't ask a person his or her age in an interview. But do you know why? Sorry, for the answer to that one you are going to have to show up July 23 for the workshop, 'Interviewing Skills for Supervisors.'"

The tone is deliberately relaxed and informal. The goal is to avoid a pre-quiz that feels like a career-threatening test. As a rule of thumb, one question per major objective is appropriate unless the subject matter is so technical and specific that the trainee won't be able to make heads or tails of it.

3 "Send my boss": Familiarize management with the content of the training.

While pouring through a stack of trainee smile sheets, you have undoubtedly run across the comment: "It was a fine course and I am glad I was chosen to come. But they really should have sent my boss, since he needs this program as badly as anybody."

So send the boss. If the doers are supposed to go to training and learn a new way of doing things, the boss had better know that new way as well. Boss training doesn't have to be identical to the training subordinates receive, but it should cover the same objectives and familiarize the boss with everything the employee will be learning in depth. This also is the time to give bosses a few techniques for supporting the trainees when they return to the job.

WARNING: Do not call your boss training "training." Call it "Executive Overview," "Managerial Familiarization," "Supervisory Briefing" or any label that will work in your organization. Be sure to cover the role the boss plays in setting expectations for employees going into a program, and a couple of ways to conduct an "expectations setting" meeting. Also, send them out the door with a handful of materials they can use both to refresh their memories and to conduct that meeting.

4 A "Can we talk?": The pre-train-ing supervisory-expectations discussion.

In a sense, this is the visibility strategy driven as far down the organization as possible — to the trainee's immediate supervisor. But there is a difference. The visibility strategy is aimed at drawing attention to the importance of the training as a whole, while the expectations discussion is focused on exactly what the trainee should, in the supervisor's view, expect to get out of the training.

To push it just a bit further, the supervisor is telling the employee exactly what the supervisor expects the trainee to get out of the training. The difference is primarily a matter of style. The discussion can cover a number of topics. Among the most commonly mentioned are: What the training will cover; why the trainee was chosen to participate (or was okayed for participation); why the training is important to the trainee and the organization; the supervisor's assessment of the trainee's strengths and weaknesses as they relate to the content and objectives of the program; specific projects or problems related to the content and objectives of the program that the supervisor would like the trainee to work on during the training sessions; and how the supervisor will help the trainee apply the new skills and knowledge when he or she returns from training.

Obviously, the supervisor's skill in setting expectations and familiarity with the program the trainee is going to attend, become important considerations here. Both imply that the supervisor must be trained in the subject the trainee will be tackling, as well as in the fine art of setting expectations with an employee.

5 **"Homework": Assigning pre-course study and projects.** Pre-training study and projects were fairly common a few years back and are regaining popularity. In the mid-1960s, trainees frequently were expected to work through a programmed text or self-study course prior to attending a program. This was an especially popular technique with technical-training people, who could assign basic content as pre-training study, and concentrate on troubleshooting, repair procedures and the like during the face-to-face or "lab" training. It was — and is — a common practice to require trainees to pass a criterion test on the pre-course material before they attended the "hands-on" part of the course. The advent of inexpensive computer-based training has prompted a rekindling of interest in the approach.

A variation on the theme is the pre-program project. Here, trainees are sent worksheets or guidelines that direct them to gather specific pieces of data on their departments; to interview a boss, subordinate or customer on a specific topic; or in some other way to pull together information for use in the program. If the program is on project management, for example, the precourse assignment might be to bring details of a project the attendee is or will be managing. The onus is on the program planner to give attendees enough guidance so that they will be able to ask the right questions and collect enough information for the project actually to become a personal case during the program.

GOOD TRAINING STRATEGIES

Call the following points "making the systems approach work," "the principles of good practice" or simply "the basics." It is important to attend to the fundamentals of good analysis and design if you hope to be in the business of providing training that solves significant organizational problems. You can't afford to do otherwise. But also bear in mind our earlier comments about the holes in this approach to "solving" the problem of learning transfer. "Good training" safeguards alone will not guarantee transfer from training room to playing field.

All that said, we can take some steps in the analysis, design and development phases that will increase the probability of transfer.

6 **"Soil sampling": The work environment assessment stra-tegy.** The good book says that all training begins with a thorough needs assessment. Dana and Jim Robinson of Partners in Change, a Pittsburgh, PA, consulting firm, suggest that a work environment assessment is critical to finding and attacking transfer problems before they have a chance to arise. The assessment, they suggest, should focus on potential barriers to transfer centered in the learner, the boss and the organization.

More specifically, within the learner, the search is for compatible and incompatible values and beliefs about the job, the way it should be performed and the employee's view of his or her own ability to change, successfully, the way he or she does the job. The Robinsons contend that if the employee's values and views are in conflict with the new way things are to be done, or if the individual does not believe he or she can master the new ways, resistance to training and use of the new skills will exist, and transfer will be doubtful.

Within the boss, the Robinsons suggest, the analysis should center on managers' and supervisors' willingness to act as coach/counselor to employees trying out new skills, as well as the willingness and ability of bosses to reward newly trained employees for demonstrating the new skills in the workplace. Without these two support elements in place, transfer becomes a much more dubious possibility.

Looking at the organization, they continue, means looking at several factors that traditionally have been associated with thwarting the development of new skills. Among them are the consequences to employees for trying out new things; the organization's physical and temporal barriers to performing new behaviors; policies and procedures that may work against exhibiting new skills; and the presence or absence of systems that give feedback to newly trained employees on the results of performing in a new way.

The assessment can be carried out in written-survey, face-to-face or small-group interview form. The strengths and weaknesses you consider when you use these methodologies for needs assessment and evaluation purposes apply here as well. Interpretation problems are inherent in paper-and-pencil surveys, while face-to-face and small-group interviews run into problems of trust and fear of disclosure.

7 **"Why are you here?": The goals and expectations opener stra-tegy.** It's nice to know where you are going before the plane leaves the ground. Airline cabin-crew people routinely remind us that, "This is Flight 467 to Juneau, AK. If you aren't interested in going to Juneau with us this afternoon, it would be a good idea to deplane at this time." The same principle applies to training. It is a good idea to make sure everyone has a clear idea of exactly where you are taking them before you begin. This is especially helpful with very long courses that will cover a lot of information and with programs that cover knowledge and skills that are somewhat foreign to the trainee population.

Two common "opener" approaches are:

• *The expectations opener.* Here the trainer begins the session with an exercise designed to elicit trainee expectations. In their book, *Games Trainers Play*, Ed Scannell and John Newstrom suggest dividing trainees into teams and having them answer the simple question, "What two or three things do you most want to learn from this course? What do you want to be able to do or know as a result of this training?"

The trainer records the expectations on a flip chart. When all the expectations have been voiced and recorded, the trainer discusses which ones the course is and is not designed to meet. If a wide disparity exists, the trainer might have to modify the program or commit suicide to atone for a faulty needs assessment.

• The statement of objective's opener. This one is fairly self-explanatory — and even has some data to back up its effectiveness. Several years ago, author-consultant Robert Mager and friends conducted a number of studies on instructional objectives. In one of the studies, a group of engineers was given a set of detailed instructional objectives and some sample test questions. The engineers then went off and taught themselves as they saw fit. The result was that they learned faster and as well as those who were taught in several traditional ways. A second study found that in classes where a written list of objectives was handed out to students, their performance on criterion tests was superior to that of a no-objectives group.

The point is that if you simply hand out the objectives of the training at the beginning of the program, you increase the chances that they'll learn what you want them to learn.

8 "The more we are together, the more...": Training groups and teams.
There are two schools of thought about training intact work groups. One side says, "The group that learns together earns together" and so on. Team-building enthusiasts are particularly fond of working with natural work groups and teams intact. Blake and Mouton's "Grid" training is based partly on the premise that people sort out their on-the-job differences during the training.

The countering view is that social relations get in the way of the training. People fear they will look foolish to peers, give the wrong answer to a question or have their performance during the learning period confused with — and evaluated against — their performance on the job.

When the issue is transfer, option one, training intact work groups, wins. "I have found that unless there is a 'support system' back on the job, deterioration of job skills is very likely," contends consultant Dean Spitzer of High Impact Training, Alameda, CA. "We tend to forget that work is a group activity, not an individual activity. I like the concept of 'critical mass.' This means that there is a threshold number of employees who should be trained in any one job or unit in order to provide the necessary support for application of new skills."

9 "A picture is worth...": The behavior-modeling strategy.
The data is overwhelming: Programs that use behavior-modeling technology in their design have a better success rate with respect to transfer of skills to the workplace. Start with the research of Stanford University social psychologist Albert Bandura, move on to the very impressive work of Arnold Goldstein and Melvin Sorcher at General Electric, and end with the research of Henry Sims and others who evaluated the transfer effects of a large behavior modeling-based supervisory training program for a California manufacturer, and you come to the same conclusion: Behavior modeling increases transfer.

Now for the bad news. First, some things cannot be effectively modeled. Behavior modeling is doing; it is behavioral. Secondly, turning on a video camera is not the same as developing a behavior-modeling-based program. In fact, videotaping is only a small part of the applied behavior-modeling process. The trainer's demonstration skills, the trainee's success in practice attempts, and back-on-the-job consequences also play a big role.

10 "First you punch in, then...": Teach daily work habits.
Sometimes we get so wrapped up in trying to teach "the big picture" and the "underlying theory" of a job or an operation. We forget one important detail — what the employee is supposed to do back on the job.

Robert Kushell, president of Dunhill Personnel Systems in New York City, has observed that, "Much is taught [to managers] on business theory and practice, [but] I know of no training ground where executives can learn the basic work disciplines: how to plan and organize their time effectively; how to develop the specific, small-scale goals necessary to the success of their long-range plans; and how to assess their productivity level accurately." That same criticism can apply to types of training other than executive and management development. The nitty-gritty how-to's of the workaday world aren't that much fun to teach, but they are critical to know.

11 "Borscht is better": Keeping theory to a minimum.
The "Every Theory in the Known Universe" survey course may be great in undergraduate business school programs, but it makes for terrible working-world training. J. Regis McNamara, a professor of psychology at Ohio University, calls it the "chicken-soup or the-more-ingredients-the-better theory of training." Dean Spitzer asserts that if anything in training comes close to resembling an experiment designed to prove that forgetting exists, this is it. When concept after theory after concept are shoveled in, the poor trainees are left to make up their minds about what applies to their jobs — that is if they can remember any of the theories, concepts and ideas, and if they can resolve the conflicts between them.

If you want transfer, Spitzer and McNamara agree, the idea is to focus on a few, related, consistent concepts and make sure they are learned well.

12 "Let me see you do it": Evaluate performance.
You have probably heard this lecture a dozen times before: "Evaluate the outcome of your training — not just how the trainees felt about it." But you've probably never heard evaluation referred to as a strategy for transferring learning. It requires you to (a) test trainees' performance at the end of training to see if the stuff was, indeed, learned, and (b) observe and retest performance back on the job to see if they can still do it and will do it in the real world.

This strategy produces several potential benefits. First, if transfer does not occur, you have some idea where the breakdown is — if not the explicit causes. Secondly, if trainees are to be performance tested, your training will be shaped in that direction. And finally, if trainees are told that their performance will be tested not only at the end of training but on the job as well, they will be alerted to the fact that on-the-job performance is an important outcome.

TRANSFER-ENHANCING STRATEGIES

We're hanging the "transfer-enhancers" label on those procedures and strategies that are included in programs not for the purpose of improving immediate end-of-training results (indeed, some of them can even detract from those results), but rather to improve later, on-the-job results.

13 "One more time!": The use of overlearning.

Overlearing, or having trainees practice beyond "mastery," is sometimes justified. Especially when the training includes some motor skills, overlearning can be quite effective after trainees go back to the job. Even if the motor-skill component is small (such as when we teach managers to praise their employees), we know that overlearning can enhance transfer. Why? How can it possibly do any good to train people beyond the point where they can exhibit adequate end-of-training behavior'?

Part of the answer is, we don't know. We just know it works — sometimes. In the laboratory, for instance, certain kinds of tasks show more transfer as the degree of original learning goes up (even beyond mastery). Research by Gordon Mandler conducted in the 1950s showed increasing generalization of both simple motor and simple verbal responses with overlearning. In interpreting such research, it helps to conceptualize performance as situation-action combinations. That is, in most training, people must learn *what* to do and *how* to do it (the "action"), and *when* or under what circumstance to do it (the "situation"). Overlearning can apply to either "situations" or "actions."

There is some logic in believing that overlearning of actions may be helpful primarily in the motor component of the action. Part of the reason seems to lie in the nature of motor skills. The movements we make continue to become smoother, more natural and easier even after we achieve criterion-level accuracy. No one who has ever practiced hitting a baseball will dispute that. The "grooved swing" is more likely to be right, more often, in the real world. So one reason for overlearning actions is to improve the consistency of on-the-job performance and its correspondence to end-of-training performance.

In order for overlearning to occur, trainees must be given plenty of time during training to practice what they have learned. This alone makes it unlikely overlearning will be used much. It is a rare training design that allows even enough time to reach criterion performance.

14 "Step into my LINK trainer": The use of lifelike situations.

Simulations, or lifelike situations, are a standard way to bring "realism" into the classroom. The justification for simulating a real-life environment comes from arguments about what facilitates transfer of training. To the extent that the "identical elements" theory of transfer holds water ("the greater the similarity between the training and operational environments, the greater the transfer of training"), simulations are wonderful ways to enhance transfer.

As usual, however, it's not that simple. Most of the research you see cited was done on the learning of simple new responses to simple situations — paired-associate learning, serial learning and recall, recognition of simple items, etc. But a lot of practical training is actually concerned with what researcher Charles Noble refers to as "human selective learning," that is, taking actions you already know how to do at the appropriate times.

So, what can we say about "identical elements"'? First, what seems to be important is that the "right" elements be identical between training and operational settings. But what are the "right" elements, you ask? Well, there's the rub. For example, if you simulate the work setting right down to the smells, then discover that the most important aspect of the job involves attending to sounds, where are you?

Donald Holding, an early researcher into motor skills and feedback, formulated a "principle of inclusion" that states: "If the training task includes most or all of the requirements present in a subsequent transfer task, then transfer performance will be high; but if this inclusion is not present, then transfer performance will be low."

In some simulations the designers seem to forget that it is people who are involved, and so don't provide for any modeling of affective responses. But people who are confronted by an angry customer on the job may be afraid or angry themselves, in response. And if the simulation doesn't take those emotions into account, its fidelity (and therefore usefulness for transfer) may be low.

15 "Imagine that": Mental imagery and rehearsal.

Clinical psychologists have used mental-rehearsal techniques with patients for years. And they work. Visualizing a feared object, such as a snake, and slowly decreasing the imaginary distance between yourself and it, really does reduce the fear of snakes.

There is also pretty good evidence that mental visualization can help increase motor skills performance. One often-quoted piece of research (which means we've never been able to locate the original study) involved three groups of kids aspiring to improve their basketball skills. Each shot 10 freethrows from the foul line. For the next week, one group did nothing, one group went to the gym and practiced shooting freethrows, and the third group sat in a room thinking about — visualizing — themselves shooting free throws. Guess what? The mental-rehearsal group did almost as well as the "practice shooting" group on a retest two weeks later.

The visualization technique has been used successfully in a number of interpersonal-skills training such as supervision, public speaking, sales, customer relations and so on.

16 "Thar she blows!": Building trigger mechanisms for back on the job.

When the lookout spotted Moby Dick and the cry went out, the crew sprang instantly into action, each member doing exactly what he had been trained to do. There was no problem of transfer of training. All that was needed was the "trigger" — the lookout's cry.

Any good training is aimed at imparting not only knowledge and skills, but the conditions under which specific skills are to be used back on the job. Once again, it is often useful to conceptualize jobs as consisting of condition-action sets: "Under X conditions, do this; but under Y conditions, do that; and under Z conditions, do nothing at all." Then it becomes clear that the trainees' ability to discriminate one job situation from another and "hook up" the appropriate set of behaviors to the situation is critical to transfer of training. One way to help trainees hook up their skills with the right situation is to teach them "trigger mechanisms" that either exist naturally or have been added on the job.

If you design a machine to flash a red light when it needs oil, that red light is a potential trigger mechanism. If you then train a person to know what that flashing red light means, and how to do what needs to be done, i.e., how to add oil, the light acts to enhance the likelihood of on-the-job performance.

But signs flashing "low oil pressure" and "add toner" are not the only kinds of trigger mechanisms. There are also natural situational triggers. Many come directly from customers. When the client asks, "Can I have the payments automatically deducted from my checking account?" salespeople can learn to respond appropriately (in this case, by assuming the sale and asking for an act of commitment).

The training task, in the case of natural triggers, is to teach people to recognize trigger situations. Naming the triggers often helps. In a sales situation, for example, we might classify a whole set of trigger behaviors on the part of prospects as "buying signals," and try to teach salespeople how to recognize them, and to respond correctly when they do recognize one.

A simple technique is to put triggers on signs or posters, reminding people to "Catch someone doing something good today," or whatever. When trainees see the poster they will be reminded of (triggered to perform) newly acquired skills. That is, you hope the poster will trigger them; hanging wall posters all over the plant doesn't guarantee anything. But one reason commonly given by trainees for not using skills they possess is, "I forgot." Triggers in the form of reminders can help overcome this kind of barrier to transfer of training.

17 **"Where's PAPA?": The Participant Action Planning Approach.** The Participant Action Plan (PAP) can be, well, a rather perfunctory exercise: "All right, class, I'd like each of us to stand up in turn and tell how we are going to use what we learned when we go home."

Just the same, when done well, the PAP can be very effective. Robert Youker of the World Bank in Washington, DC, enumerates 11 benefits of the approach: It encourages transfer by acting as a sort of MBO for the training program, increases commitment by verbalizing it, provides for practicing the skill, helps anticipate problems, encourages contingency planning, gains commitment to action, sets up an expectation for follow up, provides an opportunity for reinforcement, helps set up a supportive environment, sets up a "system" for organizational change and provides an opportunity for evaluation.

Dean Spitzer suggests the first item on the trainee action plan should be to meet with the boss to discuss the training just completed. He goes so far as to suggest the trainer send a copy of the PAP to the supervisor with a note explaining what it is and how it works.

POST-TRAINING STRATEGIES

Post-training strategies generally focus on defeating poor transfer through some form of augmentation. Refresher courses, beefed-up feedback and special attention from the returning trainee's supervisor are typical strategies. Post-training strategies and procedures are sometimes very expensive, and always very visible.

18 **"Love notes": The follow-up letters strategy.** Follow-up notes to the trainee and the trainee's supervisor after the training can produce significant gains in skills transfer, suggests Thomas Connellan of Performance Feedback Associates in Ann Arbor, MI. Actually, the process he advocates starts at the outset of the training, with a letter to the trainee's supervisor while the training is still in progress. This letter asks the supervisor to set up a meeting with the individual on his or her return from training to discuss what was learned, how the individual will use the new skill or information on the job and what support the person needs from the supervisor. The letter also asks the supervisor to schedule a second meeting three to five weeks after the first to discuss progress.

A second letter goes from the training department to the trainee two months after the training. This one asks the trainee to assess the two meetings with the supervisor, and the support received from the supervisor since the end of training.

19 **"Can we talk — again?": The post-training chat.** The post-training discussion between the supervisor and the returned trainee should center around the trainee's end-of-training action plan — if there is one — with the supervisor taking a reactive role. If no PAP or list of action items has been generated, the supervisor's role becomes a more active one.

With the supervisor in the driver's seat, the discussion should center on:
- What did you learn?
- How will it be useful to you?
- What can you do first?
- By when?
- How can I help you?

20 **"Practice, kiddies, practice!": The rehearsal-room strategy.** Very old joke:

Tourist to beatnik: "Excuse me, sir, how do you get to Carnegie Hall'?"

Beatnik: "Practice, man, practice."

The ingredient most frequently shortchanged in training is practice. Knowing about something is quite different from being able to do it — ask any armchair quarterback.

But often practice is kept to a minimum for very legitimate reasons, especially in off-site training. When lack of in-training practice is questioned, considerations such as safety, cost, time and logistical problems in setting up realistic practice situations are usually blamed, along with the ever-popular, "They always groan about role play. It's the least-liked part of the course, anyhow."

The real reason for not providing practice usually boils down to the matter of dollars. It is very expensive to take people away from their jobs to train them, and allowing them to practice what they are learning is frequently viewed as somehow being of secondary importance to cramming one more piece of new "stuff" into the program and, hopefully, into their heads.

One way around the problem is through planned rehearsal. If the training is being held near the trainees' actual work site, setting up a laboratory is a possibility. This approach works nicely for word-processing and microcomputer skills. We've also seen labs for public-speaking skills. Here, an executive with a speech to make or a press conference to hold, goes to the lab, and turns on a videotape machine, gives the speech or makes his announcement, and then reviews the tape. Only graduates of the initial training gain laboratory privileges, and part of the training is in the use of the laboratory. In the case of trainees who are from remote areas, it may be possible to set up a situation where off-line and out-of-production equipment is designated for practice work.

21. "As you remember": The refresher training strategy.

The follow-up or refresher session is a much-overlooked option for promoting transfer. Arty Trost of Organizational Dynamics in Sandy, OR, promotes the refresher session as a way of dealing with things the trainees are encountering on the job that were not considered in the training. The refresher session also gives the trainer a way to gather case material and caveats for subsequent rounds of training.

Trost emphasizes that the follow up does not provide new material; it refines and polishes skills learned in the original training session and encourages continued use." Timing of refresher training seems to be related more to convenience than to any optimum, we discovered. Periods from four weeks to four months are commonly recommended as the proper interval between training and refresher. In practice, we've seen refresher programs mounted as long as a year after the initial training.

22. "Hey! Nice job, Gladys!": The supervisor-as-coach strategy.

Several of the strategies already mentioned allude to the supervisor as an important figure in the successful transfer of new skills to the workplace. If the supervisor doesn't care for the new ways or doesn't encourage the employee to use what was taught in the training, then nothing will be different back on the job. Every trainer's nightmare (and perhaps the single most effective way to guarantee that learned behavior will not be transferred) is the one where the supervisor sits the just-graduated trainee down and says, "You know all that crap they taught you at the training center? Forget it! Around here we do things my way."

Experience suggests that while this does happen, it isn't as frequent as the nightmare might imply. It is more often the case that the supervisor isn't aware of his impact on the employees behavior — it can be hard to believe sometimes — and that even being aware, he isn't 100% sure of the best way to apply that influence to promote the use of new skills. So teach him.

Advice varies on the skills this training should build, but there are some common themes. The supervisor-as-coach should:

- State expectations of the trainee with regard to the training content.
- Set goals for using new skills.
- Give trainees feedback on their progress toward using the new skills on the job.
- Encourage and praise the trainee's use of the new skills, progress toward mastery, and efforts to apply the new skills and knowledge on the job.
- Be available to coach and counsel the trainee in applications problems that may crop up.
- Act as an appropriate model of how the skills are applied.

23. "This group gets the gold star, this one the...": The count-and-chart approach.

The results of feedback on performance can be pretty dramatic. Connellan cites instances in which simply specifying the performance level and providing precise sequential feedback on performance, along with a little reinforcement, have decreased absences, increased sales and reduced error rates dramatically.

These very basic behavioral tools work for individuals, small groups and whole departments. They can work as a follow-up to training. The only "trick" is to be sure that the performance being counted and graphed on a regular basis — daily if possible — occurs frequently enough that it can be counted and that progress toward a goal can be perceived and reinforced.

Post-training goals like "Be promoted by June" or "Start acting like a better person" are difficult to track or keep frequency counts on. In broad terms, they are goals but not performance objectives or standards.

The supervisor and the employee will have to come to grips with the problem of "indicators" — behaviors and performance that have a tangible relationship to the goal.

A twist on the chart-and-count trick is the keep-a-diary gambit. Cutting a post-training goal into behavioral measures with a meaningful frequency to track can turn out to be worse than trisecting the angle. If that's the case, try a critical-incident diary. Returned trainees end each workday with journal entries that recount their last eight hours' most memorable and heroic efforts to apply "management by walking around," "participative decision-making" or whatever it was that they learned during the training program.

FINESSING STRATEGIES

In some instances, transfer of training is a problem only because we train people at times and places distant and different from those where they're going to perform. Suppose we didn't do that; we wouldn't have so many transfer problems! The trick is to finesse the problem by not expecting the skills to be learned sufficiently — or at all — away from the job. The core idea is to bring the training as close to the job as possible through one of several strategies.

24. "Problem? What problem?": The job (re)design method.

Probably the clearest case of finessing the transfer-of-training problem is the one where you can figure out a way not to do any training at all. No training, no transfer-of-training problem. Simple, huh? Well, sometimes it actually is. As Robert Mager and Peter Pipe (and countless others) have suggested, sometimes the best way to help people do their jobs better is simply to change the job.

For example, if people on a production line are required to lift heavy objects to a workbench and are having trouble doing it without injuring themselves, we could put together a training course on "lifting heavy objects safely." But on the other hand, we could arrange it so the heavy parts are delivered to the workbench by conveyor so that no lifting is required.

We were impressed by a sign on a piece of machinery in a Caterpillar Tractor Co. plant a few years ago. It said: "This machine does the work of three people." At first we were mostly impressed at the chutzpah it took to flaunt that fact in front of the employees. Then we discovered that the signs were a positive factor in the work setting. Why? Because the three people the machine replaced had the worst jobs in the factory; workers were delighted they didn't have to worry about doing those jobs anymore.

In other cases, where jobs will not be eliminated, they still may be changed and made simpler. Automation may replace the need to perform certain of the most tedious or precise tasks, leaving an easier or livelier set of tasks for the worker. Or technology can be used to enhance the skill, speed, power and precision of a worker. This is precisely what any good tool does. Granted, sometimes this means we must train the worker to use the tool. But typically, it is easier and more efficient to learn to use the tool than to learn to do the job as well without it.

25 "Let's try that move out on the dance floor": The interim-project approach.

One way to get the training environment closer to the work environment is to bring the work environment into the training. And one way to do that is to include instances of "live work" (actual performance of job tasks in the work setting) as part of training.

If application of skills actually can be made in the work setting under work conditions, then you have finessed the transfer-of-training problem because no transferring is necessary (or, more accurately, learners actually make the transfer during the training). The trick here, as it is in simulations, is making sure that the application of skills occurs under work conditions. Otherwise, all you've done is set up a "simulation" that happens to use the physical environment of the workplace.

What researcher Shirley Harmon calls the "interim-project approach" is multiple-phase training that consists of three parts: (1) the original training workshop, (2) an on-the-job application project, and (3) a summary report workshop (to discuss the application project).

At first glance, this technique appears to be your basic "follow-up project" or Participant Action Planning Approach in another cloak. The difference is larger than it seems. Structuring training so that the project, or live work, falls between two meetings with a facilitator or instructor is more likely to benefit trainees than just sending them home with a project in their hands. With the interim-project approach, the designer can exert more control over how much and what kind of feedback and reinforcement trainees will get after they do their projects, and not count so much on supervisors and managers to handle those tasks.

There always seems to be an awkwardness and embarrassment when trying skills for the first time — awkwardness that makes it difficult to deal with someone up the reporting chain. It often works better if participants can hear about struggles, failures and successes from each other, and can work out explicitly with peers how it felt and how they think it will be next time.

Extended, spaced or "multiphase" training can often benefit from an opportunity to apply the training on the job between training sessions. To make this worthwhile it helps to provide some structure (much like competence-building activities do) for the application — rather than just exhorting the participants to "Go try this stuff out." And it usually helps to devote some time at the beginning of the next training session to reporting application experiences, and giving feedback and some kind of reinforcement to those who tried out their skills.

26 "Experience is the best teacher — (we're just lousy students)": Competence-building activities.

When we ask people who are unusually good at doing something where they learned to do it, they usually answer, "From experience." Almost nobody, in the long history of humankind, has ever said, "From the Frizblit Training Course!"

Discouraging, isn't it?

So, if people learn from experience, just what do they learn? If you practice a bad forehand swing, over and over, will you learn anything? You bet! And you'll have the hardest-to-improve forehand at the racquet club. What people learn from experience is full of good stuff (to the extent that they are good performers), but it is also full of silly stuff, superstition, irrelevancies and just plain bad habits.

John Wannamaker, the legendary Philadelphia department store magnate, was once asked, so the story goes, how effective his advertising was. He replied, "Half of it is no damn good!"

"Then why don't you get rid of it?"

"Because I don't know which half it is," was Wannamaker's answer. We suspect that what excellent performers do is like that: Half of it is no damn good, or at least irrelevant to their successful performance, but they keep doing it just because they learned it from experience — along with the crucial stuff.

What's the trick? How can you turn plain vanilla "experience" into anything like an efficient competence-building activity? You have to impose some structure. It can take these forms:

• Designate specific on-the-job "experiences" as learning opportunities (e.g., the third customer who approaches you next Tuesday; or every fourth phone call you make next week).

• Set specific learning expectations for each designated experience.

• Have the learners keep track of what they do and what results they achieve (and sometimes, how they feel about it), using a form that also serves as a job aid to remind them of what they are trying to accomplish.

• Construct a way for a second party to monitor and reinforce what is learned (through regular meetings with others who have been trained, or with an instructor, mentor or boss).

• Provide a simple recordkeeping system so participants can track their own progress.

27 "Just put this template over your keyboard and": Using job aids.

One of the most venerable methods of finessing the transfer-of-training problem involves the use of informational job aids, or performance aids. (We say "informational" to distinguish them from physical tools that aid performance.) The theory is simple: Rather than requiring people to do things they aren't good at (such as storing masses of data in their heads), you provide "external memory" in the form of checklists, look-up tables, reference manuals, flowcharts, computer databases, labeled machine parts, templates to put over their keyboards or telephones, etc. Then you don't have to train them to remember all that stuff; you just have to train them to use the job aid.

How difficult will it be for people to use the job aid? How much training in using it will be needed? You may be designing the thing to avoid training — but giving trainees something they won't or can't use properly isn't worth your while. Typically, some training in the use of job aids is necessary.

It's almost universally true that if you can replace training with a job aid, it's a good idea to do it. Exceptions include occasions when it's most effective if skills are run off automatically (so that stopping to look at something would interfere), or when looking something up would simply take too much time, or when there is so much information to be conveyed that for efficiency, people had better remember at least what they use most often.

28. "Good old OJT": On-the-job training.

Yes, this hoary old creature rears its ugly head. And you thought OJT was what you were in the business of replacing, right? It's true that some OJT has a deservedly bad reputation. Typically, it's the kind that was put in place because no one wanted to (or could) design or pay for decent training. So OJT became synonymous with "Let's just throw 'em in the water and keep the ones who learn to swim."

But there are situations where the best way to learn a job is by doing it, especially when doing the job poorly during a "break-in period" doesn't have dire consequences, or when it is too costly or complex to adequately simulate on-the-job conditions.

There are situations where poor initial performance means nothing more than doing it more slowly than highly competent people do it. If such a job can readily be learned by observing others and practicing, it may be more economical to let trainees work slowly for awhile than to take them off the job entirely for training.

In other circumstances there are prerequisite, low-level portions of a whole job that must be learned before higher-level performance can occur. Apprenticeships often begin this way, with the apprentice doing the "dirty" work that takes little skill, then progressing up to higher-level tasks. Again, if much can be learned by observing, giving a trainee something easy to do while observing the more complex parts of the job may make sense.

In situations where the amount of practice required to achieve competent performance is much greater than the amount of instruction, it may be more efficient to provide the instruction in small doses on the job, letting the trainees add new skills one at a time. Many jobs that require motor skills are like this.

On-the-job training is an implicit part of all other training. We know that we don't teach trainees everything. So how do we justify sending them out to work? By explicitly or implicitly counting on OJT to finish the job.

Here are a few recommended "rules" about using OJT. For those who will supervise apprentices during their OJT, "training" must be an explicit objective of their position; supervisors should be measured, monitored (at the very least during performance reviews), and singled out for rewards based on their achievement of training objectives.

Likewise, we think that "learning objectives" should be an explicit part of the job of the apprentice during OJT; the apprentice should be measured, monitored (more frequently than quarterly) and rewarded for achievement of learning objectives. Further, the achievement of learning objectives during OJT should receive at least as much attention from supervisors and the rest of the organization as does the performance of other job duties.

So there are the 28 techniques, strategies, methods — call them what you will — we have cataloged by combing the literature of psychology, educational research, and training and development. What did we leave out? Probably quite a bit. But like old John Wannamaker, we don't know which half.

Notes:

9 Ways to Make Training Pay Off Back On the Job

If the skills you teach in class don't get used on the job, maybe you've got one these problems

BY RUTH COLVIN CLARK

Ever observe a group of trainees a month or two after they emerged from your training program? Are the skills they learned in class being used on the job? Does your organization have a workable system for following up on its training efforts to see whether they result in better performance in the real world of the workplace?

Even after an excellent class, training frequently fails to pay off in behavioral changes on the job: Trainees go back to work and do it the way they've always done it instead of the way you taught them to do it. The phenomenon is called transfer failure. It happens because skills do not transfer automatically into job performance. In other words, the fact that you have learned how to do something a certain way doesn't necessarily mean you'll do it that way. Since the point of job-related training is to improve performance on the job, transfer failure obviously defeats the purpose.

Why does training — solid, effective training — fail to transfer? There are a number of reasons. Here are nine situations and some tips on how the problems could've been avoided.

1 Rocking the boat. A supervisor in the documentation services department previewed a training program on structured writing techniques. The program taught an unusual method for formatting written material. The supervisor liked the approach and sent four of his writers to the course. They came back to work and designed a new policy manual using the techniques they had learned. When the department manager saw the result, she promptly vetoed it on grounds that its unique appearance would draw criticism from other managers in the organization. The supervisor pointed out the advantages of the new method, but the department head was adamant. "We haven't turned out anything like that before," she said. "Things have been

> **Consider offering fewer courses so you can devote more of your time and dollars to ensuring training transfer.**

going smoothly up to now. Let's not rock the boat."

Solution: The supervisor just discovered — too late — that his own department manager, as well as other managers and supervisors, should have previewed the course with him. Front-end consultation and approval by all interested parties would have prevented tail-end failure.

Management advisory committees can be formed to set policy and to help review training courses while they're still in the development stage — or before they are purchased. If a proposed program is scrapped due to lack of management commitment, better it should happen early, before a lot of dollars are invested.

2 Mismatching courses and needs. The manager of a data processing center met a training vendor who demonstrated a very impressive course on prototyping. The DP manager asked the training department to send all employees to the course. However, the techniques applied only to about 25 percent of the employees who were building new applications. The other 75 percent were working on maintenance projects that did not require the use of prototyping techniques.

Solution: Match courses to needs systematically. Curricula that reflect the ideas of one or several line managers, working independently and sporadically, tend to be fragmented and counterproductive. Training should flow from two primary sources: (1) a validated analysis of current job tasks and the skills required to perform them, and (2) a model of the future technological directions of the organization, agreed upon by upper management.

To conduct a job analysis, first identify all major tasks and required skills. Then ask a sample of the employees currently in the job (and their supervisors) to rate the importance and complexity of each skill as well as their current proficiency in it. Concurrently, ask top managers to rate the same skills on the basis of their importance in meeting departmental objectives. Training priorities should be based on skills perceived as high in importance by managers and rated low in competency by employees and their supervisors.

This job analysis will only identify current skill needs. In any rapidly evolving technological environment you also will need to identify new technological applications to supplement the job analysis. Finally, the people in charge of training should have access to top management's strategic plans for the future so that appropriate training will be in place when needed.

3 Supervisory slip-ups. The organization offers classes on time management and other generic skills. These programs are in heavy demand, and supervisors sign up their subordinates months ahead of time. When a given employee's turn finally arrives, the supervisor sometimes has forgotten why the individual was supposed to go to that particular class in the first place. Small wonder that supervisors rarely take the time to discuss the training with their people, either before or after the class. Supervisors are counting exclusively on the training department to improve their employees' skills.

Solution: Ultimately it is the supervisor who must be responsible for the work performance of his or her employees. Training is one tool supervisors have to improve that performance. They need to recognize that training only teaches people to do things they don't know how to do: There is no point in sending anybody to a training program unless he lacks a particular skill required by the job.

Instead of abdicating all responsibility to the training department, supervisors can increase the impact of training dramatically by: (1) conducting brief pre- and post-course discussions with employees where they agree on how the skills learned in the program will be applied on the job, and (2) making specific follow-up assignments after the employee returns to be sure that the skills are applied. This is especially important when employees are attending non-technical training (time management, interpersonal skills, etc.) where the transfer challenge tends to be most difficult.

Busy supervisors will not do these things without a push. The training department should help them by teaching them how to handle those pre- and post-course activities. In addition, second-level managers should be persuaded to include planning and implementation of employee training as part of the supervisors' formal job responsibility, to be evaluated in regular performance appraisals. In other words, supervisors must be taught how to play their crucial role in training and they must be held accountable for playing it.

4 Losing track of what training employees need. In the data processing department, supervisors typically have responsibility for 10 to 20 employees at different job levels working on various project teams. In constructing their training plans, supervisors generally refer to the training catalog and use their best judgment to assign training to individuals based on their recent performance. But because the supervisors are dealing with a lot of employees who work on varied assignments that involve a large number of different skills, it's difficult to be consistent and accurate in determining each employee's training needs.

Solution: Help supervisors assess and track employees' skills by providing an automated records system. A variety of such systems are available to run on either micro or mainframe hardware. They can be programmed to list all job-related skills and provide for a competency rating agreed upon by employee and supervisor. When the individual competency ratings are matched against recommended competencies for the particular job, discrepancies are flagged and training

> **Busy supervisors will not incorporate these techniques without a push from the training function or top management.**

options matched to the job skills are generated automatically. These computer programs help supervisors make systematic training plans based on both the requirements of the job and individual assessments of employee skills.

5 Lack of a "critical mass." Employees of a sales and product support division were sent to a course on conducting and participating in meetings. But their attendance was staggered over a one-year period. By the time the last of them had attended the class, 10 months had slipped by since the first students had gone. Division supervisors found it very difficult to implement the techniques in real meetings.

Solution: Train already intact work groups. Peer group support is a major factor in determining whether newly learned skills will transfer to the job. People are much more likely to do things the new way if everybody in the work group (or at least almost everybody) is trying to do them that way at the same time.

When you train only a few people at a time from any particular group, you never develop a "critical mass" of commitment to the new skills. Without that critical mass, the status quo tends to defeat change. Furthermore, if people aren't called upon to use new skills immediately after they learn them, the skills tend to atrophy.

Whenever possible, train entire working groups at the same time. If it isn't practical to train an entire team, try setting up interdepartmental or even intercompany support networks. User groups have been formed around various computer-software applications. Why not set up user groups for other types of training as well?

6 No help applying skills back on the job. During the structured writing class mentioned earlier, most students did very well on the practice exercises they were given — but they had the instructor's help. When they returned to their jobs, the instructor wasn't there. Many had trouble applying the new techniques to actual work assignments. After a few attempts, some became discouraged and reverted to their previous writing styles.

Solution: Extend training beyond the classroom. If an intact work group is learning an important new skill, follow-up training is essential to transferring the skill. Require program graduates to work on a regular project assignment using the techniques they learned. The instructor or someone competent in the new skills should provide follow-up consultation, visiting the trainees and helping them apply the techniques to their unique job assignments. Or, as an alternative, give the graduates an assignment to work on for two weeks on the job. Then schedule transfer sessions where they meet as a group with the instructor, compare results and discuss problems.

7 The external instructor is gone. That writing class was taught by an outside consultant, and it was not feasible to arrange for her to follow up after the class.

Solution: To ensure continuing consultation beyond the classroom, consider using internal instructors — or supplementing a consultant's classroom training with an internal expert who can serve the follow-up functions.

This may mean asking the consultant to spend extra time with the person who will serve as your internal expert.

8 Training as a "day off." The training department teaches a

MEASURE YOUR TRAINING TRANSFER QUOTIENT

Here is a generic survey you could adapt to your own training situation. Send the questionnaire to everyone who has completed a given course within the past six months. (Or randomly select 100 employees who have completed the course.) Even a 50% response rate will give you a good indication of whether the training transferred to the job. Administer the survey anonymously to ensure honest feedback.

Scoring: Add up the number of responses of "3" or above to both question B and question C (i.e., one person who checks "3" to question C and "4" to question B counts as two responses). Divide by twice the total number of questionnaires returned, and multiply by 100. A score of 80% or better probably means that the skills you're teaching are transferring adequately to the workplace. A score of less than 70% suggests that you need to make some changes.

TRAINING FOLLOW-UP SURVEY

Course Title _____ Dates Attended _____
Company Division (please circle):
  Sales   Manufacturing   Customer Service   Data Processing   Other _____
Course objective _____
(Section above completed by training department)

A. At the end of this course, to what degree did you feel that you achieved the objective stated above?

VERY LITTLE		MODERATELY		VERY MUCH
1	2	3	4	5

If you circled below 3 on Question A, stop here and return the questionnaire. Otherwise, continue.

B. Since completing this course, how often have you used the skills you learned in class on your job assignments?

RARELY/NEVER		OCCASIONALLY (MONTHLY)		FREQUENTLY (DAILY)
1	2	3	4	5

C. As a result of this course, how much improvement have you experienced in completing your job assignments?

RARELY/NEVER		OCCASIONALLY (MONTHLY)		FREQUENTLY (DAILY)
1	2	3	4	5

If you answered Questions B or C with a 3 or greater, then go on to Questions D and E. If you answered Questions B or C with less than a 3, then go on to Question F.

D. Describe at least three typical ways that you have used the skills you learned in class and how your job performance has improved as a result.
_____

E. Place a check next to each reason below that might explain why you have applied the skills you learned to your job assignmments:
  _____ My supervisor discussed with me how my new skills would be used on my job assignments.
  _____ My supervisor required me to use the new skills.
  _____ I received help from others in my work area.
  _____ I was given necessary time and/or tools to apply the skills.
  _____ I received training at the right time to provide me with the skills when I needed them on the job.
  _____ The skills I learned applied directly to my job assignment.
  _____ Other: Please list other factors that helped you apply these skills to your job assignments: _____

F. Place a check next to each reason below that could explain why you have not been successful in applying skills learned to your job assignments:
  _____ My supervisor did not require me to use the skills. My supervisor did not agree with the skills I learned. My supervisor was not aware of what skills I learned.
  _____ I was not given time/tools to implement the skills on the job.
  _____ There was no one to help me implement the skills in my work area.
  _____ The skills did not seem to apply to my job assignment.
  _____ My job assignment changed so these skills did not apply.
  _____ The training was not timed right for my job assignment.
  _____ Other: Please describe other reasons you did not apply the skills to your job assignments: _____

variety of courses on supervisory effectiveness. Trainees are required to show up for class, but they aren't evaluated on their performance in the course or back on the job. Practice exercises are voluntary and many trainees choose to skip them. Most of the supervisors listen politely in class. Some ask a few questions. But rarely does anyone invest much effort in acquiring the new skills. A day in training is generally regarded as an opportunity to kick back and drink coffee.

Solution: Build accountability into your training. Competency-based training is built on specific, job-related objectives. Learners must be held accountable for reaching these objectives. Instructors should send a summary of course objectives and the trainee's performance in class to the trainee's supervisor. The organization should demand that all training courses be instructionally valid, i.e., each course should prove that people who take it and invest reasonable effort will attain the objectives.

If the course is just plain ineffective, the issue of transfer to the workplace becomes irrelevant. Likewise, if learners are not held responsible for investing effort in their own training, even the best instruction will not generate maximum benefits. Accountability in training should address both of these problems.

9 Training is not available when needed. Many organizations rely heavily on classroom training, scheduling courses on some fixed timetable (e.g., quarterly) or when there is sufficient enrollment to justify teaching the class. This means that people may be on waiting lists for several months. Knowing this, supervisors will send employees to courses as the classes become available, even though the employees will not be needing the skills in the near future.

Solution: Consider self-instructional training. When live classes are scheduled on a body-count basis, there is often a lack of coordination between the timing of the training and the opportunity to apply the skills back on the job. Self-instructional courses delivered by workbooks, video or computer-based training provide access to information when it's needed.

The drawback to self-instructional courses is that even when they're well-designed (and a lot of them aren't), they demand a high degree of motivation from the learner. There is no instructor to answer to; learners often start the courses but fail to complete them. An obvious alternative is to build or buy self-instructional courses and supplement them with live tutors to help trainees, give them regular feedback, and measure and report their progress.

All of these "solutions" demand a greater investment of time and resources — both finite quantities — on the part of the training department. You may want to consider offering fewer courses, but investing more effort to enhance transfer. Rather than offering six new courses next year, concentrate on one or two critical programs, building in the pre-course planning and post-course follow-up that will help ensure training transfer to the job.

Notes:

But Will They Use Training On the Job?

You conducted a dynamite course and sent trainees back to their jobs brimming with new ideas and skills. Think your job is over? It's just begun. Add these techniques to your training repertoire to prevent entropy.

BY DEAN R. SPITZER

One of the trainer's most vexing problems is getting trainees to transfer what they learn in a training session back to the job. Most of us are confident in our ability to teach skills, but few of us can guarantee that these skills will be used when trainees leave the protected classroom environment and go back on the job.

The work environment has so many built-in factors that deter skill application and behavior change: productivity pressures (especially when trainees have been away for some time and work has been building up); pressure to do the job like everybody else ("Who do you think you are, Joe, with those new-fangled techniques!"); and the temptation to regress back to old, more familiar behaviors. But perhaps the strongest factor which works against change is simply that new learning takes time to integrate into existing behavior repertoires. Few employees are willing to make this extra effort unless there are some pretty obvious payoffs. Trainers rarely are in a position to offer tangible incentives for using new skills on the job.

However, the situation is not hopeless. Even without control over incentives, trainers can make on-the-job application of skills easier, and provide motivational mechanisms and develop support systems for employees. Our responsibility as trainers does not end when trainees leave the classroom; that's actually only where it begins!

Try the following techniques and you will find that trainees will use the skills you have taught them. And, this use will be much more effective and effortless than either you or they imagined.

1 Personal action planning is one of the most widely used methods to increase the likelihood of on-the-job follow-through. During the course, individual trainees complete an "action plan," which identifies the steps they plan to take to apply the new skills when they return to the job. As a result, trainees make a certain commitment to action, especially if they publicize their commitment by sharing their plans with others. Ask participants to complete part of their action plans after each segment of the course; then, at the end of the course, ask trainees to review and prioritize their action plan steps.

2 Group action planning follows the same format as personal action planning. Try to form groups of trainees who will either be working together or will have access to each other on the job. This technique develops the same sort of commitment as personal action planning, but also provides a support system for trainees when they return to the job.

3 Multiphase programming involves running a training program in parts so that trainees immediately apply part of the lesson on the job. Often the lack of on-the-job skill application is caused by "skill overload." Participants just learn too much and feel overwhelmed. By dividing programs into parts, you can send your trainees back to the job with a manageable amount of new skill. They can apply these skills and return to the program to share their experiences and solve problems before progressing to the next skill area.

Multiphase programming is very successful in organizations flexible enough to permit this type of "commuter" training. However, many organizations are not receptive to the idea; they prefer the "all or nothing" approach. Try to sell this type of program within your organization. It is the best way to train.

4 The buddy system pairs program participants so that they can learn together and give each other support back on the job. Since lack of support back on the job is a major problem, train at least two people from each department at the same time. That way, some close interaction will exist after the training program ends.

When the "buddy system" is used along with small-group activities (involving people from other departments), you get the best of both worlds: trainees develop support systems and interact with people from other job categories.

5 Performance aids provide a meaningful transition from fully guided learning to independent skill application. Performance aids can include checklists, decision-tables, charts and diagrams; they give trainees a better chance to use new skills, since they provide the minimal guidance that is usually needed in the early stages of on-the-job application.

6 Recognition systems reinforce the "value" of new skill applications. Although few trainers have much control over major incentives, they can design meaningful recognition systems. Trainers can give certificates, letters of merit, "performance points" and publish newsletters, just to mention a few ideas. Recognition is a powerful incentive in a work environment that offers few other perks.

7 Training trainees as trainers takes the "pressure" off the training department; provides training in the performance environment; and motivates trainees to learn more, since they will be asked to teach other. This approach is a particularly effective way to expand limited training resources, as well as increase the likelihood of on-the-job application.

WHY IBM TRAINEES PRACTICE WHAT TRAINERS PREACH

The question of whether "soft" skill training for technicians and managers at IBM's home office in Endicott, NY, will be applied back on the job is anything but moot. Since 1982, week-long courses that cover subjects such as time management listening skills and so on have concluded with each trainee providing a signed statement and videotaped description of an action plan that explains exactly how the new information will be used back on the job.

Participants are free to choose specific elements of the course which they feel will prove most useful to them, but they have to choose something and they must commit to using it.

The emphasis on application of new skills continues in follow-up sessions two months after the main programs. Entire classes are brought back together to discuss successes and failures, and experiences are compared with the original videotapes. The overall effect is noticeably persuasive in communicating the policy that training will be applied instead of forgotten, according to Steve M. Yourst, an IBM staff instructor in Endicott.

"In addition to providing a stimulus for the trainees to formulate solid action plans," Yourst writes, "these individual presentations significantly reinforce the key points made by the instructors by having them reiterated, along with applications, from the viewpoint of the students."

In order to prepare their statements and tapes, trainees obviously have to think about the material presented in the course. Yourst includes a 15-minute period for "reflection" at the end of each day's session for them to do that thinking. "The process," he says, "significantly increases the probability that trainees will not only make a better mental connection between theory and practice, but will then go out and apply what they have learned."

— *Dean R. Spitzer*

8 Contracting with trainees is a useful motivational technique that increases the likelihood of skill application. The completion of a contract form increases commitment, especially when the trainee is reminded of it later. Some trainees may be reluctant to sign a contract, so this method can be used on a voluntary basis.

9 Ample resource access is an important follow-up to training that makes on-the-job application of skills easier. Trainers must never assume that initial training will be enough. Follow-up resources can include a hotline phone number for asking questions, audiocassettes that will serve as a refresher, summary sheets, trainer visits to the work place and other methods. Resource provisions in the work environment will enhance skill application and demonstrate your continuing commitment to trainees' welfare.

10 Follow-up questionnaires should be sent to participants after they have had a week or two to try out new skills. Evaluation questionnaires completed immediately after a course ends are almost always biased by gratitude, relief (that the course is over) and forgetfulness (about all the worst aspects of the course). After all, it is only in application that any training course can be meaningfully evaluated. Additional information and "prodding" can be added to the questionnaire to increase the probability of application. It also shows trainees that you care and are still thinking of them. Send follow-up material to trainees on a regular basis (perhaps weekly) for the first month or two after a course.

11 Follow-up contacts such as telephone calls ("How are things going...?") or personal visits serve the same purpose as a questionnaire, but do so more personally.

12 Follow up sessions give participants an opportunity to come together again to share ideas and solve problems. This is particularly useful when the multiphase programming method is impractical. These sessions invariably produce a positive response, as well as provide the opportunity for follow-up course evaluation.

These methods will greatly enhance your effectiveness as a trainer. It will certainly increase the likelihood that trainees will use the skills you so expertly teach them. Program follow-up should not be viewed as an "optional extra." It is an essential part of any effective training course. A trainer must have an arsenal of techniques to avoid "training entropy" in the performance environment. The methods discussed in this article should give you just such an arsenal.

Measuring Back-on-the-Job Performance

To survive a recession or budget cut, find your dollar value

BY J.B. CORNWELL

The most foolproof way I know for a trainer to protect his or her job from the sometimes terminal effects of hard economic times is to document bottom-line results. Better yet, document the dollar value of those results, and show upper management a significant "profit" on investments made in training.

What are bottom-line results? For our purposes let's define the bottom line on training as the on-the job performance of trainees after training. To document the actual influence your training program had on that performance, it's necessary to establish, and document, a baseline. What was the performance level before, or without, training? For those of you who protest that your training program was designed to change something other than on-the-job performance, I'll broaden the term "performance" to include manifestations of attitude, knowledge, appreciation or whatever intangible you sought to influence in the first place.

(If you can't describe some visible, measurable evidence that would indicate that your training program works, stop reading — but figure out why the devil you wanted to do the program at all!)

The size and sophistication of your organization — the number, nature and accessibility of your students — and the nature of the job your students need to perform will all determine what methods you'll use to measure the final effects of your program. Regard-less of differences in all those factors, however, there are some constants. There are certain questions that you will want answered, even though you may use very different techniques for gathering the answers.

Let's review some of the basic questions and some of the options for defining them more specifically.

STUDENT'S POST-TRAINING SURVEY
Three to six months ago, you completed the Training Program, _____. The purpose of this survey is to determine how well the program prepared you for the job.
Attached is a list of the tasks covered in the program and a guide to code the answer sheet below. The information you provide will be kept in strictest confidence and will be used to improve the content and quality of training. Thank you for cooperation.

Coding instructions

For each task/learning objective for the program you attended, write in the number(s) of the appropriate statements under the letters designating the subject.

Example: If the task is #1— The learner will be able to adust a spark plug gap to the correct clearance— and if you do this routinely on the job but differently and with a different tool than that suggested in training, you would place a 3 in the box for task #1 under subject A (see code sheet) as below.

TASK #	A	B	C	D	E
1.	3				
2.					
3.					

A. I am doing this task regularly on the job.
1. After training I only needed practice.
2. After training I needed to learn this task on the job. I didn't learn it in training.
3. I am doing this task differently than I learned in training because:
   a) Work conditions don't allow me to do it as I originally learned it.
   b) It doesn't work the way I learned it.
   c) I figured out a better way.
   d) My supervisor told me to do it differently.

B. I rarely do this task on the job.
1. I learned it in training, but I don't get enough practice to keep sharp. Each time it comes up, I have trouble.
2. I get enough practice and stay sharp.
3. I didn't learn it in training. I had to learn it on the job.

C. I don't do this task on the job.
1. The job doesn't call for it.
2. I get help when it comes up because:
   a) I didn't learn it.
   b) It's too difficult for me.
   c) It comes up so rarely I forget how.
   d) I was assigned a different job.

D. How I learned this task.
1. I could do it successfully before the training.
2. I learned it effectively in the training:
   a) Because it was taught well.
   b) But I could have learned it easier from a manual or instruction sheet.
   c) But I could have learned it just as well on the job.
3. I learned it with difficulty because:
   a) The training was confusing.
   b) There wasn't enough practice.
   c) There wasn't enough explanation.
   d) There wasn't enough reference material.

E. Because of attending this program.
1. I feel better about my job and the company.
2. I feel the same as I did before.
3. I'm impatient to get ahead.
4. I feel worse about my job and the company.

---

1 **How accurately did the training program address the exact requirements of the job?** Assuming that the program was designed to train students how to do a job or how to do it better, how closely did it match the actual job the students were called on to do after the training? This question raises some sub-questions: Did the program address all the things the students needed to learn to be able to perform to standard? Were the things not addressed easy and convenient to learn on the job or to figure out when the need arose? Were things presented that weren't needed in the program? If so, weren't they needed because the student already knows how to do it, the job doesn't require it, or the student could have learned it quickly and easily on the job?

Note here that the answers to these questions shouldn't be "contaminated" by answers to later questions. At this point, all you want to know is whether or not you set proper specifications for the program, not whether it worked.

Probably the simplest way to obtain answers to this first question (and subquestions) is to survey students and their supervisors by means of questionnaires. Where practical, one-to-one interviews, observations, and statistical analyses of work-reporting data can be used to enhance your findings. If you've specifically defined performance objectives for the program, supply both students and supervisors with copies of those objectives, along with the questionnaire so they can comment on the relevance of each item separately and specifically. The more specific the answers, the easier it will be to determine what, if any, changes are appropriate.

2 **How successfully are the students performing each item learned in the training program?** Don't let answers to this affect your interpretation of answers to Question 1. Here you want to learn whether or not your students are successfully doing the things they (should have) learned in the program and, if not, why not. Actually, the "why not" is of critical importance. Sub-questions are: Did the student learn the task in the program and then forget how to do it? Did the student not learn it successfully? Can the student do the task but isn't because of conditions, environment or management? Could the student do the job at first but didn't get enough practice to maintain his or her skill?

One pretty reliable way to determine if the students can do the tasks learned is to have them retake your final exam. There's some risk here, of course, that your exam doesn't validly measure what you intend it to measure; performance tests are more reliable than paper-pencil tests to measure whether people can do things. Students frequently do things differently from the way they learned to do them because they lack management support and because they learned inappropriate techniques in training — that is, the way they learned to do it is exceedingly difficult or doesn't

---

SUPERVISOR'S POST-TRAINING SURVEY

Three to six months ago, _____, one of your subordinates, attended the training program _____. The purpose of this survey is to gather data about how well the program prepared him or her for the job.

Attached is a list of the tasks covered in the program and a guide to code the answer sheet below. The facts you provide will be used to examine the objectives and methods of the program design and the techniques of delivery. They will provide opportunities to improve effectiveness and efficiency.

Coding Instructions

For each task listed for the training program, insert a number corresponding to the correct statements about that task in the appropriate subject box.

Example: If the task is #1— The learner will be able to adjust a spark plug gap to correct clearance— and if (s)he does this successfully but uses a different tool and technique because the tool used in training isn't available, you would place a 4 in box C for task #1, as well as appropriate codes in each other box in the survey.

TASK #	A	B	C	D
1.			4	
2.				
3.				
4.				
5.				
6.				

A. This task is:

1. A routine daily part of the job.
2. An occasional part of the job.
3. An unusual part of the job.
4. Not part of the job.

B. Performing this task is:

1. Extremely important; an error would be catastrophic.
2. Important, but occasional errors are tolerable.
3. Of routine importance; errors can be easily corrected.
4. Not very important; errors make little difference.

C. Since attending the program, my subordinate:

1. Has performed this task successfully.
2. Needed additional help to learn this task.
3. Is performing this task, but differently than taught because:
   a) We have a better way.
   b) Conditions don't allow us to do it the way it was taught.
   c) (S)He doesn't like to do it the right way.
4. Has not performed this task because:
   a) (S)He didn't learn it.
   b) (S)He forgot how before the occasion to do it arose.
   c) (S)He hasn't needed to do it.

D. Since attending the training program, my subordinate's general attitude seems to have:

1. Improved a lot.
2. Improved slightly.
3. Not changed.
4. Deteriorated slightly.
5. Deteriorated alarmingly.

---

work in the real job environment.

Here again, well-designed questionnaires to students and supervisors, supplemented with observation, interviews, and analysis of any available work-reporting data, usually provide as much reliability as you can get without a large budget dedicated to quality control. If you do have a large budget, actual observation of work as it's being done is probably the most reliable, time-consuming and expensive method of measurement available.

3 **What consequences have occurred "other than those intended?"** Training programs influence students in many ways, besides teaching new or improved ways to do defined tasks. Sometimes we specifically intend to apply some of these influences in order to, say, reduce attrition, grievances, or accidents. If that's your intention, you'll want to know what happened. Did attrition decrease? How much? Is that more, less or the same as the target? Question 3, then, essentially asks, "What may have happened that we didn't expect — good or bad?" Training programs that have no goals related to morale, attrition, absenteeism, grievances, human and customer relations, and so on, quite often affect some or all of those factors. The changes they produce aren't always beneficial.

For example, a training program may provide necessary skills and stimulate ambitions for a more responsible and higher-paying job than the one the student supposedly is being trained for. The result may be that the trainee exhibits undesirable behavior stemming from his or her frustration. On the other hand, training programs can positively affect employee behavior, in addition to satisfying stated objectives related to job task skills.

It's important to find out — from supervisors, management, personnel records, or wherever you can collect evidence — what side effects the training program may be causing. If possible, try to get these sorts of data from two sources. The first will be the control group, people who did not attend the training program. The second source will be people who participated in the program. This information will be most useful when it reports on the behavior of a large number of people over the same time period — trained people versus untrained people during the same three month period, for example.

Use the accompanying sample surveys as a set of data collection instruments, including a post-training student questionnaire, supervisor questionnaire and supporting forms. The design of these instruments includes several assumptions, the most important being that the organizational climate will influence students and supervisors to take the time to fill them out accurately. Unfor-tunately, in many organizations, the return rate would be less than 10%. Should you wish to vary this format, consider the possibility that the people you're attempting to survey won't take the time to fill out your questionnaires.

A far simpler format is more likely

With some creative accounting, any documented increase in productivity can be expressed as a bottom-line payoff of training.

---

to get responses, but the information will be more general, harder to compile and analyze, and less likely to suggest specific changes. A one-pager that asks the following questions will give you less information than the examples, but general answers are always more useful than specific silence.

• What tasks do you need for the job that weren't presented or that you didn't learn successfully in the course?

• What tasks did you learn in the course that aren't needed on the job?

• What did you learn that has been most useful on the job?

• What did you learn that has been least useful on the job?

Finally, a word about expressing results in dollars. If your learners are sales reps, it's not too difficult to determine dollar value of results with this sort of model: Untrained sales reps average $100,000 per year in sales, and trained reps average $150,000 per year. Therefore, the return on the cost of training one sales rep is $50,000 in revenue. (That's income, not profit, but it is a net increase resulting from training.)

With a little creative accounting, any documented increase in productivity or decrease in nonproductivity, such as attrition, can be expressed as increased income or decreased cost to your organization. In other words, as bottom-line results of training. To reach that bottom line, you must find out how your students are performing on the job and how training influences that performance.

Notes:

Chapter 4

Measuring the Payoff of Soft-Skills Training

Why Soft-Skills Training Doesn't Take

Do our 'interpersonal skills' programs really build skills?
Do our role plays miss the point?
Have we built a house of cards?

BY JAMES C. GEORGES

Good technical trainers have very high batting averages. They can start with an average group of people and turn most of them into skilled technicians. In fact, the standard definition of a successful technical-training program is one in which 90% of the learners master 90% of the skills being taught. And that means — as far as good technical trainers are concerned — that trainees can demonstrate skilled performance not just in class but in a real job situation.

Similarly, good tennis or golf coaches can coax dramatic improvements out of just about anybody. Few people would doubt that those coaches are building valuable skills — that their coaching produces visible improvements in the athletes' performances in tennis matches or golf tournaments.

"Soft skills" training, on the other hand, is much more a hit-or-miss proposition. When we teach subjects that fall under the headings of management, leadership, interpersonal communication, problem-solving, and consultative sales techniques, we have a lousy batting average. In most organizations, we're lucky if 20% of the people who graduate from our courses go back to the job and use the techniques we taught them to improve their "games." The other 80% may try out their new "skills" a few times, but they quickly revert to their old patterns.

We warned them, of course, that doing things the new way might seem clumsy at first. We encouraged them to stick with it: "You'll have to practice these skills back on the job to make them your own. Draw up an action plan for integrating them into your behavior... They'll start to pay off for you eventually." We urged their bosses to support them for practicing the new skills, even if their performance suffered somewhat in the beginning.

But in the real world, people simply don't stick with behavior that

Suppose we conducted soft skills training in the way coaches build the skills of world-class athletes or musicians?

makes them feel artificial and maladroit, especially if it causes their performance to suffer in ways that hurt.

Most trainees will drop the new techniques like hot potatoes the moment the idea of a temporary dip in performance becomes concrete — as soon as "My performance may suffer a little at first" turns into "Hey, I'm losing sales with this technique," or "I'm actually alienating people by stumbling through this formula."

What's more, it may be that the only reason we have even that pitiful 20% success rate is that about 20% of our trainees were already skillful performers when they walked into class. Somebody who is naturally good at giving effective feedback to subordinates, for instance, will be able to take just about any reasonable set of principles we present and make them work. After all, when it comes to soft skills, we know there are "naturals" and self-taught masters out there. Almost everything we teach about communication and leadership and so on comes from studying those masters.

Why are we so much less effective at teaching "people skills" than we are at teaching technical skills or at teaching people to play tennis? Perhaps it's largely because we don't really do any skills training in "soft" subjects. We just call it skills training. What we actually deliver is knowledge training; we pass along information about a particular behavior.

Knowing about how something is done is not a skill. Being able to describe the steps involved in completing a task is not a skill. The ability to perform those steps in a clumsy, disjointed way is not a skill.

It's not what you do but how well you do it that determines whether you are skilled. You have a skill only when you are able to do something skillfully.

That seems so self-evident that it shouldn't need to be said. But it does. Because when it comes to soft-skills training, skillful performance is the one thing we don't build or teach. Instead, we tell trainees they'll have to achieve it on their own, through practice, back on the job.

Sure. Back on the job — the last place where they can afford to look awkward, uncertain and incompetent, as people do in the early stages of learning to master any new skill.

Steps

When we teach soft subjects, what we really do is "steps" training. It works like this.

First, pick a subject or process and break it down into a series of steps. For example, here are five steps in a rational procedure for problem-solving that's older than Plato: (1) define the problem, (2) seek options and alternative solutions, (3) gain agreement on the most acceptable solution, (4) commit to a plan of action, (5) observe the results and follow up with appropriate actions.

Second, discuss the steps in class to see that everybody understands what they are. If possible, show them a videotape (a behavior model) of someone demonstrating the steps.

Then conduct a role play or two so the trainees can practice using the steps. All trainees should prove that they understand what the steps are, and roughly what they look like in practice. The point is not to achieve a smooth, convincing, skilled performance. Who has time for that? We're happy if everyone can achieve a forced, artificial approximation of what a human being might look like and sound like while using these steps skillfully in a real situation.

Finally, make everyone promise to practice the steps back on the job until they come smoothly and naturally get their bosses to promise to reinforce this practice. If they aren't getting enough support from their bosses, bring the trainees back for more sessions. Show them a different videotape. Stage more role plays. Then sing, once again, the soft-skills training theme song: "Now go back to work and make these skills your own."

What's wrong with this picture? The essential problem is that the steps aren't the skill. Skill is what it takes to execute the steps successfully. That's why program graduates who use perfectly valid procedures fail so often to achieve the results they desire. Whether the subject is sales, supervision or whatever, any logical set of steps is doomed to fail if the person's demeanor is too mechanical, too tentative, too pushy, too righteous, too unconvincing.

Leave the trainees with the impression that the steps are the skill, and you've encouraged them to discard the steps when they experience repeated failures back on the job — as most of them will, at first. People aren't stupid. They protect themselves. A step-by-step procedure that isn't comfortable and doesn't seem to work will not be used. Not even if management "buys into" the training program enough to do a little bit of coaching and reinforcing. Busy managers don't have time (and often don't have the skill) to do enough coaching.

Another weakness of that standard "skills training" process lies in those role plays. A few role plays will not build a skillful performance. Most role plays are designed, in fact, only to ensure that the trainees have grasped what the steps are. That's why the language and performances seem so artificial. Role plays aren't designed or even intended to produce the sort of smooth, natural performance that would be required in order for the steps to work in a real-life situation. Provided the trainees attempt to execute the steps, however clumsily, they graduate from the course and are deemed to have a new "skill."

Nonsense. The only thing they have is new knowledge about certain step-by-step behaviors. Good technical trainers would consider it criminal to throw a novice machine operator into a real production process if the novice could perform only a clumsy — even counterproductive — impersonation of a person actually able to operate the machine. But when it comes to people-skills training, that's

Most "soft" programs don't transfer because we fail to give trainees the appropriate skills practice.

standard procedure.

Then we all stand around and engage in endless arguments about why soft skills so often fail to "transfer" from the classroom to the workplace. We have a long list of excuses: Management failed to reinforce the new skills, the company's culture wouldn't support them and so on. Sometimes these arguments are true; but if so, the training program should not have been run in the first place.

In truth, the No. 1 reason for transfer failure is that most of the "soft" programs we run don't give trainees any genuine skills that they can transfer to the workplace.

Real Skills

Suppose we conducted people-skills training more in the way that world-class coaches build the skills of athletes, musicians and karate experts? Or the way a good private coach might train a politician or a top business executive to field questions from the news media? Whether you're talking about Jack Nicklaus, Mary Lou Retton, Ella Fitzgerald, Bruce Lee or a presidential candidate, much of the training they received was patterned along these lines:

• First, find out what the learner needs to accomplish. Then present the appropriate skill model in plain language, explaining the "what to do's" in the fewest possible words. These "what to do's" are the smaller elements in the overall model.

• Show examples of the whole skill model. Then show examples of the first smaller skill element. Videotaped behavior models are great, but any clear example would do. Check the trainee's understanding until "Do you know what to do?" is no longer an issue.

• Now shift the emphasis away from the "what to do," that is, away from the "step." Explain that the step is not the skill. The skill lies in how well you execute each step, and ultimately in how well you integrate the steps into a skillful performance.

• Drill each single skill element. (A drill is not the same as a role play. More on this in a minute.) Keep drilling each element until both learner and coach can see that the learner has mastered it well enough to succeed in a real-life situation — that is, until the learner performs competently, consistently and confidently.

• After each skill element has been drilled to mastery level, move on to the next element. Finally, combine the skill segments and drill the entire skill model. By the time you get to the whole model, this will be relatively easy to do, since little will be new to the learner and any weak areas will have been strengthened in previous drills. (In a traditional role play, by contrast, the whole skill model is the first thing practiced and critiqued. The learner's performance is riddled with weak areas.)

• Finally, for reinforcement back on the job, do not rely solely upon the trainees' bosses to provide encouragement and additional coaching. Instead, teach the trainees — during the training program itself — how to coach each other. During the drills, trainees should alternate between the roles of learner and coach — just as gymnasts "spot" and critique each other while they practice a difficult move, then a series of moves. This not only helps logistically (one trainer cannot simultaneously coach 30 individuals through the sorts of drills we're talking about), but also improves each person's learning. The old maxim that you learn by teaching is true. Once trainees return to the job, they will be more accessible to one another for coaching and reinforcement purposes than one boss can be to a whole group of people. By all means, get bosses involved. Just don't count on them to provide all the necessary support

What's the difference between a drill and a role play?

Take a golf lesson with me. I'll show you a series of steps, covering everything from driving off the tee to putting. The first three steps will be: how to grip a club, how to align your feet and shoulders to the target and how to swing side-to-side so as to strike the ball squarely. Once I've shown you the whole series of, say, 15 steps, we'll want to give you some practice.

The "role play" model for that golf lesson would be for you to go out and play nine holes of golf, bearing in mind the 15 steps I described. I would coach you and critique your performance only after you finished the ninth hole.

To "drill" you, on the other hand, I'd take you to a driving range. You'd work only on the first three of the 15 steps in the total skill model. But in less time than it would take to play nine holes of golf, you'd hit several hundred balls. And you'd get immediate, continual feedback about your performance on every swing. Once we were satisfied with your driving, I'd take you to a putting green. And so on.

Suppose we had only enough practice time for you to play four nine-hole rounds. Shall we go ahead and play those rounds, according to the role-play model? Or do you think you would develop more skill and confidence as a golfer if we devoted the same amount of time to the drilling model, perhaps ending with one nine-hole round? Professional golfers build their ability to drive and putt and escape from sand traps by drilling those skills, not by "role playing" them.

Drills are short, repetitive experiments. And repetitive, coached practice is the best way to develop skillfulness. You can get a lot of drilling done in the time it takes to complete one full role-play.

Drills also build confidence, because drilling is the fastest way to master each particular skill element. And confidence comes from the knowledge that you can do something well and do it consistently and predictably under a variety of circumstances. Confidence builds "ownership" of the skill. And ownership must occur during the training course for the skill to transfer to the real job.

Doing It with People Skills

How would you drill people to perform a "soft skill" consistently, predictably, smoothly and confidently? Let's take a particular skill element that might be taught in any number of courses, whether the topic is interpersonal communication, effective supervision, sales, negotiation, leadership or how to conduct a performance review. The element is the ability to maintain self-confidence and poise even in the face of resistance, that is, resistance from the client, the subordinate, the peer or whomever.

Training works best when it's tied to real goals that the trainees really want to accomplish. So have each

---

Repetitive drills build real skills — right here, right now.

---

learner pick a real situation to work with: trying to sell the Mark VI electric widget to a customer, trying to enlist the support of a peer from another department in some project, etc. Tell the learner to make a specific request for the coach's commitment or support (for example, ask the coach to buy the product or to lend his wholehearted support to the learner's project, etc.). The learner makes essentially the same request a number of times, but each time the coach expresses a different type of reaction: refusal, resistance, indifference, hesitant interest, acceptance, enthusiastic support, etc.

Coach and learner immediately discuss and critique the way the learner handled each of the coach's reactions. If they find that the learner has trouble maintaining composure in the face of, say, a challenging or distrustful reaction, then they drill heavily on handling that reaction. The coach challenges and the learner responds to the challenge, over and over again. These are not role plays, but brief, repetitive exchanges. The learner experiments with different ways of responding to the coach's challenges.

The two aren't experimenting in the dark here. They have the recommended "steps" and techniques to work with. But since they're drilling a particular skill instead of working through an entire role play on "giving a performance review" or whatever, they can isolate the learner's specific weak points and work effectively to strengthen them.

You can use drills to build any number of specific skills that might fit into a variety of soft-subject courses: the ability to negotiate or inspire a change in another person's point of view, the ability to end conversations at the most productive point or at the point of maximum commitment. Whatever skill element you're teaching, the advantage of repetitive drills over the standard role play is that well-executed drills build genuine skillfullness — right here, right now.

Take another generic skill element: the ability to establish conversational rapport. The true "skill" is being able to do it without resorting to artificial feedback techniques. In the real world, credibility is the issue. So the question is not, "Did you remember to acknowledge that you took the other person's point of view seriously?" That's the step that you demonstrate in a role play When you try to use it, unconvincingly, back in the real world, you may well find that you just annoy and alienate people.

The question is, "How believable were you while you were acknowledging that you took the other person's point of view seriously?" That's the skill. And unless you have developed it naturally, you're likely to build it only in the low-threat environment of a training program, and only through repeated drills that focus on your personal believability. You won't build it in a few role plays by doing an awkward impersonation of the woman in the videotape. And you won't build it back on the job.

When it comes to interpersonal-skills training of all sorts — be it for managers, salespeople or anyone else in the business world — plenty of organizations do a perfectly adequate job of imparting valid knowledge about effective behaviors. So why does this training have such a spotty batting average?

Let me say it one more time: Knowing about how something is supposed to be done is not a skill. Skill is the crucial element that turns knowledge into behaviors that succeed in the real world. If the so-called skills you've been building in class seem to vanish when people get back to the job, the first question to ask is whether you were building any genuine skillfulness at all.

ROI of Soft-Skills Training

Want to find out if your team-building course contributes to the bottom line? Here's a way

BY JUDITH PINE
AND JUDITH C. TINGLEY

You're sitting at the conference table with some production line managers. You say: "The problem-solving courses have reduced rework by 12%, resulting in a savings to the company of $500 a week. The cost of training your team was $5,000. That means you'll see a return on your training investment of 400% over one year."

Suddenly, the phone rings and snaps you out of your daydream. Reality returns. The fact is, the results of "soft-skills" training — in subjects such as problem-solving, team-building, communication, listening, stress management — are notoriously difficult to measure.

Soft-skills trainers seldom attempt evaluations designed to calculate return on investment (ROI). Trainers, as well as some line managers, generally prefer to think training is "good" whether it accomplishes anything measurable or not. Training goals are often stated in terms that make measurement difficult if not impossible: become a better listener, improve quality, reduce stress. Maybe trainers fear that soft-skills training doesn't produce an outcome that can be tied to the bottom line. Perhaps some simply don't know how to conduct a results-oriented evaluation and calculate return on investment — though the training literature is full of models and cookbook formulas that explain how to do it.

So things have stood for many years. But now the picture is changing. The recession, the epidemic of corporate downsizings, the flattening of organizational structures and the popularity of total quality management are sweeping away some of those old attitudes about the evaluation of training. Today, trainers are under increasing pressure to direct their efforts toward satisfying their internal customers — and many of those customers want to see a measurable, bottom-line impact from training. This translates into an effort to tie training directly to the business

Team members needed to improve their communication skills and share responsibility for tasks and team goals.

results that management is emphasizing — increased productivity, fewer errors, higher employee morale, a stronger bottom line.

Plenty of technical trainers already conduct return-on-investment evaluations. Now soft-skills trainers are beginning to ask the tough questions that link training programs to the operational results of the organization: "How do we know that training makes a difference on the bottom line?" "How can we measure the effects of training on attitudes, behavior and performance, and translate that effect into dollars saved or dollars gained?"

The Model

We set out to demonstrate that all four levels of Donald L. Kirkpatrick's classic evaluation model could be applied to soft-skills training. Furthermore, we wanted to prove that this is not an overpoweringly difficult undertaking, but something that a couple of ordinary trainers (namely, us) could do.

About 30 years ago, Kirkpatrick proposed that the efficiency and effectiveness of training can be evaluated or measured at four different "levels":

Level 1. Measurement of participants' reaction to the training at the time of the training.

Level 2. Measurement of participants' learning of the content of the training.

Level 3. Measurement of participants' use of their new skills and knowledge back on the job.

Level 4. Measurement of the company's return on the training investment.

Very rarely is a serious evaluation of a soft-skills program carried beyond Level 3. We wanted to apply all four levels of the model to soft-skills training in a contemporary setting.

The Study

We conducted this study at Garrett Engine Division, the Phoenix division of Allied Signal Corp. that manufactures jet engines. As part of a total quality manufacturing effort, we conducted a two-day course in team building with intact work groups, the maintenance teams that repair manufacturing machines.

Each team consisted of a first-line supervisor and hourly employees who represented all the trades commonly found in a maintenance department: electricians, mechanics and plumbers. All of the teams reported to the same manager and all were measured on the same performance criteria.

The team-building course included information and experiential exercises on communicating effectively, synergy in teams, stages of growth and change, characteristics of effective work teams and problem-solving on specific work issues. In other words, the program was neck-deep in the sort of "soft" material that is usually considered too squishy to evaluate in terms of ROI.

We chose an experimental group, which received this team-building course, and a control group that did not receive the training. We felt this design would increase the probability that any change that occurred was a result of the training rather than an artifact of circumstances. To be more specific, we used a quasi-experimental design described by Campbell and Stanley in their classic text, *Experi-*

mental and Quasi-Experimental Designs for Research.

We began with four similar maintenance teams. The primary function of each was to maintain equipment used in the manufacturing process. We randomly assigned two of these teams to the experimental group and two to the control group. The teams were similar, but not equal, so we gave pre-tests to both groups to create pre-training benchmarks. Our thinking was straightforward: If the groups are similar prior to the training, and one group experiences training while the other doesn't, we can say with considerable confidence that any differences in performance that appear after the training are a result of the training.

Selecting and Measuring Outcomes

The key to determining a training program's return on investment lies in selecting the outcomes to be measured and linking the training to those outcomes. In *Training for Impact*, Dana Gaines Robinson and James Robinson emphasize the need to draw a clear, causal relationship between the skills and knowledge you're developing through training and the operational outcomes you want to measure. In other words, you need to be confident that if, after the training program, the costs of some business process go down or the revenues it generates go up, this is indeed because people have begun to do the things they were taught to do in the course.

In practice, this means that if you're designing a training program that you intend to evaluate at Level 4, you must start with Level 4 considerations and work backwards. First, what business outcomes do you want? Then, how should people behave in order to achieve those outcomes? Then, what do you have to teach them in order to enable and encourage them to behave that way? Then, how will you know if they learned the things you were trying to teach them? Finally, how should you go about teaching these things?

What kinds of operational results should you measure? An organization's mission and strategic plan determine the outcomes it considers valuable. Management, employees and trainers should all be involved in deciding which specific outcomes to measure. Outcomes may be related to increased productivity, quality, inter-

TABLE 1
CHANGES IN PERFORMANCE

	Response Time	Completion Time	Total Down Time	Estimated Cost
Experimental Group				
Before Training	4.8 hours	13.6 hours	18.4 hours	$1,341
After Training	4.1 hours	11.7 hours	15.8 hours	$1,156
Control Group				
Before Training	4.4 hours	11.6 hours	16.0 hours	$1,165
After Training	4.4 hours	11.7 hours	16.1 hours	$1,211

nal or external customer satisfaction, or a myriad other choices. But whatever the outcome, it must be measurable, it must be linked to the training, and you must be able to translate it into money saved or earned.

At Garrett, we chose decreased downtime of equipment as the desired outcome. We also measured

> **The key to determining ROI lies in selecting outcomes to be measured.**

job response time and completion time. Response time refers to the amount of time it takes the equipment maintenance people to respond to a call for service. Completion time is the time required to complete the job. The company already tracked this data routinely, so it was easy to acquire a measure of response and completion time two weeks before and two weeks after the team-building training.

Once we had determined the desired outcomes for Level 4, we moved back to Level 3. At Level 3 you're trying to link Level 4 outcomes to the behaviors the training was designed to elicit. For example, a Level 4 outcome for a soft skill like assertive communication might be increased productivity and savings resulting from shorter meetings. A Level 3 outcome would be that the trained people use assertive communication techniques in meetings.

In the Garrett study, we postulated that if a work group behaved in ways characteristic of a good team, they'd be likely to respond to and complete jobs more quickly. This is the link between behaviors at Level 3 and outcomes at Level 4. In particular, team members needed to improve their communication skills and share responsibility for tasks and team goals. We found a nationally normed team assessment instrument and used it before and after the training to determine how the members perceived their team's performance in these areas.

Once we determined the Level 3 behaviors we wanted, we decided what knowledge, skills and attitudes had to be learned in the training to develop these behaviors. This is a Level 2 outcome, a measure of the content taught. In the Garrett study, we gave team members a paper-and-pencil test after the training to evaluate their knowledge of effective team qualities, characteristics and behaviors.

Finally, we measured the participants' reaction to the training at Level 1 to find out if they considered the training useful, well-presented and informative. This involved the standard "smile sheet" that asks participants to evaluate the course, the delivery, the instructor and whether course objectives were achieved.

Evaluating the Results

A statistician who specializes in evaluating education helped us analyze the data. His task was to determine statistically whether differences on post-training measures could be considered a result of the training rather than the result of chance. He found that the program was effective at all four levels of evaluation.

Only the group that went through training was measured at Level 1. Trainees gave high ratings to the course and its instructor. They agreed that the objectives of the workshop were clear and had been achieved.

At Level 2, a post-test found that participants' knowledge of team-building concepts did improve, compared with both their pre-test levels and with the scores of the group that didn't receive the training.

To measure Level 3 outcomes, skills and knowledge used on the job, we asked both the experimental and control groups to complete a team assessment instrument after the training. Training participants improved their pre-training scores in team communication, sharing responsibility for tasks, alignment on team goals and rapid response. In other words, people who participated in training considered their teams more effective after the training; they said behavior had changed in accordance with the workshop's teachings.

Was the training effective at Level 4? Did this new behavior have an effect on the bottom line? Were costs reduced, profits increased or service improved?

We measured actual changes in performance on two variables: job response time and job completion time. Table 1 shows before and after figures for the experimental and control groups. Prior to the team-building course, the people in the experimental group were slower to respond to job requests than those in the control group. After the program, the experimental group responded more quickly. The control group stayed about the same.

A similar improvement occurred in job completion time. Prior to the team-building course, people in the experimental group uniformly took longer to complete jobs than those in the control group. Yet after the program, training participants were completing the average job 1.9 hours quicker than they were before. (Interestingly, the control group showed a slight increase in completion time, which resulted in an increase in cost per job for the control group. We attribute this increase to random factors that can affect any measurement process.)

The machines serviced by these maintenance teams are used 24 hours a day, seven days a week. The maintenance department had established a "burden rate," or the cost of machine downtime, prior to this study. This rate was the figure we used to evaluate the return on investment of the training. Clearly, if performance improved — i.e., the maintenance teams cut their response and completion times — then equipment would be down fewer hours and money would be saved.

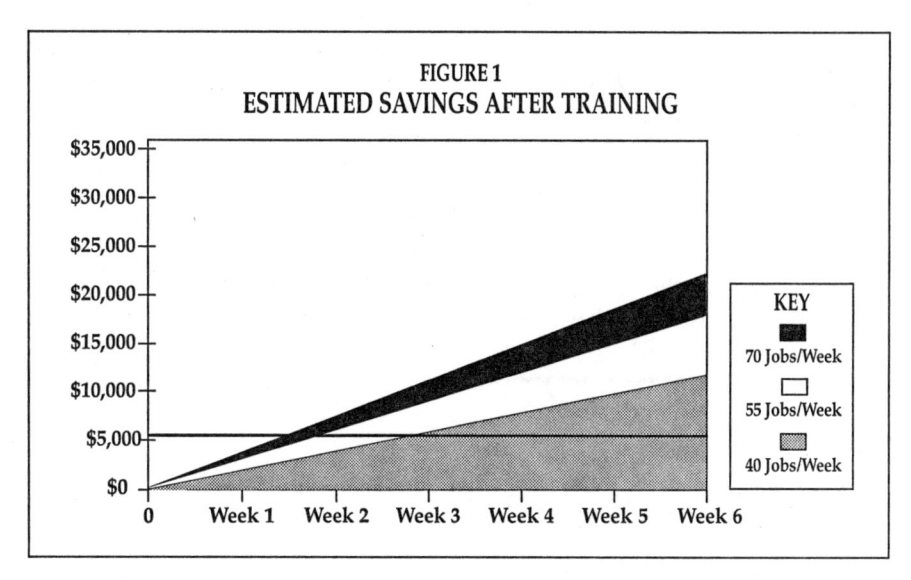

We estimated the average response and completion times per job for the experimental and the control groups, both before and after training. Then we calculated the average total downtime per job. We used these estimates to figure the average cost of downtime per job, also shown in Table 1.

The average cost of equipment downtime per job for the experimental group after team-building training was $1,156. The average cost per job for the control group during the same period was $1,211. Thus, we can estimate the savings per job that resulted from the training is $55 ($1,211 minus $1,156).

The most conservative way to estimate the return on training investment is to compare the post-training performance of the experimental group with the performance of the control group. Obviously, if both groups — or neither group — improve, we can't conclude that training made a difference. In this case, we can attribute the markedly improved performance of the experimental group to the training.

> **Whether or not you can demonstrate true ROI, the results will still help you develop more effective training.**

A less conservative way to estimate ROI is to measure the experimental group's performance before and after training. Using the figures in Table 1, if you subtract cost per job before training from cost per job after training, you'll end up with a more impressive $185 saved per job.

How fast do these savings add up? We estimated the total cost of this team-building training at $5,355, which includes presentation time, materials, overhead and participants' time off the job. The average number of jobs per week per team was 55, with 40 jobs representing a light week and 70 a heavy week.

Figure 1 illustrates return on investment of the training over time. The horizontal line represents the fixed cost of the program ($5,355). Each sloping line represents estimated savings at the end of a given week. The steepest line represents savings given heavy workweeks, while the middle and lower lines represent average and light workweeks, respectively. When a sloped line crosses the horizontal line, savings have exceeded the cost of the program. If we assume average workweeks, program costs are recouped within two weeks.

You can also express ROI as a percentage. In the Garrett study, we calculated the ROI after four average workweeks:

$55 (average savings per job)
x 55 (jobs per week)
x 4 (number of weeks)
= $12,100 (benefits)
− $5,355 (cost of training)
= $6,745 ÷ $5,355 (cost of training)
= 1.25 x 100
= 125% ROI

What we don't know is how long the training effect will last. To project

**FIGURE 1
ESTIMATED SAVINGS AFTER TRAINING**

KEY:
- 70 Jobs/Week
- 55 Jobs/Week
- 40 Jobs/Week

any long-term savings, we would need to continue to assess job-response and completion times of the trained group and the control group.

Just Do It

Soft-skills training can be tied to productivity measures — even by relative novices to the concept of ROI evaluation. We found Kirkpatrick's model a clear and useful guide to carrying out a systematic four-level evaluation.

Doing this kind of evaluation dramatically improved line management's perception of the training function, as well as our understanding of internal customer service.

Why feel threatened by the idea of determining ROI for a soft-skills program? Try it as a pilot project. Whether or not you can demonstrate a return on investment, the results will help you develop more effective training and improve your relationship with line management. Even-tually, you'll be able to demonstrate, indisputably, in bottom-line terms, training's value to the organization.

Notes:

How to Make Level 3 Evaluation of Soft-Skills Training Pay Dividends

BY DAVE ZIELINSKI

With all the demands on a training function's time, doing a Level 3 or Level 4 program evaluation can seem almost masochistic. Few departments without dedicated program evaluation personnel have the luxury of time or dollars to evaluate training transfer to that depth.

But Vickie Shoutz, a human resources planning representative with Hutchinson Technology Inc., a computer components manufacturer, found some long-lasting benefits from a Level 3 evaluation she did in a tooling department. Those benefits made the additional time and dollars put toward the evaluation more than worthwhile, she says.

The evaluation was done for an interpersonal skills training program delivered to 150 tool-and-dye makers. The program, Employee Interaction, created by Pittsburgh-based Development Dimensions International (DDI), features modules like communicating effectively, handling conflict, and other interpersonal skills. Tooling department managers had requested the training following growing reports from some internal customers that dealings with the tooling department were often strained and marked with miscommunication.

The Pre-Training Work

The important thing is to design evaluation steps into the process as you design the course itself, not after the fact, Shoutz says. She and colleague Julie Page worked with James Robinson of the consulting firm Partners in Change to develop the evaluation protocol. "He worked with us off and on throughout the process, giving us some topnotch advice about when to do Level 3 evaluations — and when not to — and how to carry them out," Shoutz says.

Shoutz's program involved two pre-training steps:

1. Administering surveys designed to establish a baseline of interpersonal skill levels. Frontliners, team leaders, and supervisors in the department — and maybe most importantly, the tooling group's internal customers — were all asked to rate the group's interaction skills. There were self-assessment surveys, as well as assessments of peer, subordinate, and supervisor skills. Skills rated included two-way communication in one-on-one interactions, clarity of information provided, detail provided in interactions, responding with empathy, ability at dealing with conflict, and team-to-team interaction skills.

2. Holding focus groups to gather more qualitative data. In this step, Shoutz interviewed another set of front-liners, supervisors, and internal customers. "This information was critical — it rounded out the picture, and gave us some concrete examples of interaction problems and their causes," Shoutz says.

The Post-Training Work

Some three to four months after

EVALUATING SOFT-SKILLS TRAINING

Suppose you run a group of managers through a training course on a "soft-skill" topic like leadership or coaching or negotiating. And suppose you'd like to know what effect the course really had on their ability to lead or coach or negotiate.

Measuring the impact of soft-skills programs is notoriously difficult. If you just count the number of times the trained manager "exhibits key behaviors" — complimenting subordinates, say, or using certain catch phrases from the program — you may be measuring useless trivia. Compliments don't please subordinates if they seem insincere, for instance, and a manager who uses all the right catch phrases sometimes comes across as an android from Seminar Hell.

In short, you don't really care whether trainees can stand up and "demonstrate four leadership principles" as taught in the course. Rather, you want to know whether they're any more effective than they were to begin with in particular kinds of situations that call for the quality you are defining as "leadership."

What to Do?

Mohr Development Inc., a Stamford, CT, consulting firm, recently tried out an evaluation scheme you might consider adapting for any of a variety of soft-skills courses. The task was to evaluate the effectiveness of a packaged course on leadership that Mohr delivered to 15 managers in a client company over a three-week period. These trainees were all technical-project managers in the company's research and development area; their subordinates were engineers and technicians.

The evaluation technique was to videotape the trainees handling simulated leadership situations both before and after the training, and to have judges assess the tapes. At least, that's the skeleton of the technique. There's more to it, explains Mohr chairman Bernard Rosenbaum.

Three scenarios were chosen for the simulations, and two real technicians were trained to play the confederate roles opposite the student-leaders. The scenarios

Continued on p. 94

the training ended, the same groups were asked to rate the group's interaction skills on paper surveys and in focus groups. Using a scale of 0% to 100%, the pre-training surveys had shown the tooling group used the required interaction skills only 50% of the time. The post-training surveys showed employees were using those skills approximately 75% of the time, Shoutz says.

Training also followed up with supervisors six months after training to reinforce use of those skills, and to inquire how they believed the training had paid off. "Managers were still talking up the program results six and nine months following it," she claims.

Total tab for the effort? About $110,000, including needs analysis, program customization, survey design and data collection, consultant fees, trainer costs, and participant costs. Shoutz estimates she, Page, and some others spent about 800 hours on the evaluation.

The discovery of work environment problems was an unexpected benefit of the process. The tooling department works in two separate buildings. Those in one building complained in evaluation focus groups that its shadowy, cramped nature made the environment depressing, and affected their ability to be model communicators. The folks in the other building, working with more natural light, high ceilings, and more ample work space, reported no such problem. Management has since addressed the problem with building design changes.

Continued from p.93

were designed to represent three things the company agreed a leader should be able to do well:

1. Initiate change. In this case, that meant presenting a nonnegotiable and undesirable change to the subordinate.

2. Convert ideas to action. Identify a technical professional's undeveloped idea that otherwise might go unnoticed, and encourage him to develop a plan to test its feasibility.

3. Delegate responsibility. Specifically, delegate a responsibility the subordinate doesn't want — at least, not initially.

Two days before the training began, each of the 15 project managers was videotaped handling one of those situations. The scenarios were assigned at random and left untitled to prevent the managers from predetermining how they were supposed to behave. Then, one week after the training, each manager was again videotaped, this time handling a different scenario (to minimize any practice effect).

To ensure that everything else remained constant, only two "confederates" were used in these scenarios — one male, one female, both trained to be consistent in their presentations and in their responses. Each manager interacted with one of these confederates in the pre-training session and with the other in the post-training taping.

In the post-training simulation, managers were not specifically instructed to use anything they had learned in the program. They were simply told to handle the situation as effectively as they could.

Three managers from the client company served as judges to rate the performances in the videos. The judges received unlabeled pre- and post-training videos in pairs, viewed them in random order and rated them on coded forms. The judges were given a day of practice in "using rating scales specially developed for judging leader-subordinate simulation behaviors, which resulted in a high degree of inter-rater reliability," explains Rosenbaum.

("Aha!" cries the alert reader. "There's the skunk in Rosenbaum's rosebush! These rating scales are designed to reward behaviors and phrases taught in Mohr's course, so naturally the post-training videos score better — even if the trained manager couldn't really sell the confederate a dollar bill at half price!" Calm down, now. Your reflexes are in good shape, but you're jumping the gun.)

The judges were asked to do two things. First, they were to guess which tape showed the pre-training session and which the post-training one. This they were able to do with 100% accuracy, proving that the students' behavior did change in some way following the training.

Second, for each tape, the judges were to assess the degree to which the leader involved the subordinate in the discussion, the degree to which the leader would be likely to achieve his or her objectives, and the overall effectiveness of the approach used in each situation. In that last pair of ratings — likelihood of achieving objectives and overall effectiveness — lies this evaluation method's defense against the charge that judges are just counting catch phrases or superficial behaviors. Assuming the judges are impartial toward the training program, you're getting their honest opinion of the effectiveness of the trainee's performance in real-world terms.

In this program's case, average post-test ratings were significantly higher than pre-test averages in all three of those categories.

Mohr isn't suggesting that this method replace other evaluation tactics, such as asking graduates directly whether the things they learned were useful back on the job. But if you're after "hard evidence" that somebody's behavior changed as a result of soft-skills training — and that this change was either good, bad or indifferent — you might give the video method a try.

Chapter 5
Evaluating Management Development & Sales Training

Measuring the Impact of Management Development

Management training is a billion-dollar business. But measuring its bottom-line payoff isn't a simple task

BY RON ZEMKE

Management development and management training are large and growing budget items. Large budget items inevitably provoke questions about cost justification and ROI. Many CEOs are beginning to ask about expected payoff and proof of tangible results. In short, management wants to know: "What are the measurable, bottom-line results of management training and development?"

The mandate is clear: "Get ye hence and measure the worth of management training." But to paraphrase the Bard's Hamlet, "To measure! Perchance to know; ay, there's the rub..." And the rub, of course, is to find a meaningful measure of the relationship between management training and that vaunted bottom-line.

To answer the question, "How do you evaluate the results of management development and training," we polled a number of activists in the management training and development field. Though we found differences in the way some approach the evaluation process, all preambled their answers with specific qualifiers.

1. Management development and management training are two different topics. The difference became apparent as we talked with Malcolm Warren, director of manpower development, Dayton Hudson Corp. Warren sees management development in holistic, big-picture terms. "For any organization," he contends, "management development relates to a set of costs and benefits accruing from the way it acquires human resources to fill positions or complete tasks.

"The organization has only two options: Hire already developed talent from the outside or develop the talent inside. Obviously, one part of the organization's return is a consequence of choosing the best option. Cost reductions drop directly to the bottom-line. The out-of-pocket costs of the outside acquisition are easy to determine — search, relocation, orientation, etc. Also determinable is the risk cost. Outside acquisitions run a higher risk of failure than internal choices who are known by the organization and who know it."

Implicated in this global view of management development is the position that management training is only one management development activity. And while management development is hardly an optional activity, given the costs and risks of management personnel acquisition, management training is an activity about which decisions can be made rationally and outcomes weighed and evaluated.

2. Training is only one element of many which lead to job performance. Be it operating a derrick or directing operations, every individual's performance must be viewed in the context of the organization. Say, for example, that the organization teaches a management-by-objectives philosophy. But suppose the organizational culture punishes managers who try to decide, plan and manage by objectives, and rewards those who dramatically and successfully fight fires. Given these conditions, any new manager in his or her right mind will soon be reporting for work figuratively garbed in hard hat and red suspenders.

Larry Wilson, CEO of Wilson Learning Corporation, Eden Prairie, MN, put it this way: "The idea, at least in part, is to train managers to manage, efficiently and effectively, the existing organization. It's not sensible to train a person to manage an environment or organization that doesn't exist. It's like training a pilot to fly a 747 and then sending him off to build the plane. It won't happen. He needs the skills and the plane to do the job."

Scott Parry, president of New York's Training House, makes a similar observation: "If training is to be effective, we must prepare the environment as well as the individual. We must take inventory of the reinforcers and constraints that will help or hinder supervisors and managers as they try to apply new concepts and skills gained in the classroom. We must then equip trainees with the tools and techniques for dealing with them."

3. The bottom line on the P&L statement is probably not the best measure of management training. While it may be an appropriate measure of the whole management-development effort, it rarely assesses a specific management-training program.

Dayton Hudson's Warren makes the case for expecting a measurable relationship between management development and bottom-line results: "The costs of an effectively managed development process must be found significantly lower than outside acquisition over time. The benefit to the organization from effectively investing in human resources is simple to figure. Simple, that is, if we accept the notion that the managerial workforce of our organization contributes directly to its bottom line.

"Although we can argue about all the other variables — changes in the market, economic conditions, degree of contribution, etc. — ultimately the payoff will be a higher return on the investment in management resources. In my opinion, then, the bottom-line measure of management acquisition and development is the organization's earning before taxes, less the actual cost of management acquisition and development, divided by the compensation and benefit costs for the management workforce. If this margin improves over time, the acquisition and development process is paying off."

Dr. George Litwin, vice president of the research and communications division of Boston-based Forum Corporation, basically agrees with this bottom-line-of-the-P&L opinion.

"To me," he says, "the only sensible place to measure the results of a training effort is at the bottom line. By this I mean such things as growth in sales revenues and profits or the increase of market share, acceptance of products and services by customers, or the maintenance of a strong professional employee group which is reasonably stable and demonstrating the skills necessary for success."

But Litwin then points out a Catch-22 in depending on such a long-term measure: "Our experience with this kind of bottom-line measurement is that it is a lagging indicator of what's going on in the organization. That is, what the bottom line shows is the effectiveness of organizational units and their managers at an earlier time. We find that traditional bottom-line results lag by six months, a year or even two years behind the actual performance of the individuals involved. So, the first problem in measuring training results is to get some short-term indicators.

The trick, then, is to find something to measure — some indicator — which all parties will agree has a "known," or "logical," or "easily inferable" relationship to what the organization is trying to accomplish.

But What Indicator?

As one would expect, all our respondents insisted that no management training activity should begin without first determining what changes or improvements the experience should provide.

Our experts offered no vehement opinions about the one best indicator to measure or how to measure it. As Richard Grote, president of Dallas Performance Systems Corp., explained, "It doesn't make much difference. The decision to measure, not the specific method of measurement, is the critical factor. When management makes the decision to measure the results of management development activities and follow that commitment with action, 80% of the job is done."

Once agreed that the organization's management must know and clarify what results they are trying to obtain, our respondents differed somewhat about which short-term indicators they preferred. Litwin, known for his research in climate and attitude, says trainee attitudes toward the organization and the job are worth watching. As he puts it, "The most immediate indication of change in an organization is revealed in the beliefs and expectations of the people in the organizational unit. The first place you would see change would be in people's beliefs and expectations about what they are doing and about the success they might have. The reason we know that's a short-term indicator is that these beliefs and expectations are subject to change as a result of an organizational program. We also know that beliefs and expectations really lead to the arousal of motivation. They kick off the motivational surge which is what often leads to a period of high performance."

Wilson offered another viewpoint. "There is a difference between the objective and the purpose of a business. Usually the objective is to make a profit and stay in business. But the purpose of a business is to solve problems, or provide a service, or in some way help the customer. One way to really understand the impact of management training, or any training, is to clarify and measure that purpose or mission on an ongoing basis. By continually measuring your impact with the customer, you develop an unbiased, third-party opinion of how your organization is doing and how the things you do internally impact that mission."

The third most frequently mentioned indicator and method of measurement was the individual-performance contract. Essentially this is an agreement between the training participant and his or her boss about which performance differences should occur following training and how these differences will be recognized and measured. As James R. Cook, Practical Management Associates, Woodland Hills, CA, suggests, "No matter how good the training may be or how much learning occurs, the transfer of material from classroom to work is strongly influenced by actions and attitudes of the trainee's boss. Of course, other environmental elements, such as peer group expectations and organizational structures, are important, too. But the effect of these is often contingent upon, and mediated by the activities of the boss."

Scott Parry emphasizes that by using the personal performance contract in conjunction with training, we take advantage of "that most basic law of learning: People learn, not by being told, but by experiencing the consequences of their action."

Grote notes two other advantages of a boss/subordinate agreement about what the training should provide and how the results will be measured. "First," he suggests, "the boss is more likely to support the subordinate's use of the new behaviors if he and the subordinate have discussed implementation beforehand. Second, management support of management development is likely to increase, since to measure the results of management development, management must heed it, must make the decision that it is worth measuring.

Alchemy or Science?

A final, moderating viewpoint on the evaluation and measurement issue comes from Psychologist Chuck Bates, who teaches business and management courses at North Island College, British Columbia. Bates cautions that most current measurement and evaluation methods suffer from their susceptibility to the Halo or Placebo Effect. If you tell a manager that your seminar will make him a better manager and later ask him if you were right, you will invariably receive a positive answer. Often the manager will sincerely believe something good happened, but will be hard pressed to identify a specific change.

"What's the solution?" Bates asks rhetorically, and answers: "The alchemists provide a useful analogy. Most of them spent their lives trying to turn lead into gold, just as we squander our lives trying to turn bad managers into good ones. But a few alchemists had a better idea. Instead of shooting for the big prize, they limited themselves to studying only that which they could measure. They found the melting points of compounds and isolated a few elements. Their activity was mundane, but they laid the foundations for modern chemistry. The fellows trying for the flashy transmutations contributed nothing, and wasted their lives. Science has advanced only as fast as its measurement technology has advanced. "Someday, management development will be a science, too."

And as the opinions shared by our experts suggest, we aren't there yet, but we're getting closer.

How to Get the Most Out of 360° Feedback

Managers who find out how others see them:
(a) become willing to change
(b) become defensive and vindictive
(c) go back to business as usual

BY GARY YUKL AND
RICHARD LEPSINGER

Feedback from multiple sources, alias "360-degree feedback," is currently something of a rage among training professionals. Consultants and practitioners alike tout it as the optimal tool for enhancing leadership and management capabilities, particularly when a company is trying to develop a more open, communicative culture.

More than many developmental tools, 360-degree feedback can prompt real, measurable changes in managers' behavior. The reason is simple: When people receive honest, specific feedback from their bosses, colleagues and subordinates, they often come to understand how their behaviors affect others — and the need for change in some of those behaviors.

Yet like other "magic bullets," multi-rater feedback often fails to bring about the advertised effects. Too often, 360-degree feedback is a one-time event that is forgotten as soon as managers return to the hectic world of work. When this occurs, the problem usually lies with the type of feedback that's being asked for, and how it is gathered, displayed, interpreted and acted upon.

Generally, the process works like this: Questionnaires are used to gather information about managers' behavior from those in a position to witness it on a daily basis: direct reports, colleagues, bosses, and sometimes suppliers and customers. Managers then receive feedback reports that summarize the responses given on these questionnaires. In most cases, participating managers also get the chance to discuss the feedback they've received during workshops conducted by a facilitator.

Many stumbling blocks can blunt the effectiveness of this process. Most fall into two categories: the design and administration of the questionnaire, and the design and facilitation of the follow-up activities. You can increase the likelihood that real behavior change will result from your 360-degree feedback intervention if you follow these recommendations.

The Questionnaire

In selecting a feedback questionnaire, look for the following qualities:

- **Well-researched:** Empirical research should show how each behavior itemized on the questionnaire is related to managerial effectiveness. Solid evidence that the behaviors are relevant for success increases managers' interest in getting and using the feedback. Providing feedback on behaviors that are not actually linked to effectiveness is a waste of time and money.

- **Behavioral:** The items on the questionnaire should describe specific, observable behaviors. People have difficulty giving accurate feedback when the descriptions of behavior are vague and general (such as "structures the work roles of direct reports"). The items should describe concrete behaviors: "Explains what results are expected when a task is assigned," or "Tells you when a task you are doing needs to be completed." Specific items like these provide the basis for feedback that is easier for managers to interpret and use for improvement.

- **Positive:** Behaviors should be described in positive rather than negative terms. Avoid questionnaires with items like, "Yells at you for making a mistake." Better wording would be, "Helps you understand the reasons for a mistake and how to avoid making similar mistakes in the future." Some direct reports will be leery about reporting that their boss does something that is ineffective (even if he does so only occasionally); they are more likely to say he does not use an effective behavior frequently. Moreover, a questionnaire full of negative items tends to make managers feel defensive and less likely to participate voluntarily in the feedback process. Finally, feedback about ineffective behavior does not tell people what they should be doing — only what not to do.

- **Personal:** Whenever feasible, behaviors should be described in terms related to the individual answering the questionnaire. It is better, for example, to ask for a response to "This manager praises me when I carry out a task effectively" than to "This manager praises direct reports who carry out a task effectively." Respondents shouldn't be expected to hazard guesses about a manager's behavior with others. This kind of wording also gives a more accurate picture when the manager behaves differently toward different people. Of course, such wording is not appropriate for behaviors that involve more than one person ("Holds a special celebration after the group successfully accomplishes a project") or for behaviors the manager performs alone ("Reviews performance reports for the organizational unit").

- **Multidirectional:** Managers tend to behave differently with people depending on their organizational relationship with them. For example, our research indicates that managers use different patterns of influence behavior when they are dealing with

> Action planning encourages managers to take control of their lives and decide for themselves how to become more effective.

direct reports, with colleagues and with bosses. That's why feedback from different perspectives provides a more complete picture of a manager's behavior. But don't solicit 360-degree feedback about behaviors that are used exclusively in one type of relationship. Delegating, for example, is something managers do with direct reports. Colleagues and bosses generally will not have firsthand knowledge of a manager's delegating behaviors. Thus, you may need different versions of the questionnaire for respondents with different relationships to the manager. Each version should include only the behaviors that are relevant in that kind of relationship.

Administering the Questionnaire

A successful feedback system depends on enlisting the cooperation of a sufficient number of respondents who have knowledge about the manager's behavior. Managers need guidelines for how to identify appropriate respondents and gain their cooperation.

Some useful guidelines:

• **Select respondents carefully.** In most cases, the participating managers select respondents to fill out the questionnaires. This gives managers a greater sense of control over the process and increases the likelihood that they will accept the feedback. Some trainers worry that managers will distribute questionnaires only to their friends, but even friends will usually provide honest responses if they know their feedback will be held in confidence.

Still, advise managers to select a representative sample of people who are most critical to their effectiveness on the job. Also encourage them to identify people who are in a position to provide accurate feedback — ideally, those who have interacted with them on a regular basis for a year or more. Respondents should have had the opportunity to observe a manager's behavior for at least four months.

• **Ensure an adequate number of respondents.** The number of respondents should be large enough to ensure adequate sampling and to protect the confidentiality of the sources. You'll need at least three completed, usable questionnaires from subordinates, for example. Because some people invariably fail to return the questionnaire, the initial sample should be larger than the number of responses needed.

People asked to complete questionnaires also need guidance to help them provide accurate feedback:

• **Explain how the data will be used and ensure confidentiality.** People who are afraid of adverse consequences will be reluctant to fill out a behavior questionnaire, and, if they do complete it, they probably won't provide honest answers. This problem is especially acute when direct reports are asked to describe the behavior of a boss who is defensive or abusive.

To gain cooperation from potential respondents, explain the purpose of the survey, how the results will be used, and how confidentiality will be

> **Gather information about managers' behavior from those in a position to witness it on a daily basis: direct reports, colleagues, bosses and sometimes suppliers and customers.**

ensured. You might want to explain in a cover letter that the questionnaire results will be used to provide feedback, and emphasize that individual respondents' answers will remain anonymous. (One way to protect confidentiality is to ask respondents to mail their completed questionnaires directly to an external consultant who will analyze the results and prepare the feedback report.) Feedback should not be reported if there are too few respondents to protect individual confidentiality.

The boss's feedback presents special problems if it is displayed separately from other feedback. Obviously, the boss's feedback won't be anonymous. Although the power relationship reduces the risk of adverse consequences, the boss may decline to participate in the process out of a desire to avoid embarrassment or to avoid the perception that this is some kind of formal performance appraisal. It should be easy to get the boss to cooperate when the purpose of the feedback is purely developmental; the boss is able to provide relevant and unique information about the participant's behavior.

• **Help respondents avoid common problems in rating.** It's difficult to remember how much or how often a manager used a given type of behavior over the past several months. Instead, raters may base their responses on their general feeling about the manager. Thus, you may get a "halo effect" — that is, a manager who is well-liked may be given high ratings on all scales, regardless of her use of particular behaviors. Conversely, a manager who is strongly disliked may be rated negatively even on those behaviors that he performs often.

Another common bias ("attribution error") occurs when a manager who is known to be effective is rated highly on any scales the rater believes are relevant to effectiveness, regardless of the manager's actual behavior. For example, a manager may work well with individuals, but do little to build team spirit.

When raters fall victim to these biases, their feedback becomes less useful. Even managers who are very effective in general can benefit from identifying areas for improvement, but you'll have a tough time pinpointing their weaknesses if the feedback is biased.

You can alert raters to these biases, and urge them to rate each type of behavior independently. An even better solution is a short training session that teaches respondents to rate behavior more accurately. But rater training is costly and may not be feasible unless your organization plans to collect behavior ratings on a regular basis.

The Feedback Report

There are many different ways to summarize respondents' feedback, some of which are more useful than others. In general, however, the feedback report should:

• **Clearly identify feedback from different perspectives.** Behavior descriptions from different perspectives — direct reports, colleagues, bosses — should be presented separately. Aggregating feedback from different sources tends to make it more difficult to interpret. For example, if a manager tends to use consultation frequently with colleagues but seldom with direct reports, aggregate data will obscure that the manager treats people differently based on their relationship and position in the organization.

- **Compare feedback from others with the manager's own perceptions.** Most feedback reports compare what others say about a manager's behavior to self-ratings by the manager on a parallel questionnaire. Just going through the process of rating themselves helps managers understand the behavior scales better. Comparing their own ratings to those of others also helps managers interpret the feedback. A high level of agreement among the various raters confirms that the manager's self-assessment is probably accurate; large discrepancies suggest that someone is not perceiving behavior accurately.

Managers often rate themselves higher than others rate them. For example, a manager may indicate that direct reports are frequently praised for their accomplishments, whereas the direct reports report that they receive little recognition from the manager. This is exactly the type of discrepancy that should get the manager's attention and probably indicates a weakness to be addressed.

However, it's important to explore the reason for a discrepancy rather than jump to conclusions about it. Self-ratings may be higher because the manager is biased, his behavior may not be visible to the other raters, or the other raters may have interpreted the items differently.

A discrepancy in the other direction may also occur, but this is less common. For example, a manager may rate himself lower than others do on inspiring subordinates to greater efforts, perhaps because the manager does not realize the extent of his positive influence as a leader.

- **Compare the manager's ratings to norms.** It is difficult for a manager to know whether her score on a specific behavior is high or low without some basis for comparison with other managers. For example, our research shows that managers, in general, use rational persuasion very frequently when they try to influence others. Yet a below-average score on this behavior will not be obvious without the use of norms. Ideally, norms show where a manager falls in the distribution of scores for a large sample of managers. One good way to do this is to use a percentile score that indicates how many managers in the database got lower scores.

- **Display feedback for items as well as scales.** Most behavior scales or categories consist of several items. The behavior scale of "mentoring," for example, may consist of items such as: "Offers helpful advice on how to advance your career"; "Provides you with opportunities to develop your skills and demonstrate what you can do"; "Encourages you to attend relevant training programs, workshops or night courses to develop greater skill and expertise"; and "Provides extra instruction or coaching to help you improve your job skills or learn new ones."

Some feedback reports provide feedback for the scales, but not for the separate items that comprise them. Both types of feedback are useful.

> **Just going through the process of rating themselves helps managers understand the behavior scales better.**

Item feedback helps managers understand the behavior scales because the items provide specific examples for each category. Feedback on individual items also reduces problems caused by missing responses. Once the scale scores have been computed, the fact that different respondents skipped different items that make up the scale is camouflaged. Omitted responses may be counted as "never does" or not counted at all, but either way, blanks distort the overall scale score. Reporting results for individual items provides a more accurate picture of a manager's behavior and makes the feedback easier to interpret.

The best form of item feedback is a mean score for each item (the ratings from all respondents on the item are totaled and divided by the number of respondents). Some feedback reports also present the range of scores (highest and lowest), and even the distribution of answers from different respondents (how many people in each group selected each response). Again, the score distribution should not be shown unless there are enough respondents to protect the anonymity of individuals.

- **Provide feedback on recommendations.** Feedback questionnaires typically ask respondents to describe what the manager does, not what the respondent would like the manager to do. We have found that asking respondents for recommendations provides a useful supplement to feedback about observed behavior. In particular, these recommendations should show how many respondents said the manager should use the behavior more frequently, the same amount or less. This information helps managers interpret their behavior feedback and identify their strengths and weaknesses.

For example, even though a manager has a moderately high score on a behavior such as delegating to direct reports, some people may prefer even more delegation. Without the recommendation it would be hard to discover this opportunity for improvement. Occasionally, respondents think the manager should use a behavior less, although this does not happen as often if the questionnaire describes only positive behaviors. Because of the extra time required to complete a questionnaire that includes a section on recommendations, these questions should focus on scales rather than individual items.

The Feedback Workshop

Sometimes managers receive only a written report on 360-degree feedback, but it's better to have a facilitator explain the feedback and help managers use it to the best advantage. A feedback workshop with 15 to 20 managers is an economical way to use a facilitator. A number of workshop activities can help participants understand the feedback, accept it, and use it to improve their effectiveness.

- **Explain the purpose and benefits of the feedback.** Both the managers themselves and the people completing the questionnaire are more likely to cooperate if they know the feedback is to be used only for developmental purposes and not for evaluation of current performance.

- **Explain the underlying model of leadership and management.** The behavior questionnaire should be based on a theory of effective leadership that identifies behaviors important for managerial effectiveness. This theory should be explained to managers early in the workshop so that they have a basis for interpreting the feedback and focusing on its most important aspects. A good theory also helps managers understand the need to modify their behavior, depending on the specific situation and their objectives and priorities. If developing subordinates is a high priority, for example, more delegation is appropriate. Obviously, managers should delegate assignments more frequently to someone who is competent and trustworthy than to a person who is inexperienced or irresponsible.

• **Involve managers in interpreting the feedback.** In some feedback systems, computer programs provide a narrative interpretation of the feedback and tell managers what they must do to improve. Managers who are responsible for making decisions about millions of dollars of company assets may understandably resent having a computer tell them to change their behavior. With some assistance from the workshop facilitator, most managers are quite capable of evaluating their feedback and determining its implications; they also know better than anyone else about special circumstances that have affected their results. Moreover, allowing managers some room to interpret their results increases the likelihood that they will accept the feedback.

• **Emphasize strengths as well as weaknesses.** Research shows that people are more likely to reject feedback if it is consistently negative. The workshop facilitator should help managers keep a balanced perspective by stressing positive as well as negative feedback. The facilitator should emphasize that the feedback is intended to give managers a sense of what behaviors they should continue, not just what they should be doing differently. The facilitator also should be prepared to provide advice, encouragement and support to managers who are concerned about correcting weaknesses.

• **Ask each manager to develop an improvement plan.** Feedback is more likely to result in behavior change if each manager develops a specific improvement plan. This action planning encourages managers to take control of their lives and decide for themselves how to become more effective. Moreover, in combination with a leadership theory to guide the process, the action planning will help managers learn how to analyze the specific needs of their leadership situation.

Follow-up Activities

The benefits of a feedback workshop are more likely to be realized if supporting activities follow it. Useful follow-up activities include training, coaching and assessment of the feedback's effects.

• **Provide opportunities for skill training.** Skill training allows managers to learn how to improve their behavior, not just what behaviors need to be improved. You can tell a manager he needs to use influencing and inspiring behavior, but if he's not good at influencing and inspiring people, he's highly unlikely to get better at it without training that teaches him those skills. Training will also increase a manager's confidence about using the behaviors back on the job.

The feedback workshop can be expanded to two days to include a day of skill-building, or training can be provided in separate sessions at a later time. Considerations of time, logistics, participant needs, and the type of behaviors involved will determine the best approach. A combined feedback and training workshop takes longer to conduct, but the cost of travel, facilities and trainers may be lower for a combined workshop than for two separate ones.

• **Provide support and coaching.** Individual support and coaching for managers will help them apply what they have learned. One approach is to hold a follow-up session four to six weeks after the feedback workshop to review progress, discuss any difficulties the manager may be having, and provide encouragement and coaching. An alternative approach is to have managers meet with their bosses or with a human resource manager to review progress on their improvement plans.

• **Assess the effects of the feedback workshop.** One way to assess behavior change is to hold review sessions to discuss how well the managers have implemented their improvement plans. Another approach is to conduct a follow-up survey among the people who responded to the questionnaire for a specific manager six months to a year after the feedback workshop to assess the amount of behavior change. This way, the company gets valuable information about the return on its investment in feedback workshops, the facilitators get information they can use to improve the workshops, and researchers get an opportunity to learn more about leadership and training.

With all these benefits, you'd think it would be common practice to conduct follow-up evaluations of feedback and training workshops. Unfortunately, systematic evaluation is the exception rather than the rule. This situation may improve, however, as companies become more interested in measuring the return on their investments in training and development.

Over the years, we have learned a lot about using feedback effectively, but we still have much more to learn. Thousands of feedback workshops are conducted every year, but few studies evaluate them. We need more research to discover what works well and what doesn't.

Companies that conduct feedback workshops have an unprecedented opportunity to evaluate the effect of variations in how feedback is collected, presented and used. Many academics would welcome the chance to collaborate with practitioners in this area. It is time to begin exploiting the opportunities we have to advance our knowledge about this increasingly popular form of management development.

Teaching Johnny to Manage

Why doesn't most management training 'take'?
Maybe because it has no connection
to real life in your company.

BY ALEX MIRONOFF

In most organizations, teaching Johnny to manage has been a difficult, haphazard and often unsuccessful exercise. After years of watching several major corporations struggle with a variety of dubious approaches to management training, I venture to suggest an embryonic solution to the problem.

As a way of analyzing the management-training muddle, let's apply — informally and unmethodically — the Kepner-Tregoe principle of comparing a defective object with a similar object that does not have the defect. In this case, the similar, defect-free object is technical training.

Management training, in most organizations, differs from technical training in two important respects: (1) Management programs tend to be vastly more controversial and entertainment-oriented than technical courses, and (2) They don't word. At least, they don't work very well, considering the amount of money you're pouring into them.

I propose a seemingly simple solution — "seemingly simple" because, like most concepts involving management training, it is much easier to talk about than to apply. I've seen this one applied successfully, however, so I can offer a concrete example. First, though, let's look at technical vs. management training and observe some critical differences between the ways we approach them.

In Search of Reality

You could argue — lots of people do — that teaching people to manage is different from teaching them to use a personal computer. You could assert that managing people is a more complex activity, that people are really hard to understand, that management is a "soft" science, and so on. But in fact, PCs also are quite complex. I don't really understand how they do what they do. And I could develop training that treats PC operation as though it were a "soft" science. This last observation gets to the heart of the critical difference between our traditional approaches to technical and management training.

In management training we usually attempt to teach things that do not exist in the organization.

If we strip away the surface distinctions between technical and management subjects, we are left with the fact that in management training we usually try to teach things that do not "exist" in the organization. We teach ideas and behaviors that participants and top management alike view as nice to know, but essentially irrelevant to getting the job done. In technical training, on the other hand, we teach facts, ideas and behaviors that everyone clearly understands from the outset are intrinsic to the successful performance of the job.

Our personal-computer example is particularly apt here. A few years ago, when the hype for PCs was at its zenith, we saw an onslaught of generic "computer literacy" programs. They were designed not to teach people how to use any specific hardware or software applicable to their jobs, but rather to teach "bits," "bytes" and random snippets of programming languages to people with no real need or desire to know In technical training, such programs are aberrations, quickly corrected. Generic computer-literacy courses flourished briefly, then died

Can you imagine a company today spending vast sums of money to put its people through PC-training courses on hardware or software applications that the company does not have, does not intend to get and may not even believe exist? Is there a single profit-oriented organization in the country today that would consider funding a program such as "Concepts in Personal Computing"? Is there a training director who would dare ask for that finding?

In most businesses today, before trainers teach anybody anything about PCs, the company will have decided how they'll be used, who will get them, what brand will be the company standard, what software will be purchased and so on. Once management has made these decisions and committed itself to a course of action, trainers can teach the relevant concepts, procedures and skills. Employees usually will leave the training program with better capability to use the equipment that, you will recall, already is sitting on their desks and for which they have specific work applications. While we can certainly debate the design or effectiveness of the training program, there is no question about its relevance to the employees' jobs.

The picture is quite different for the typical management training program. First, companies regularly budget for courses with such nondescript titles as "The World of Management," "Effective Business Writing" or "Delegating to Motivate." These staples are routinely developed, purchased, or even worse, farmed out to fly-by-night seminar sponsors in the naive hope that Johnny will somehow see the light and be transformed. He'll stop flogging his people even though his own manager continues to flog him. He'll stop writing ponderous reports in tortured, bureaucratic language — even though the company considers such language "businesslike" and rewards people for using it. He'll become a better manager — whatever that is.

Second, the people who design management training courses ordinarily go to great lengths to avoid content that suggests there are right and wrong ways to manage. In this scheme of things, weaknesses are merely strengths amplified to a gross degree. Every management style is basically OK — even Attila's. Who knows when the fifth century will make an encore?

By contrast, when we teach PC operation, we show participants the three equally acceptable methods for issuing a particular command — and we tell them clearly that any other method will fail.

Most companies do not realize that they have effectively delegated policy-making in the critical area of acceptable management practices to the training department and to academic management theorists. And this is something that can not be delegated; trainers and academics have no authority to enforce the policies they establish or to reward Johnny for following them. The result is a costly, pointless exercise that raises two questions: Why do organizations persist in supporting this kind of training and what should they be doing instead?

Sticky Wickets

Part of the answer to the first question lies in the pervasive assumption that every civilized company provides management training. But I believe the plethora of generic programs that have no roots in organizational reality are a direct result of management's discomfort with making decisions about people issues. While managers are used to making decisions about products and equipment (often to a level of detail they would do better to avoid), they seem considerably less decisive in the unpredictable area of handling people. They would rather delegate this onerous chore to someone foolhardy enough to volunteer. Enter the human resources development department.

Having dropped this sticky wicket into someone else's lap, management wants to hear no more about it other than how many bodies were put through the training cure and at what price. Management's tolerance for more of the same then becomes a function of the company's current profit-and-loss picture ("Can we still afford this?"), the occasional trainee reaction ("I got a lot/nothing out of it") and, ultimately, the resulting change in performance ("If this training is so good, how come Perkins still acts like a horse's ass?").

It isn't surprising that so many management trainers spend no more than two to three years in the job just about long enough for the company to figure out that the training isn't taking and that it needs to be delegated to someone new.

This leads to the second question: What should companies be doing about management training? The answer is that they should do management training the same way they

> **Companies need to conduct management training the same way they do technical training.**

do technical training. They should train people only in concepts and skills that complement the existing hardware and software.

In the management realm, "hardware" and "software" refer to an organization's mission, values, policies, procedures, standards of performance — in other words, the sum of all those management decisions that give the organization its unique shape and distinguish it from a mere collection of people, housed together and engaged in some loosely related and — one hopes — profit-making activities.

Absent a clear mandate that defines the management philosophies and behaviors that best serve the organization's mission, trainers are reduced to presenting conventional wisdom or the musings of this season's management guru. If that's what is happening, then all of the methodological decisions that trainers agonize about are moot. Lectures, behavior modification, experiential exercises, video, computer-based training — they all make equally little sense or impact if participants do not recognize that the content is a formal, visible standard within the company

The acid test of a proposed management program is whether it conveys your senior management's actual position on a particular issue. It must be backed up by the personal examples of people at the top, by a plan of action and by a way to measure results.

For example, if you, as the trainer, are asked for a program on effective delegation techniques, your first question should be: What is this organization's policy about delegation?

Nobody in the executive suite can tell you? Nobody has time to talk it through with you so that you can prepare a valid program? Somebody does tell you, but you know from experience that the policy you're hearing about is a fantasy that bears no relation to the way things really work in this organization? Then you may as well forget the training. You have no subject to teach — that is, not if you're looking for any kind of significant, practical, high-impact outcome. If you merely want to prolong the agony, go ahead and design or buy a course on effective delegation. But start planning now for your next career move — or for an exciting future in court reporting.

Case in Point

I promised a concrete example of a training program that avoids the trap of being a nice-to-know in-house version of Management Sciences 101. The example comes from the company I work for.

It came as a pleasant surprise to find senior managers at Provident Life and Accident Insurance Co. who were eager to tackle people issues, and to use the human resource function in general and the training division in particular as vehicles for doing so. I repeat... To use the training department, not to delegate the policy function to it.

Last year, the Provident revised the performance planning and appraisal process. Top management planned the revision and determined the values that would underlie the new process, as well as its essential design features.

The performance planning and appraisal system was tied into revised job descriptions. Every employee had a written statement that described the accomplishments necessary to perform the job well. These statements would be the basis for the appraisals. Guidelines were prepared for the personnel policy manual that showed how to complete appraisal forms and conduct appraisal interviews. Only then was a training program developed to teach managers how to conduct performance appraisals.

All managers and supervisors

attended the program during a two-month period. Chairman and CEO H. Carey Hanlin attended the first program and demonstrated his support by telling participants "...the group that has been least effective are the people at the top...and the inadequacy of our performance appraisals begins with me...so I'm looking forward to participating in this program, too."

He spoke to virtually every class thereafter. He talked about his belief in the importance of the appraisal process and what he would like to see done differently in both the writing and delivery of future appraisals. On occasions when schedule conflicts made a personal appearance impossible, a videotape of his talk was shown.

The program included a comic video based on performance appraisal war stories from the company's employees and showed typical, unproductive approaches to the appraisal process. Videos showed executives conducting various phases of an effective appraisal interview. Critiques and role plays followed.

We also used the standard "how-to" exercises — how to write performance standards and supporting comments, how to interpret ratings and so on. But throughout the program, we made it clear to the trainees that this was the Provident's performance planning and appraisal system, and one of their major responsibilities as manager was to use it effectively. What's more, they would be held responsible for using it effectively.

The result was a program not in "Good Ways to Coach and Counsel" or in "Principles of Effective Performance Appraisal," but in the specific values, policies, systems and procedures to which the organization had committed itself. Coaching and counseling were covered, but not as freestanding topics. Principles of human relations were covered, but as a subset of a company system that already embodied those principles. The program didn't even have a properly jazzy name. It didn't need a name.

The course did not include evaluation forms or other internal measurements. The outcome of the program and the means for measuring its success became the appraisal forms themselves. More than 60 percent of the forms the human resources department received after the program contained significant new information on the employees' performance, while only 15 percent of reviews held prior to the program had had any written comments at all. The comments written in reviews conducted after the program tended to be precise and behaviorally or quantitatively phrased, while prior comments had been unspecific at best and, at worst, judgmental and accusatory.

For once it was possible to decipher what managers were really trying to tell their people. Fewer employees complained about the way managers handled performance-appraisal interviews. When complaints or poorly completed appraisal forms surfaced, human resource staffers — who now had the backing of senior management, as well as program and policy materials — directly questioned the responsible managers. The gap between training and application had been closed.

What About Johnny?

My underlying assumption is that Johnny really isn't doing a good job of managing. But don't blame Johnny. Chances are he was promoted into a management position after displaying good technical skills and an ability to think and talk in ways that led someone to believe that he had "management potential." Don't blame the training department, either. It probably has exposed Johnny to half-a-dozen courses explaining how ideal managers should think and act in a theoretical world.

The blame for Johnny's inadequacies as a manager lies squarely with the top managers of his company, who neglect their responsibility to define, update, communicate and demonstrate the organization's mission, values and management standards so that Johnny can understand them and the training department can elucidate them.

Training can only elaborate on that which already exists; it cannot create new behavior for an environment that will not support it. The sad truth is that precious few top managers are willing to take a stand on what constitutes desirable and undesirable management practices. Even fewer will go so far as to bring their reward and sanction system into line with their stated positions. That's one big reason why the solutions I'm proposing are easier to talk about than to do.

In a routine planning session with the senior management team of a previous employer, for example, I was amazed to discover that those managers put no stock whatsoever in the concept of situational leadership. Project managers, they maintained, should not be asked to adapt their leadership styles under any circumstances; it might unsettle them and make them even less effective than they already were. Why was I shocked? Because these same people, had sponsored about five years worth of management classes based on the Hersey-Blanchard situational leadership model. Nor did this discovery deter the training group from continuing to present Hersey-Blanchard as the way to go. The situation did not bother the executives much either, since they instinctively understood that nothing happening in training programs could possibly have an impact on the real world anyway.

The odd little marriage of convenience between training and top management at this company continued until downturns forced a purge of all "nonessential" functions. Training went first and the executives followed in due course. What these executives failed to recognize was that they were paid their handsome salaries to make tough decisions about which management norms would best serve the organization's mission. They were responsible for managing the corporate culture. What the training department failed to recognize was that it was neither authorized — nor paid— to make such decisions.

I fear this farce is being repeated in boardrooms across the country. The key questions for these executives are: Which management concepts and practices do you really believe will best advance your organization's mission? What is your role in ensuring that they are effectively defined, communicated and practiced?

Even less-than-optimal management approaches — if they are consistently understood, supported and communicated throughout an organization — can be taught and implemented with more effect than highly pedigreed academic theories that have no credibility in the company's ruling circles. If top managers would take the time to think through their beliefs on what management concepts and practices are essential to success in their businesses— just as they do when they decide which types of products and services to sell — training departments would be capable of achieving considerably more success in teaching Johnny to manage.

How Do You Know It Works?

Have you been asked to prove your management training is working? Are you stymied? This method can help

BY MATT HENNECKE

I sank uncomfortably into the too-soft chair in the marketing vice president's office and felt grateful for the momentary reprieve granted by his ringing telephone. While the VP upbraided an underling long distance, I rehearsed my plan for selling this corporate kingpin on the management training curriculum I had devised.

I had heard stories about the VP's brutal questions and the way he had methodically dismantled the proposals of others who had dared sit in this same chair. But I was ready. I had done my homework. I was prepared to reap the glory that had eluded so many before me. My plan was foolproof and I was young and overconfident. For the hundredth time I looked for holes in my logic and for the hundredth time felt sure my proposal could stand up against any onslaught.

I knew the VP would be impressed with the executive overview of the management needs analysis I had conducted within the company. I would recommend specific training programs. In response to his questions I would talk about standard deviations, random samples and all the other statistical mumbo jumbo I had learned in school. In short, I would blow his socks off with my iron grasp of needs analysis, training design and curriculum development.

I braced myself as his telephone conversation ended and he swung around and launched his barrage of inquiries about my proposal.

"Have you got the results of the management survey you conducted?"

"Yes, sir. Right here," I said, fumbling with the manila folder. He took the folder from me, opened it and began to scan.

"What training programs are you going to develop based on these results?"

"Well, I'm convinced we need to address the needs of our lower-level managers first," I said confidently. As you can see from the survey results, they need training in these areas. "I pointed out two or three indicated needs.

The questions continued to come hard and fast for the next 15 minutes. My logic was inescapable. My answers were convincing. My head was beginning to swell. And then, just as victory seemed assured, he asked the one question that put to flight my army of facts and logic.

"How are you going to prove that these programs are effective?"

Hit close to home? Make you squirm a bit? While this is a fictional scenario, many training professionals can probably sympathize with any unfortunate who is asked to prove the effectiveness of a management training program. As a profession we've gotten pretty good at assessing management training needs and developing programs to meet thems, but we have largely failed in our efforts to prove we have accomplished what we set out to do.

Most management trainers don't really know if their efforts are effective, and still fewer know how to evaluate a program's impact. But the day is coming (and already has arrived for some training departments) when we will have to convince others of our worth and justify our existence. I believe we can do it, but first, let me hedge a bit.

The approach I describe here is designed to prove behavior change as a result of training interventions, not bottom-line dollar impact on the company. Management is largely behavioral, and we may never be able to untangle causality enough to prove the impact of management training on the bottom line. But we can measure whether or not our training programs are changing a manager's behavior. If top management isn't satisfied with that, we'd better start dusting off our résumés.

Laying the Groundwork

Before you can begin to prove the behavioral effectiveness of your management training efforts, you need to lay some groundwork. Three components should be built into your training programs: a way to track attendance, specific objectives and peer-subordinate questionnaires.

Tracking System

Your first step should be to introduce a tracking system so you know who has and who has not attended your management training programs. Such data, while sometimes tedious to gather and maintain, is the foundation upon which program effectiveness is based.

Why? Because at some point in your efforts to prove the worth of your training programs, you will need to compare the behaviors of a target group (managers who have been through your training programs) with the behaviors of a control group (a similar group of managers who have not been through your training programs). Tracking provides the means for making such comparisons. If you aren't already doing so, start distributing attendance sheets at all of your training programs.

Program Objectives

Whenever I develop a management training program, I begin by deciding what the outcomes or objectives of the program will be. Similarly, when I purchase a training program I look at the outcomes promised by the vendor. I ask questions like, "What will the manager be able to do as a result of attending this session? What new beliefs, new knowledge and new skills will a manager possess as an end result?" Often, the promised outcomes are inflated, nebulous and unmeasurable. Less often they're clear, concise, behavioral and measurable. We shouldn't be surprised, however, by the diversity of training objectives because outcomes come in three varieties: affective, cognitive and skill/behavioral.

Training programs with affective outcomes attempt to change values and beliefs. As a result, their effectiveness is difficult to prove. "Rah-rah" motivational sales programs with balloons, funny hats and inspirational speeches are of the affective variety. They may have value, but the value may not be lasting or easy to measure.

Training programs with cognitive outcomes attempt to improve a person's knowledge by providing information. Such programs have objectives that identify what people will know as a result of attending a training session. Technical training programs often have cognitive outcomes and as a result are fairly easy to evaluate that is, you can test to see if the knowledge has been learned. If you are teaching someone the four steps for completing a form, you can measure their knowledge before, during and after the training to prove the effectiveness of your training efforts. You can even test periodically to see whether the knowledge has been retained. You cannot prove, however, that a person's new knowledge will produce a related change in skill level or behavior. Unfortunately, many management training programs impart information without attempting to change behavior.

Training programs that have skill and behavioral outcomes or objectives promise that trainees will be able to do certain things or behave in certain ways. Here again, the outcomes of technical training programs are fairly easy to observe and therefore to evaluate. It's easy to measure the speed and quality of an assembly line operator before, during and after a training program. All you need is a stopwatch and some quality standards. However, the behavioral outcomes associated with effective management are not nearly so obvious or measurable. Demonstrating that a manager is an effective delegator or motivator is much more difficult than demonstrating that an assembly line operator is maintaining quantity and quality standards.

So what does this all mean? Because management is largely behavioral, management training programs should emphasize skill and behavioral outcomes rather than affective or cognitive outcomes. Instead of making our managers aware of the theories of motivation (a cognitive outcome), our training programs should teach them specific motivational skills and behaviors. A manager who actually can motivate others is more valuable to a company than one who only knows the theories of motivation.

Try to rework or rewrite all the outcomes of all of the management training programs you have developed or purchased to reflect specific, observable behaviors; then deliver on those promises by teaching specific skills and providing ample practice. For instance, change the outcome of your motivation program from: "Upon completion of this program, participants will be aware of the complexity of motivation," to "Upon completion of this program, participants will be able to make positive reinforcement statements to their employees." Deliver on this rewritten objective by teaching managers how to phrase performance statements that will motivate their employees.

Peer-subordinate Questionnaire

The final component of the system for proving the effectiveness of your management training efforts may raise some eyebrows (and some blood pressures), but it is a powerful and, more importantly, reliable means of finding out how a manager is actually managing. My suggestion is a peer-subordinate questionnaire. Before you bail out, consider the following: Effective management is largely behavioral; therefore, training for managers should be behavioral; therefore, to evaluate management training we should find out if our training efforts are producing new behaviors.

Why a peer-subordinate questionnaire? Because it is a more reliable indicator of behavior and performance than self-assessments or boss assessments. According to Gary Latham and Kenneth Wesley, authors of *Increasing Performance Through Performance Appraisal* (Addison-Wesley, 1981), self-assessments and boss assessments of managerial performance consistently have proven to be unreliable, whereas peer and subordinate assessments of performance consistently have proven to be reliable and valid.

Consider this question: Who is in the best position to evaluate a manager's ability to manage — the manager, the manager's boss or those who are managed? Again, research shows that a manager's subordinates and peers can evaluate her ability to manage better than she can and better than her boss can. They are not merely observers of managerial behaviors; they are the recipients. Peer and subordinate evaluation of performance also is more reliable simply because more people are doing the evaluating, The more people who observe and evaluate the behavior; the more accurate their collective assessment will be.

Your peer-subordinate questionnaire should tie questions directly to the specific behaviors you are trying to teach in your management training programs. For instance, if an objective of your motivational training program is to teach participants "How to provide positive feedback to employees," then you include a question on the questionnaire such as, "To what extent does this manager provide positive feedback to employees?" The questionnaire provides the mechanism for proving that the behaviors you are teaching are, in fact, being observed by those who are in the best position to do so.

Putting It All Together

Once your tracking system is up and running, and your training program is teaching new behaviors, you can begin to use your peer-subordinate questionnaire to gather data to use for comparisons.

Let's say, for example, you want to see if the motivation program you conducted six months ago is having a demonstrable impact on the behaviors of the managers who attended. Select a target population of managers who went through the motivational training session and compare their collective and individual scores from the peer-subordinate questionnaire against a control group of managers who did not attend the motivation session. One word of caution: Don't use the same managers for your target and control groups when you evaluate other training programs. Instead, use your tracking system to help you select different groups of managers. This helps you avoid contaminating your results.

If your training programs are truly creating changes in behaviors, then the ratings received by the target group in both the motivation and leadership sections of your peer-subordinate questionnaire should, on average, be higher than the ratings received by managers in the control group.

TYING TRAINING TO THE BOTTOM LINE

We all know that an effective training department is one that ties its goals to the corporate strategy. But how does a training department create and maintain a curriculum that meets individual skill needs as well as overall strategic goals?

Let's face it: With suggestions and ideas coming from human resources development (HRD) personnel, employees, managers and outside experts, a curriculum can become a mishmash of overlapping and unfocused programs. Steven J. Zlotowski and James E. Peters of the Strategic Management Group Inc. (SMG), a consulting firm in Philadelphia, recommend using a two-dimensional "training matrix" to help focus and synthesize ideas into a training plan that addresses the skill needs of employees at every level.

One dimension of the matrix consists of the skill areas needed to advance the company's goals; the other lists the various groups of employees to be trained. The first step is to identify the target groups that need to develop specific types of skills. For instance, on the matrix in the figure here, a senior manager needs to develop competence in strategy formulation and management skills; a professional employee needs to focus on functional expertise and technical skills. Both need to concentrate on communications skills and personal development.

The next step is to develop programs and courses to address each skill area. And keep in mind that a particular skill area will mean different things to each target audience. For example, communications training for executives might include courses in public speaking and how to communicate the strategic plan. The course lineup for entry-level managers would cover topics such as team building and conducting performance appraisals.

In a SMG staff paper, Zlotowski and Peters recommend following a few basic strategies to develop and implement a curriculum that meets the goals of the matrix:

• **Reinforce fundamental skills.** This type of training ensures that employees have the basic skills they need to perform their jobs efficiently. It includes three distinct categories: nuts-and-bolts skills, such as training the clerical staff to use a particular word processing package or teaching new engineering techniques to a group of design engineers; people-management skills, such as developing the ability to communicate effectively with subordinates; and managing the "economics of the job," such as learning to give employees a financial perspective on the impact of their jobs.

• **Enhance individual excellence.** Provide employees with an understanding of the organization as a whole, and the direction in which it is moving. This orientation encourages them to think in terms of what needs to be accomplished instead of just performing tasks. It prepares them to handle uncertainty and accept greater responsibility, to think of themselves as idea-contributors rather than simply order-takers.

• **Accept bottom-line accountability.** Set benchmarks for measuring progress toward HRD goals. Assess each program in terms of how much trainees improved a particular skill — be it calibrating widgets or conducting selection interviews. These skill areas, in turn, contribute to results such as increased efficiency, lower turnover and improved customer service.

Bottom-line accountability is a philosophy, not just a dollars-and-cents measurement, say Zlotowski and Peters. It's a philosophy that can only exist if the HRD department supports and responds to the company's operating needs. It is by fulfilling these needs that training boosts profitability.

SIMPLIFIED TRAINING MATRIX

Group	Strategy Formulation	Functional Expertise	Communications	Management Skills	Technical Skills	Personal Development
Executives	✔		✔			✔
Senior Management	✔		✔	✔		✔
Middle Management	✔	✔	✔	✔		✔
Entry-Level Management		✔	✔	✔	✔	✔
Professional/Technical		✔	✔		✔	✔
Supervisory			✔	✔		✔
Operators/Manufacturing					✔	✔
Office Staff/Clerical					✔	✔

Is It Really Leadership Training?

You really want to teach your people to be more effective leaders? Then define leadership as the ability to get whole-hearted followers

BY JAMES C. GEORGES

Imagine being on the receiving end of a typical seminar on leadership. "OK, trainees, we have now covered all the materials. You've learned to parrot the labels we attached to what we told you are the key characteristics of numerous heroes in sports, politics and business. You've filled out two do-it-yourself psychological profiles, so you can now label your own leadership styles. You have been exposed to six different theories of leadership, as articulated by noted researchers and authors. We have fed you a smorgasbord of information culled from some old courses on management and communication that we found lying around — all of it jazzed up with the latest leadership jargon. You have studied situational strategies for exercising influences. You've got notebooks full of helpful reminders about how to do everything from run an effective meeting to conduct a legally defensible performance appraisal.

"Yes, I think that's everything. Now, of course, you'll have to go back to the job and practice all of these skills in order to make them your own. Work at it. And good luck!"

Practice these skills? Good luck, indeed. Luck is exactly what the graduates of most "leadership development" courses will need. Because they didn't learn the first thing about how to lead.

How do I know? How can you know? It's easy.

First, ask the trained people to give you a specific definition of leadership. What is it, and how do you know when you're demonstrating it? If you get a vague answer ("communicating a vision") or a lot of different answers, begin to worry.

Second, check the confidence levels of several trained people while they are performing a leadership skill that they supposedly learned. If they perform tentatively or unconvincingly, your concern should grow. They may have understood the concepts, but

> **If trained people have difficulty giving you a specific definition of leadership, you're in trouble.**

they didn't learn how to function effectively as leaders.

Finally, the best and easiest test of all: Observe the trained people at work. Do they get more followers after the training? That is, do they succeed in attracting the wholehearted support of others for whatever courses of action they favor?

No followers? Then no learners. That is the pure and simple measure of leadership.

Attracting Followers

A distinction often drawn between managing and leading is that leadership commands the follower's head and heart. That's true. "Followership" is always a decision based on both intellect and emotion. But this tends to draw us into a wonderland of abstractions, where "leadership" stands for every desirable quality under the sun.

If we really want to talk about leadership as a discrete skill — or set of skills — that can be improved by training, then the point of effective leadership training is: how to get a wholehearted follower, or followers, for any given course of action. Period. That's it. It's not how to be the best person you can be. It's not how to get more productivity out of people. It's not how to be a better supervisor or a better communicator or a more creative thinker. It is how to get from others their genuine "buy-in" — support, enlistment, ownership — for a given course of action. That is likely to result in any number of benefits — better teamwork, for example. But teamwork isn't leadership either.

Leadership is some ineffable quality? It's hard to pin it down? It's difficult to measure the impact of a leadership training course? Nonsense! Define leadership as what it is — obtaining followers — and you have a supremely measurable skill. You can always tell if and when you're successful at leadership. You can tell every time you commit yourself to an idea, a project or a course of action, and try to win someone else's support for it. If you got a wholehearted follower, you succeeded at leadership. If all you got was compliance or surrender, you failed. If you got increased resistance, outright opposition or apathy, you failed miserably. No followers means no leadership — not on this issue at this time.

Leaders at Risk

In other words, leadership places you at risk. It's something you can lose at. You often have to compete for followership, and the leader in any situation is the one who ends up with the followers. But the current direction of training tends to make competitiveness a dirty word — that is, when it means something that you, personally, do. The art is to make all sides win. But we're kidding ourselves if we think we can shy away from winning and still be effective leaders.

Do you really want to teach your company's people to be more effective leaders? Define leadership as the ability to get wholehearted followers. Stick to that point and build your curriculum around it. There's plenty of valid information out there about how to practice leadership as a skill.

Some of it may even be buried in the course you're teaching now.

Are Sales Training Results Measurable?

A dozen experts offer their answers to this controversial question

BY RON ZEMKE

It is very "in" these days to talk a tough bottom-line game. But HRD people in general and sales trainers in particular have long been sensitive to the need to prove their training and development efforts have a bottom-line payoff for their organizations.

Our 12 experts know full well that this concern is more than an academic interest or an ego trip for the sales trainer. There are jobs and budgets at stake. Big budgets.

The total yearly sales training expenditure (counting direct expenses, indirect expenses, and missed sales opportunities) for most Fortune 500 companies runs easily into the millions.

And as Homer Smith, president of the National Society of Sales Training Executives (NSSTE), reminded us, "During economic periods such as the one we've just come through, sales training departments that cannot prove their profitability invariably feel the austerity ax."

It's a simple law of survival: In a crunch, the frills go. If sales training can't prove its profitability, it's a frill. When the sales training function isn't being effectively measured, the sales training budget is just as vulnerable as the advertising budget, suggests Sales training consultant Jack Snader, president of Systems Corporation. John Wolf, president of John Wolfe Institute, reminds us of the executive who complained that half of his advertising wasn't doing a damn bit of good; but he didn't have any idea which half.

A budget crunch makes his reduction formula easy: "Cut it by 50 percent." The only irrefutable way to combat this sort of whimsy is with hard data.

But Measurement Isn't Easy

To be sure, a problem identified can be a problem solved. And, if a lack of measured results is the problem, the solution is to go measure some results. Right? Not necessarily, contended some of TRAINING's panel of experts, who were quick to add that a lack of measured results doesn't necessarily point to a lack of effort or will power. "No trainer, in good conscience, could remain in his job if he didn't believe that his or her efforts made a contribution to the company's profitability," asserts George J. Lumsden, manager of sales training at Chrysler Corp. But, Lumsden goes on, "measuring is often difficult or impossible. Do a lot of training in a bad market, and sales go down. Do a little training and have a hot product, and sales go up. On a short-term basis, it is hard to evaluate training's relationship with profitability, except in those rare and unique circumstances where exceptionally rigid controls can be applied and the results carefully monitored."

And upper management is often uneasy with the call to spend money proving an already expensive program's worth. According to F.C. "Bud" Rebedeau, president of Kielty Rebedeau and Associates, "Every sales trainer has had the experience of involving line management in the program design to the extent they *know* the process is excellent and won't allow the delay necessary to test it on a control group. 'It's good they all need it now. Take it to the field,' is the mandate given."

In addition to this "permission to prove" problem, our experts point out two other make-or-break considerations. A measurement effort can go bust if the "what to measure" and "how to measure it" questions aren't attended to carefully from the outset.

As Russell Baker pointed out in one of his columns in the *New York Times*, when it comes to "bottom-line thinking," one person's bottom-line is often another's middle muddle. This sage counsel in hand, we looked to see exactly where our experts placed the bottom we're supposed to be measuring.

Each of our experts had a number of specific suggestions regarding measures of sales training effectiveness. NSSTE president Homer Smith and Jim Evered, manager of marketing education and development at Redman Industries of Dallas, together suggested 26 potential indicators of training impact (see accompanying article on p. 115). Of the more than 30 indicators suggested by the total, five are strictly money measures.

How to Look at It

The emphasis of panel members tended to be on the development of continuous measurement systems for obtaining input on the effectiveness of a sales training effort. None of our experts was willing to advocate measuring only one indicator or measuring results only one way. As Larry Wilson, CEO of Wilson Learning Corp., puts it, "We've grown beyond the mentality that called for doing one big, mind-bending experiment or test which was supposed to prove that process or product A is better than process or product B.

"When someone asks if A is better than B, we know that saying 'it depends' is really the most honest answer there is."

Bearing in mind this preference on the part of every panel member for multiple indicators and continuous measurement, it was still possible to find differences in preferred measures and methods among the experts we polled. Four basic tactics could be distilled: experimental, critical incident, problem-solving and MIS.

The Experimental Approach

This emphasizes comparing trained and untrained, or pre- and post-trained people (or some combination of both) on one, two, or more measures of sales performance. The indicators measured are usually agreed upon ahead of time by a joint sales management and training group, and the results are compared in some statistical fashion after a reasonable period of time has passed,

The New Training Library ———————————————————— *Evaluating Training's Impact* **113**

during which the trained people have had a chance to show their "new stuff." While most of the panel members mentioned this quasi-scientific approach (which is the technically correct term for this sort of research), all were less enthusiastic than they would have been a few years ago, having become cognizant of the shortcomings of uncritically transporting the laboratory experimenter's tools into the "real world." There are so many possible variables in the sales situation that both positive and negative correlations can occur by chance, especially if you're only measuring a single outcome, such as sales closed, cautioned many of the panel. Put another way: You can't necessarily rely on statistical results to prove your program's worth.

Ian E. McLaughlin, president of Training and Education Consultants Inc., brings the point home with this story: "When I was training director for Del Monte Corp., I once ran a before-and-after test to prove the value of a district training program. We did an outstanding needs analysis, put on a terrific program and the results were topnotch. The following three months saw this district move to the top third in sales of the item we wanted to see an improvement in. I turned in a report showing dollar increases and everything else I could think of.

"Then the deluge! The product manager claimed credit for his support of the effort. The local sales manager said he had concentrated his efforts on the item after our workshop, and he claimed credit. The regional sales manager said obviously if headquarters wanted a sales workshop on one item, it must be important, so he exerted pressure on the item. All in all, I learned several lessons from the episode:

"First, as training director I should never purport to take sole credit for increased sales results — and sometimes maybe not even a little bit of the credit. Second, profitability is never a one department or one action result. Training should be built into marketing plans just as are advertising and promotional activities. Training is part of the total action plan, not a poor relative and not a panacea. Third, a better measurement for me is having a trainee return home and a few weeks later write, 'Hey, I followed your ideas and I just closed the biggest sale of my life! Thanks!'"

George Lumsden's advice was a bit more blunt: "Our training department would no more lay claim to the fact that we were responsible for Chrysler's resurgence in the current year any more than we would accept blame for our problems a year ago." A good touchstone, to say the least.

Another problem with treating a sales training program as an experiment is the hidden costs of such an evaluation. Although John T. Golle, president of Gelle and Holmes Corp., strongly recommended cost/benefit studies ("Proper evaluation/valida-

---

Your best ROI measures may be testimonials from employees about how training helped boost their performance.

---

tion studies are crucial in helping top management decide where resources are best applied and what the ROI will be as a result"), he also emphasized that management must be aware of the costs which will be incurred: "There are two definite costs associated with the measurement of sales gains. One is the cost of analysis — EDP charges, time spent, and related out-of-pocket dollars. The second cost is the cost of opportunity loss. Sample and control groups have to be allowed to run at least six months. This means that the company is not benefiting in total should an improvement be validated. One of our clients discovered at the end of their six months' validation period that they were 'losing $75,000 per day' by not having the entire company trained."

"Scientific measurement may not be wholly necessary," argues John Wolfe of John Wolfe Institute. "Sales training is rarely an isolated activity. Usually it's employed — along with advertising, promotion, public relations, etc. — by management that is farsighted enough to recognize the value of all these marketing tools."

Take American Express as just one case in point, says Wolfe. "At one time, years ago, they almost went out of the credit card business because their competition seemed invulnerable. Then they decided (under new division management) to turn things around. So they hired a new topflight ad agency; they upgraded their personnel; they embarked on an aggressive PR program; and they hired me to train their salesmen. Result? Within a year their billings had increased $53,000,000! What part of that $53,000,000 increase was I responsible for? Darned if I know!"

The Critical Incident Approach

Some sales trainers prefer to solicit and collect specific incidents or stories of improved performance from the trained population to show the effectiveness of their training efforts. At first blush, this may seem a self-serving, "war stories" ploy. It can, however, when applied under the proper controls, be most useful. Dr. John Flanagan developed the concept of the critical incident technique during World War II when he was looking for methods of improving Army flight training. When his approach (as improved by industrial psychologist Marvin Dunnette and others) is used, quite a bit of evaluative information is generated. Larry Wilson sees a well-designed sales indicator or incident collecting system as "one way to break out of the activity-reporting trap" and as "a potent way of systematically and logically tying results to objectives in an ongoing fashion."

Moreover, as Chrysler's George Lumsden believes, this collecting of apocryphal data can make an impression on management: "In 1975, when the automotive industry was struggling for each sale, we produced and put on a special training program for retail salesmen. One feature of this program was that each student, at the close of the conference, was given a textbook and a workbook. He was to read the text, complete the workbook, and send the final quiz in for evaluation. A certificate was promised.

"The student response was greater than we anticipated. We plowed through the papers and issued the certificates. And with each certificate we also sent a card asking two questions. 'How many cars have you sold since you attended the conference?' 'How many of these did you sell as a result of ideas you picked up at the conference?' This put a measurement of sorts on the program — a measurement we were happy to have.

"Salesmen would report, 'I have sold 32 cars since the training program. I sold 12 as a direct result of ideas picked up.' Or, 'I have sold 12 cars since the program. All 12 were sold as a result of the training I got because I was brand new when I attended.' Or, 'I sold 16 cars since the training...maybe two of them as a result of what I learned.'

"We took them all — good and bad. The average net gain was 6.5 cars per salesperson. Multiply that by the nearly 2,000 salesmen who attended, and if that doesn't show up on the bottom line, we'll quit training. The data impressed us, and our management, too."

The Problem-Solving Approach

Many of the 12 experts interviewed take a very hard stand against generic training and the "training-for-training's-sake" approach to sales training. Commensurate with that view of sales training, they see the attempt to evaluate a "training-cause-it's-good-for-you" effort as just another piece of the cosmetic cover-up. "Bud" Rebedeau frames the philosophy of the problem-solving approach this way: "The contribution to profits is easily measured if the sales trainer is involved in identifying, quantifying, and solving high-priority problems. These kinds of things easily lend themselves to pre- and post-measurement. A program specifically designed to correct one or two of these problems at a time — dramatically and with high visibility — contributes to bottom line. The 'rifle approach,' with pre- and post-documentation of facts, is impressive at budget time. Courses in general salesmanship and sales management can't compare."

J.D. Staunton, director of manpower resources development for National Starch and Chemical Corp., expresses the view this way: "The key to measuring the results of sales training is the development of 'needs objectives.' If training programs are based on clear objectives that have been developed by careful needs analysis, and which are directly related to profit-producing performance or behavior, then the results of training will invariably be quantifiable."

The problem-solving approach is bound up with the concept of "front-end analysis." As Jack Snader puts it: "All too often, we find that many clients have requested our doing a training program for which there is no real training need. By doing a "front-end analysis" we find that we can frequently show a client that there is no real training problem and thus the performance problem can be solved by a change in the environmental or administrative systems and procedures or by reevaluating some motivating factors affecting sales performance.

The most concise statement of how the problem-solving approach to sales training functions came from Paul H. Chaddock, director personnel development and management man — power planning at J.L. Hudson Co: "For a sales training department to make a measurable contribution in terms of bottom-line impact, it must be allowed — and willing — to accept the role of a performance problem analysis agency, not a purveyor of prepackaged programs. Within the context of this specific role, the contribution sales training makes to bottom-line *can* be measured. According to Hudson, the measurement rests on five assumptions:

1. Sales training as a function is most effective in impacting bottom-line results when it is aimed at changing behavior to create specific performances required by the organization.

2. Some unsatisfactory human performance is caused because people do not know how to perform.

3. When people do not know how to perform, some type of learning/training experience is appropriate. This assumes that the training is designed against performance objectives which, when operating, produce organizationally required results.

4. If people in the organization know how to perform but are not performing, training them (as described in Assumption No. 3 above) will probably not change those results for any sustained period of time.

5. However, if the sales training department does analyze organiza-

---

WHAT TO MEASURE TO DEMONSTRATE THE EFFECTIVENESS OF SALES TRAINING

Making a hard-data connection between your training and the black ink on the P&L isn't easy — but clearly necessary if your long-term goal is to have HRD efforts considered as integral parts of the company's or division's operating activities. Demonstrating that connection requires measuring the right activities. What to measure? *TRAINING*'s panel of top sales executives offered the following criteria as thought-starters for deciding what you might measure to demonstrate the effectiveness of your training:

- salesforce turnover
- sales volume
- absenteeism
- average commission per sale
- product mix
- average sale size
- number of calls
- calls-to close ratio
- customer complaints
- reduced training time
- implementation of promotional activities

- new accounts per unit time
- percent of objections overcome
- volume increase for existing accounts
- volume of returned merchandise
- improvement of call quality
- improvement in rank position of the trained unit
- reduced cost of training
- sales-to-travel ratio

- new-to-old account ratio
- competitive investigations
- sales-to-phone call ratio
- complaint letters
- compliment letters
- development of new product demand
- customer satisfaction ratings
- items per order
- redits-to-collections ratio

tionally required results in terms of current employee behavior and its causes, sales training is in a position to identify causes of undesirable or inappropriate performance. By recommending solutions for line management to consider, sales training can impact bottom line results.

"If these assumptions are valid, then sales training personnel can impact bottom-line results by designing learning in training experiences or by making operational recommendations to line management."

The Management Information System Approach

A few of our experts suggest that measuring the effects of a single training program per se doesn't address the complete issue. This viewpoint holds that looking at the impact of sales training, or any other development activity, should simply be part of an ongoing performance tracking and feedback system. Clark Lambert, manager of professional development at Doubleday and Company sees measurement of bottom-line impact as simply part of such a personnel management philosophy: "The training department is no different from any other operating group of a company. Any worthwhile professional development program for sales personnel is probably doomed to failure, unless the basic principles of good management are observed....*planning, implementation and control.*

"Assuming you start with a carefully defined program based upon a sales need," says Lambert, "and all other factors have been considered (such as costs, training time required, degree of difficulty, etc.) it is now mandated to build in new or revised measurement tools." The following short-term and long-term measurement factors are the sorts of things needed for tracking a program:

1 Attitude: Observation of the trainees, both during the training period and several weeks afterward.

Done through the regional and district managers, and reported to home office via call reports (a short-term measure).

2 Sales performance during sales call (after training): (A) Observed Perfor-

---

Performance doesn't improve without feedback, and that applies to sales training in spades.

---

mance: When manager makes a call with the salesperson, and later completes evaluation form for home office; (B) Non-observed: Salesperson reports specifically on success that is achieved using new training skill via call report.

3. Sales conferences: Through the use of role-playing at conferences, the new skills can be observed and positively reinforced.

4. Through revised call reports: When you build a sales training program with specific learning objectives, make certain that your weekly field call reports reflect this. If your forms are obsolete, redo them. Nothing is more motivating for a salesperson who is becoming more proficient than to be able to report it and be acknowledged for it by the home office. You must know beforehand what types of measurement will be needed, then tailor your continuous and short-term control devices to provide yardsticks for performance analysis. In my book, that's how you look for a definite contribution towards the bottom line."

So Where Does that Leave Us?

Clearly, it is possible to measure bottom-line results of a training effort. Just as clearly, "the profitability of sales training must be measured if an organization conducts such an activity," summarizes Man Master, general manager of the career training products division of Westinghouse Learning Corporation. "Otherwise," says Master, "there exists no justification for the existence of a training function."

But just as surely, as Master and the other panelists admit, there is no one best way to do it, only the way that works best for what you are trying to accomplish. The thread that ties our experts' opinions most closely together is that the effort must be made if we want to get better at what we do. Performance doesn't improve without feedback, and that applies to sales training as well as to individuals.

Lest you take the challenge of measuring the bottom-line on next week's seminar too seriously, though, George Lumsden offers this important perspective: "Training is not like a paper napkin — use it, and it's used up. Training has a residual quality that makes it more valuable as time goes on. It's often stored away for future use. It's often re-woven into a functional item far different from what was originally intended. If we train only for immediate and short-term results, we are missing some long-range potential. Training does show up on bottom lines — if not tomorrow, at least next year!"

Notes:

Build Plenty of Evaluation into Your Sales Training — Early

A demanding training schedule — with frequent evaluations — can help you determine the winners and losers early in the game

BY BRIAN O'HARA

Sales trainees must be more closely evaluated during training than any other employees in a company. That's because it's often difficult to relate their performance the first few months to their potential energy and ability levels. And that's why you need a demanding training schedule — with frequent evaluations — to give you insight into what kind of a person you hired. If trainees perform poorly on tests, do not demonstrate an ability to learn, and prove to be more "takers" than "givers," fire them now and save yourself months of frustration and payroll costs. Regardless of their track records, these trainees may not be able to sell a particular product line, adapt to the new employment environment or relate effectively to the new boss.

Here, then, are some ideas that can help you successfully train and evaluate your next new salespeople. First, you must consider how you can convince the trainee of the importance of the skill to be learned. One way is to relate success stories of people the trainee has already met in your organization who are using this skill. Display the irresistible logic of the skill through role playing. Show materials your company has generated based on its belief in the utilization of this skill.

What approach is most likely to motivate the sales trainee to master various skills? You should impress on the trainee that skill competency will be closely evaluated and tested. Stress how mastering a particular skill will improve chances of promotion.

The logical sequence for demonstrating the execution of a certain skill begins with outlining the necessary points involved in skill mastery. Test the outline. Teach all facets of product knowledge associated with the skill. Tell success stories that relate to the skill. Role play, with the trainee assuming the role of the salesperson.

Show Is Better than Tell

How, when, and where will you show the trainee how to perform this

> **Stress to sales trainees how mastering a particular skill will improve their chances of promotion.**

skill? The most widely used approach is videotaped role plays. Most trainees realize, however, that role playing sessions are, at best, simulated. Although the positive results of the sales presentation appear to be realistic, they do seem somewhat artificial. On the other hand, a successful sales call with the trainer has a strong impact on the trainee.

What will you look for when you work with your new salesperson? While experienced salespeople should be measured purely on results, the trainee should be measured solely on technique. Is he practicing proven techniques the way they were demonstrated? Does he follow the proper sequence you outlined? Is he attentive to detail, and does he react properly to changes from the prospect?

How will you determine if the trainee continues to perform adequately? The salesperson's reports should indicate both successes and failures. Occasional follow-up conversations with his prospects should indicate whether he is performing properly. Written tests in sales meetings will indicate if skills and techniques are being properly employed.

Stick to the Basics

1. Keep in daily contact with the new trainee for at least the first six weeks. Get him to tell you about his sales calls in detail — what things worked and what things didn't. Review successes and failures and the reasons for each.

2. The most effective training occurs daily on the job. The salesperson employs the skills he has learned during training and grades his results after the sales call. He must constantly evaluate his own performance. To become a "pro" he must perform well and know why.

3. Trainers can only partially solve training problems. Don't assume that the trainee's failure in a particular area is your fault. Remember, the burden for performance is on the trainee, who has to prove himself. Make it clear during training that he has an obligation to discuss any problem areas with you and that he's totally responsible for his own success.

4. Separate product training and sales training. Product training must revolve around features, advantages and benefits. It also emphasizes the technical aspects of the product. Sales training revolves around techniques, success stories, demonstrations and philosophy. Don't confuse the two; personality needs are entirely different.

Chart Progress

Progress reports tell the salesperson exactly where he stands and what he must do to improve. Daily and weekly reports help you monitor activities and guide your trainees to success.

Don't be afraid to ask for the basics and to emphasize their importance.

YES, YOU CAN EVALUATE BOTTOM-LINE RESULTS

BY RON ZEMKE

One school of thought holds that training outcomes should be measured solely on the basis of in-class learning and trainee satisfaction. Those holding this viewpoint contend that the multitude of variables affecting bottom-line outcomes makes attempts to calculate return-on-investment from training an unrealistic effort. The opposing view, the "bottom-line results" school, holds that: (a) the only training results important enough to measure are economic impact results and (b) difficulty in measurement is no excuse for not measuring.

Which school of thought you adhere to depends a lot on the assumptions you make about management, appropriate staff-line relationships, accountability, teamwork, survival and what you think you can get away with in that order.

Regardless of your allegiance, a study comparing evaluation measures should interest you. The study, conducted by Gary Rosentreter, manager of training and organizational development, Brown and Williamson (B&W) Tobacco Co., Macon, GA, compared the utility of four economic indices in evaluating the results of an interpersonal communication program.

The population for Rosentreter's study was 68 department managers, each of whom supervised a small first-line work group (16 - 38 people).

Managers were assigned randomly to training or no training conditions. The managers assigned to the training condition met in small groups (10 - 12 individuals) with an instructor, three hours a day for a week, and studied communications. The purpose of the training was to develop communication skills for goal-setting. The specific objectives were to:

• Increase self-awareness of personal communication style.
• Help identify effective responses in communication.
• Build a repertoire of responses to feelings and expressions of interpersonal communication.
• Build a response repertoire that was specific, confronting and respectful.

The methods used to meet the objectives were filmed speakers and case studies, simulations, role plays, lectures and group discussions.

Rosentreter measured results using what Campbell and Stanley call a "pre-test/post-test control group" design. Specifically, Rosentreter measured:

• Employee turnover.
• Employee tardiness.
• Number of "level-two" employee grievances.
• Department manager's performance appraisal ratings.

These measures were taken before training and six months after training for both the trained and nontrained groups. Rosentreter found:

• Significant difference in employee turnover between managers who received communications training and those who did not.
• No significant difference in hours of employee lateness, number of level-two grievances or managerial performance appraisal.

Rosentreter proceeded to test the economic benefit of the change in turnover. The Brown and Williamson personnel department calculated the cost of replacing an employee to be $62.33. Thus, the estimated total incremental cost savings to B&W from the lower turnover rate during the six months after the training was $3,429.80. The cost of the training was $1,300.00. The total incremental cost savings for the six-month period was, therefore, $2,129.80.

Though the training was popular and had some significant performance outcomes — for example, decrease in turnover in the work groups of trained managers — the actual economics of cost versus savings give the "go/no go" decision an added dimension.

The importance of Rosentreter's study is not, as he emphasizes, the actual outcome in terms of the change — or lack of it — in the four indices studied. It is, rather, the fact that both important managerial performance outcomes and economic criteria can be used to evaluate the benefit of a training program.

(Originally reported as "Evaluating Training by Four Economic Indices," in *Adult Education: A Journal of Research and Theory*. Vol. 29, No. 4, Summer 1979.)

Chapter 6
Using Technology to Enhance Evaluation

If Used Correctly, Technology Can Reduce Cost of Evaluation

Technology can help you measure training's impact more cost-effectively — but you must change the way you think about evaluation first.

BY ELLIOTT MASIE

If we're honest, we know that much of our training evaluation is intuitive and focused more on the process than the outcome of learning. The majority of training evaluations are really perception ratings: Did the instructor cover the material? Were the handouts effective? Even an end-of-class test or exercise only measures "in-class" learning, not actual learning transfer or the ability to perform a new task back on the job.

The problem, of course, is money and time. It's expensive to effectively measure transfer, and it takes a considerable amount of work on the part of the training department, the learner, and the learner's manager.

Fortunately, technology can help you measure training's impact more effectively, but you must change the way you think about evaluation first. Here are a few examples:

Multi-Point Continuous Assessment

The training department of a major banking institution sends new hires an e-mail message each day for three months containing a question about their job, computer system, or corporate policy. Some of these test items require the employee to ask their manager or colleagues for additional information, thereby extending the learning process. The answers are due within 24 hours and a copy is sent to their manager.

Knowledge Mapping

A software-based "knowledge map" is provided to each new employee prior to a training event. This is a database of literally hundreds of skills and information sets that are expected of them. The first step is for them to mark the items that they feel they know already. Marking some of these items triggers an immediate test question to verify their

> **Training managers may soon have an "on-screen map" of each learner that indicates her progress through certain training modules.**

knowledge, other items ask them to indicate their level of confidence in knowing the item. The knowledge map is then used throughout training. Employees revisit it at each major module and at the end of class. The learner is asked, with the manager verifying, to update the knowledge map six weeks after the class is over. Additional training needs are collected at that time, including examples of how they have used knowledge sets on the job.

A knowledge map can be constructed using a simple CBT authoring tool, or even developed in a database or groupware environment.

In-Class CBT

In a traditional classroom, the same exercise or practice activity is used with all students. This allows for easier classroom management, but a new computer-based classroom model is emerging that will have an impact on assessment. During practice segments in a computer-based classroom, the learner is actually proceeding through a CBT program of testing and reinforcement that allows the instructor to gather more data on the actual levels of accomplishment for each learner.

Watch for these improvements in the computer-based classroom model:

- **Electronic trainer administration tools.** Trainers will soon have an on-screen map of each learner that indicates their progress through the exercises and the types of items that need additional remedial time.
- **Post-class CBT disks.** These would allow the learner to continue to practice and test their knowledge. They could be linked into the e-mail model described above.
- **Project-based CBT questions.** In an ideal world, the manager of each learner would provide a real-world project that could be incorporated into the CBT database. The learner would actually work on and answer questions related to this assignment.

Certification

This is one of those movements that has tremendous potential, but equally enormous risks. The potential lies in our ability to hold learners and their managers, as well as training professionals, truly accountable for the outcomes of training. If we were able to test each learner on their actual transfer of knowledge, we could make better training investment decisions. In addition, we would be able to link learning transfer to performance assessment and compensation.

The risk lies in our ability to actually measure transfer. Technology-delivered testing often leads us to rely too heavily on multiple choice exams, where test-taking skills can be as important as the knowledge set being tested. Premature testing is often employed, where the learner is tested at the end of the class, rather than after using the skills on the job.

In the future, certification will be a blend of continuous assessment, portfolio evaluation (for example, a collection of examples of the learner's work projects), and managerial observation. Technology will be used to drive this process, to make it easier and to provide multiple points of assessment.s

HOW KEYPAD RESPONSE SYSTEMS CAN IMPROVE YOUR TRAINING EVALUATIONS

BY SCOTT HEIMES

Distance learning instructors are discovering that keypad response systems can be invaluable training evaluation tools, and many are beginning to use the technology in traditional classroom courses.

Keypad response systems allow instructors to eliminate written final tests and the associated hours of number crunching required to compile scores and determine course effectiveness. They also provide instructors with instant feedback throughout a course so they can adjust class material to suit the exact needs of the students.

Fiona Law, business and computer consultant at CompuTouch Ltd., uses the OptionFinder interactive keypad system made by Option Technologies Inc. to poll students throughout a four-day software workshop. Questions are projected before the class on an LCD projection panel that is linked to a PC, and everyone is asked to respond anonymously using their handheld keypad. "This makes the feedback timely, and ensures a high response rate, but doesn't take up a lot of time," says Law.

The responses of all participants for each question are instantly displayed in graph form on the projection panel so students can see how many people responded to each of the options, and instructors can tell how well the material is being absorbed by the group.

"Right away I can identify which concepts need further work and how widespread the haziness is," says Law. She uses this feedback to determine whether the whole class needs further review on specific material or whether to meet with the few who are having problems at a separate time. It also helps her develop the most efficient delivery method for the student population and shape course material for future workshops.

Reduce Training Time by 35%

Gary Connor, director of sales training for Pitney Bowes in Atlanta, has shaved 35% off his delivery time by using the Respondex keypad system from Socratec. He gives students a pretest before each learning module to determine whether they need to cover the material and how much time they need to spend on it. The system can be automated to skip a section if a large percentage of the class got the pretest answers right, or return to the subject matter if a certain number of students fail the post test, says Connor. He can also program it to randomly choose students from the class to answer a question or have it seek out a specific student profile — someone who got the last three answers wrong for example.

Connor and Law say using a keypad response system for training evaluation offers many advantages:

- **Keypad systems give you instant feedback.** As soon as students answer a question, the information is immediately compiled and reproduced on screen in a graph format. There is no collection of paper surveys and collating of results, and no hounding participants to return their surveys, says Law. Preparation time is less than a written questionnaire and questions can be augmented according to student participation and comprehension during the workshops.

- **Questions are posed while the instructor still has time to do something about it.** The immediate feedback during a session allows instructors to customize each course to fit student needs and perfect course material.

- **Participants see themselves as part of a group.** Showing graphs of how many people got the right or wrong answer lets students know they aren't alone in their confusion. "It encourages people to ask for help or clarification," says Law.

- **Response rate is much higher.** Although not everyone may answer every question with an electronic evaluation, the response rate is often 100%. The system tracks every question and answer, and can also print out individual reviews for each student with test scores and specific learning deficiencies.

- **Retention rates improve.** Connor has seen a 15% to 25% increase in retention with the keypad system. Students pay closer attention because course material is more focused on their needs.

Training Tip

If you are going to use a keypad response system for evaluation during course delivery, make sure you have a plan to deal with unexpected data. For example, if you discover half of the class doesn't understand the material, have alternative activities for them to work on. Or, if everyone already knows the information, be prepared to jump ahead to study more complex training material.

Technology Makes Level 3 Evaluation Feasible and Friendly

BY DAVE ZIELINSKI

Try as they might, most trainers still struggle with evaluating programs beyond Level 1 (smile sheets) or Level 2 (pre- and post-training testing) with any enduring success. Measuring how training directly affects job performance (Level 3) and organizational results (Level 4) still requires a formula of one part science, two parts leap of faith. And that's without even factoring in the considerable — but increasingly scarce — time needed to create, tally and report on evaluations.

But Texas Instruments (TI) is among those boasting success at Level 3, having completely automated evaluations for the thousands of training classes it offers worldwide each year, says Yvonne Torres O'Brien of TI's corporate learning institute in Dallas.

A Wired Company

TI's old Level 3 evaluation methods were labor-intensive and sporadic. They relied on paper forms, phone or personal interviews, and manual number crunching. There was little consistency from training unit to training unit — and even within training units — because evaluations were all done a little differently. And because they were so time-consuming, some course managers and instructors sometimes skipped doing them.

The new evaluation system is based on a sophisticated communications infrastructure, a prerequisite for a project of this scope. TI's internal communication system is used by all employees for e-mail, logging project hours, registering for training classes, and keeping in touch. In its broadest outlines, the new evaluation system works like this:

When employees sign up for training classes on-line, where a comprehensive listing of classes is maintained, the information is automatically entered into the Training Education Management System, or TEMS, which maintains a complete record of all employee training activity. All employees are required to complete at least 32 hours of training (soon to be

Texas Instruments is boasting success at Level 3 — and saving valuable time — with automated evaluations.

40 hours) per year, so employees pay close attention to the system.

TEMS is networked with the new evaluation system, which automatically sends an electronic message to employees 90 days after they've completed a training class; 90 days is the system's default setting. Individual course managers can specify shorter or longer periods based on when they think a level 3 evaluation should be done. The message asks employees to complete an on-line course evaluation.

Filling out the evaluation is voluntary, but if the quantity of responses isn't high enough to ensure statistically valid data, the training group has other options — including enlisting top management to encourage participation, or, if necessary, making the evaluation a requirement before employees receive credit for a class.

The evaluation form is the product of input from several TI training organizations, which realized inefficiencies in separately developing their own level 3 evaluation templates. Combining efforts to create one corporatewide system that allowed apples-to-apples comparisons of courses seemed a more useful approach.

The evaluation form, however, doesn't take a generic one-size-fits-all approach. It does include the expected multiple choice questions about how frequently skills learned in training are used on the job, the difficulty involved in transferring those skills, how performance proficiency has changed, and more. But it also allows instructors to add specific questions related to learning objectives for individual courses. More important, it gives employees up to 220 lines to make comments on the degree of difficulty they encounter using new skills, how environmental factors (on-the-job support of new skills) are limiting skill use and other areas.

That's significant, since the new system's reporting process is also completely automated, including capturing employees' essay-style comments. It's not unusual for course managers and instructors to receive reports that contain a page or two of statistics and 20 pages of comments from trainees. The whole thing is done on-line, is more time-efficient, and provides feedback that is consistent regardless of course — with results generated in a few days.

Evaluations are completely anonymous and aren't used to make judgments about employees' training progress, O'Brien says, which encourages more honest feedback.

A Big Improvement

O'Brien says the new system is proving more cost-effective because there's no paper involved and less time is needed to use and maintain it. And perhaps even more valuable is the giant database on training effectiveness being created. The system is available for all of TI's training classes, and generates tens of thousands of evaluations for all types of training, from soft skills to hard technical skills.

The data can be sliced and interpreted in a variety of ways, says O'Brien, giving TI a unique macro-level window on what training works and what doesn't. Entire types of training could be shed if TI gets convincing evidence the courses have little on-the-job impact. "We hope to make all sorts of hard decisions using this data," says O'Brien.

DELIVERING EVALUATION FORMS VIA COMPUTER NETWORKS

BY SCOTT HEIMES

More training managers are reporting multiple benefits from delivering course evaluation forms via electronic means. Not only do their response rates typically rise, but the act of receiving, completing, and then returning the survey via e-mail attachments gives students additional computer skills practice.

Dave Ferguson, senior project manager of training and performance support at GE Information Services in Rockville, MD, is among those expanding his use of e-mail to deliver evaluations. This group recently created and sent an Excel evaluation worksheet, formatted to look like a paper-based evaluation form, to employees who had completed a five-day training course. The forms were sent four to five weeks after graduation.

The course involved training employees of a GE client company how to use computer hardware and a variety of software tools. Particular focus was given to a new sales automation software package.

At the class conclusion, a level one "smile sheet" evaluation was done, but Ferguson wanted more detailed data on training transfer. Because using spreadsheets was part of the course, he created an evaluation in spreadsheet format that was sent to trainees as an attachment to an e-mail message. "Since participants had all learned to use e-mail — including using attached files — we thought this was also a good test of their new skills," he says.

The survey asked trainees to rate their skill levels in 50 specific skill areas taught in class, using a scale of one to four (from "can't do at all" to "can do easily"). Skills rated included things like creating memos within the e-mail package, entering formulas or text in spreadsheets, building a list of planned customer visits in Excel, and transmitting sales data electronically to headquarters. "We also added 10 questions about the frequency of use, or how often trainees said they were having to use these skills," Ferguson says. "We wanted data on how important some skills were to performing well day to day."

Survey Received 50% Response

Some 1,150 of 2,200 students who were sent surveys responded — a 50% plus response rate that thrilled the training function. Perhaps most impressive was that given three different ways of returning surveys — print out and mail, print out and fax, or return via attached e-mail file — over 80% of these previously computer-averse students chose the latter method. "We believed this was the most difficult of the three vehicles, so the respondents surprised us with this testimony to the skill they acquired," Ferguson says.

Returned forms are tallied in a large Excel database that allows Ferguson to run detailed breakdowns of data based on a number of indicators and create graphs and charts that trainees' managers have found valuable.

Sprint Asks Managers to Rate Training Services Via E-mail

At Sprint's University of Excellence, the telecommunication company's training, assessment, and OD arm, Karen Mailliard, director, decided to change her approach to evaluation.

Instead of sending director-level clients a lengthy paper-based survey to rate the UE's services at year-end 1995, she decided to send them just one question via e-mail. She asked them, "How would you rate the contribution UE made to your unit's success in 1995 on a scale of one to seven?"

"Previous to 1995 we had sent these directors a 20-question year-end survey that asked them to rate all of our many services," she says. "But this really simplifies it."

The one-question survey supplements other evaluation done throughout the year at lower levels in the company by the UE, including quarterly report cards from internal customers.

Respondents sent many unsolicited comments along with their numerical feedback, Mailliard says. "Some of it was 'we still need help in this area,' so we got more work out of the surveys. Everyone who responded received a follow up phone call from us."

RECOMMENDED RESOURCES FOR MANAGERS

MAIL ORDERS TO:
LAKEWOOD BOOKS
50 S. Ninth Street, Minneapolis, MN 55402
800-707-7769 or 612-333-0471
Or fax your order to 612-340-4819.

UNCONDITIONAL GUARANTEE

Examine and use any of the resources on this form for a full 30 days. If you are not completely satisfied, for any reaon whatsoever, simply return and receive a full refund of the purchase price.

Please send me the following publications:

Qty.	Title	$ Amount
_____	Creative Training Techniques Handbook, Vol. 2. By Bob Pike. $49.95.	_____
_____	Creative Training Tools. By Bob Pike. $14.95.	_____
_____	Making Training Work. By Berton H. Gunter. $27.00.	_____
_____	67 Presentation Secrets to Wow Any Audience. By Dianna Booher. $22.95.	_____
_____	Dynamic Openers & Energizers. By Bob Pike. $14.95.	_____
_____	Managing the Front-End of Training. By Bob Pike. $14.95.	_____
_____	Motivating Your Trainees. By Bob Pike. $14.95.	_____
_____	Optimizing Training Transfer. By Bob Pike. $14.95.	_____
_____	Powerful Audiovisual Techniques. By Bob Pike. $14.95.	_____
_____	The HR Handbook, Edited by Elaine Biech and John E. Jones, $59.95	_____
_____	101 Games for Trainers. By Bob Pike. $21.95.	_____
_____	101 More Games for Trainers. By Bob Pike. $21.95.	_____
_____	TRAINING Magazine. 12 issues/yr. $78 U.S., $88 Canada, $99 Other Int'l.	_____
_____	Creative Training Techniques Newsletter. 12 issues/yr. $99 U.S., $109 Canada, $119 Other Int'l.	_____
_____	Training Directors' Forum Newsletter. 12 issues/yr. $118 U.S., $128 Canada, $138 Other Int'l.	_____
_____	The Lakewood Report on Technology for Learning Newsletter. 12 issues/yr. $195 U.S., $205 Canada, $215 Other Int'l.	_____

SUBTOTAL — **Subtotal:** _____

In Canada add 7% GST #123705485 (applies to all products) — **Add GST:** _____

In MN add 7% sales tax; in WI add 5% sales tax
(does not apply to newsletters) — **Add Tax:** _____

Add $4 for first book; $3 each additional book
for shipping & handling. — **Add S&H:** _____

TOTAL — **Total Amount Enclosed:** _____

❏ Check or money order is enclosed. Check payable to Lakewood Publications. (U.S. funds on a U.S. bank)
❏ Please charge: ❏ VISA   ❏ MasterCard   ❏ American Express   ❏ Discover

Card # _____ Exp. ___/___ Signature _____
(Required for Credit Card Use)

NAME _____
TITLE _____
COMPANY _____
ADDRESS (No P.O. Boxes) _____
CITY/STATE/ZIP _____
PHONE (_____) _____ FAX (_____) _____

H607